P9-BHX-869

DUNĂREA NOASTRA ROMANIA, THE GREAT POWERS, AND THE DANUBE QUESTION 1914-1921

Richard C. Frucht

EAST EUROPEAN MONOGRAPHS, BOULDER
DISTRIBUTED BY COLUMBIA UNIVERSITY PRESS,
NEW YORK

1982

EAST EUROPEAN MONOGRAPHS, NO. CXIII

$\overline{DR}_{263}$ $\Big/ 35,329$
$F78$

Printed in the United States of America

For Su, Kristin, Mom and Dad

TABLE OF CONTENTS

PREFACE

Few issues in European diplomatic history have been so routinely overlooked as the Danube Question. Despite the fact that for a century the issue vexed the foreign ministries of Europe, generally it is given consideration by historians only in relation to the larger diplomatic problem, that is, the Eastern Question. After 1918 and the "end" of the Eastern Question the importance of the Danube received little attention outside the immediate Basin states.

Western historiography of the post-World War I period is limited therefore to the works of Hugo Hajnal and Joseph Chamberlain, both of whom wrote during the 1920s. Although their studies are excellent, they are based on limited documentation and stress a Eurocentric point of view that fails to address the important changes that took place after the war regarding the administration of the Danube.

By nature, the creation of institutions designed to guarantee freedom of navigation on international rivers requires the delicate balancing of riparian and nonriparian interests. The riverine state must surrender part of its jurisdiction over the waterway to an organization composed of all nations which border the river. The agency must in turn address both the sovereignty of the individual state and the vague concept of internationality. Nowhere was the resolution of these seemingly disparate ideas more difficult than over the question of the Danube.

During the nineteenth century the Danube was an integral factor in the Eastern Question. Due to the river's strategic and economic importance, Europe's statesmen after 1856 tried to internationalize the waterway. They failed to reach any agreement regarding the river's administration except for the area between the Black Sea and the Romanian port of Galați, that is, the maritime Danube. From 1856 until 1914, the European Commission of the Danube, the regime devised for this sector, was the sole regulatory agency in operation on the river. Composed of members of the European powers and Romania, the Commission supervised commercial activities both as a means of assuring a smooth flow of commerce as well as preventing any single power from obtaining a preponderant influence over such a vital economic artery.

With the end of the First World War, the destruction of the eastern autocracies that for centuries had dominated the river politically and economically, and the subsequent national upheaval that took place throughout the Danube Basin and Eastern Europe, control of the Danube no longer could be considered the exclusive concern of the great powers. The individual riparian states, caught up in the nationalistic fervor that marked the postwar period, were unwilling to allow outside influences to regulate the river.

Although the war removed many of the reasons for continued great power involvement in river affairs, the peacemakers at Versailles, instead of creating a single agency for the entire river, reinstated the European Commission with full authority over the Danube delta and established a second body, the International Commission of the Danube (with full great power representation), for the rest of the waterway. Responsibility for formalizing the new administration fell to a special Danube Conference held in Paris in 1920. The events and outcome of that meeting not only established the formal rules of navigation that governed the Danube until World War II; it also marked a major confrontation between the great powers and the individual riparian states of the Basin.

Romania represents the focal point at which all areas of confrontation converge. A member of the European Commission after obtaining independence in 1878, Romania consistently fought against the influence of the powers on the river. The destruction of the European Commission as a functioning agency during the war left Romania in complete charge of the maritime Danube. After 1918 Romania hoped to preserve its control over *Dunărea noastră* ("our Danube"), an objective that set the stage for a clash at the Paris Conference between the Balkan state and its wartime allies.

The Danube Question after 1914 thus acts on two levels. On the one hand, the question of internationality dominated the discussions both at Versailles and later at Paris. On the other hand, the application of the principle of internationality depended on national priorities. The resolution of the Danube Question therefore involved a serious policy dispute between the great powers (who sought to retain their former prerogatives) and the individual Basin state, as represented by Romania.

During the preparation of this study, many people gave generously of their time and talents. Special thanks must go to Professors Barbara and Charles Jelavich of Indiana University for their aid and encouragement, and Nelson Lankford of the *American Historical Review* and Steven Sowards (also of Indiana University) for their editorial assistance. My appreciation also must go to Jim Sand and Linda Ray, graduate students at Northwest Missouri State University, for their help in proofreading the text. I would also like to acknowledge the assistance of three members of the N. Iorga Institute of History in Bucharest, Drs. Paul Cernovodeanu, Ion Stanciu, and Cornelia Bodea, and Mr. N. Fotino of the Romanian office of UNESCO; their efforts enabled me to obtain the use of archival materials previously inaccessible to non-Romanian historians. Finally, there is Su; however, in this case nothing I can ever say or write will be sufficient.

Richard Frucht
Northwest Missouri State University

CHAPTER I

THE DANUBE QUESTION: BACKGROUND

In August 1920, representatives from twelve European countries gathered in Paris to draw up a navigational treaty, a *Statut Definitif*, for the Danube River. Just as World War I destroyed the equilibrium in Europe, so too did it upset order throughout the Danube Basin. Therefore, the framers of the Versailles accords authorized the convocation of this special Danube Conference as an important link in the overall peace process and as a means toward resolving the Danube Question, a diplomatic issue that had perplexed Europe's statesmen for a century.

Ostensibly, the Danube Question involved the vague principle of internationality of rivers. Although no definition can be considered definitive for this term, which has been subject to broad interpretation and little consensus, Georges Kaeckenbeeck's *International Rivers: A Monograph Based on Diplomatic Documents* succinctly analyzes the concept of internationality as defined and understood at the time of the conference. As such, his interpretation will serve as the model throughout the course of this study.

Kaeckenbeeck defined as an international body of water any river which flows through or along the territory of two or more states. Only a river that is navigable solely within one country may be held subject to exclusive jurisdiction.[1] The seventeenth-century Dutch legal theorist, Hugo Grotius, presented the first discourse on international law, arguing that anything inexhaustible cannot be used to the exclusion of others. Thus the declaration and guarantee of a river's internationality act as protection against potential economic hindrances imposed by individual nations. These obstacles may take the form of discriminatory tolls against ships or goods of a particular country, restricted use of ports, or excessive

1

tariff barriers. Internationality guarantees the right of passage to all vessels causing no harm to a riparian state. According to this concept, rivers should act as economic highways for the flow of goods; therefore, ships would be exempted from all forms of taxation, save uniform fees for the use of port facilities.[2]

The riparian states would thus work in concert to facilitate trade rather than act counter to the interests of commerce by virtue of their sovereign control of the territory along the river. Sovereignty and property cannot be considered synonymous.[3] When a river passes through or along territories, the states acquire certain common interests *ipso facto*, the regulation of which does not violate sovereignty.[4]

In order to ensure the perpetuation of this division between property and sovereignty and to protect all common interests on the river, certain fundamental laws of navigation must be formulated. These rules may be devised bilaterally among the states themselves or through a general conference. No laws may be enacted unilaterally however, and all arrangements with regard to international rivers are a matter of negotiation to be recorded in treaties.[5]

Every solution must address both the ideal of internationality and the question of sovereignty. Even though the riverine state must surrender some authority for the good of all trading nations, no country will "allow itself to be stripped of an elementary right of protection of its welfare and integrity."[6] Every agreement must be mutually satisfactory to all parties, with no one nation or special interest receiving an inordinate share of privileges, actual or perceived. To ensure harmony between riparian and nonriparian states, a commission, composed of equal representation from among the riverine countries, should be formed. This agency could also grant membership to nonriverine nations with economic interests on the river. Once created, the central body would be entrusted with overseeing the administrative operations of the river, from the establishment and collection of tolls to the construction of port facilities.

A potential conflict remains, however, between the interests of nations taken collectively and the sovereign powers of one state in particular. Thus, an executive commission, especially one composed of "nonriparian powers may be objected to as infringing on sovereignty."[7] In order to be justified the agency requires genuine proof of advantages to all delegations concerned. The establishment and duties of such an executive commission was the central question involving the Danube.

Definition and application of rules of internationality vary according
to time and the requirements of foreign and economic policies, that is,
national self-interests. As such, because the Danube Question was a diplomatic concern, other, more basic issues were at stake than the simple
desire to guarantee freedom of navigation on the river. The formation
of any foreign policy is based on numerous complex factors. For the
parties interested in the Danube, four predominated: the geographical
importance of the river, territorial nationalism, political exigencies, and
trade and other economic considerations. "Internationality" was thus
but a facade behind which diplomatic efforts promoted national policies.

During the nineteenth century, the role of the Danube in European
affairs was part of the larger Eastern Question that vexed the foreign
ministries of Europe; the Danube issue was molded by the dictates of
ministers formulating policies designed to stabilize southeastern Europe
and that, of necessity, required constant great power presence and supervision within the Balkans. Regulations governing the Danube reflected
those policies. But the pattern whereby great power diplomacy clashed
with the principles of sovereignty and territorial integrity did not end
with World War I. Although the cast of characters changed, the basic objectives, methods, and confrontations of the earlier epoch remained. The
riparian nations sought to retain maximum control of the river within
their own territories. The great powers, on the other hand, continued
to believe that only strict regulation and supervision of the Danube (which
included the active participation of France, Great Britain, and Italy, as
well as any other "interested" nonriparian state) could ensure stability
and thus definitively establish the elusive concept of internationality.

Historically, the question of the Danube has been among the most
complex of all the problems concerning rivers considered "international"
in character. No other river flows through or along so many disparate
nations. Between the Treaty of Paris in 1856 and the outbreak of World
War I all attempts toward internationalizing the waterway failed, save
for the creation of a European Commission of the Danube, which regulated traffic between the Black Sea and the Romanian port of Galaţi.
This situation was due, in large measure, to the rivalries among the great
powers and fears that one of them might obtain a dominant position
on any administration governing the river. After 1918, instead of creating
a unitary regime for the Danube in conformity with the prevailing views
of internationality, such as Kaeckenbeeck's, the framers of the Versailles

treaties authorized the formation of two separate and distinct regulatory agencies: the old European Commission of the Danube to regulate all maritime traffic and a new International Commission of the Danube to operate on the rest of the river. Because of their different functions, the composition of the two organizations would be dissimilar; only the members of the European Commission could sit on both agencies. This provision called into question one of the basic tenets of an international regime: no nation or group can receive an inordinate share of privileges or representation in the regulation of a waterway. Therefore, when the issue of the Danube's future was decided at a special *Conférence internationale pour l'établissement du Statut Définitif du Danube* in 1920, the debate centered not only upon the type of administration that would govern the river but also upon the prerogatives to be given each commission and its respective members. Furthermore, with the great powers receiving representation on both organizations, the conference was dominated by friction between riparian and nonriparian interests. The former, seeking to protect their own territorial sovereignty and develop their national economies, confronted the commercial interests of the more advanced states of Western Europe; the latter, in turn, sought to maintain the rights and privileges of river administration obtained during the nineteenth century. Therefore, the political and economic nationalism that characterized the history of the Danubian Basin during the interwar years clashed with the *status quo* diplomacy, which was based on the maintenance of past prerogatives, employed by the powers.

For the Danube Question, Romania represents the focal point at which all areas of confrontation, both theoretical and actual, converged. The reason lies in the geographical relationship of Romania to the river. One-third of the waterway either flows exclusively through Romanian territority or forms a border with its neighbors. All major rivers within the country connect in some manner with the Danube. More importantly, the river acted as Romania's economic lifeline. Dependent on the export of primary products, Romania needed a good transportation network. During the years that comprise this study neither roads nor railroads were adequate to handle the commerce. Instead, the nation's limited transportation system linked the producing areas with the country's rivers; small boats then carried goods to and from cargo ships on the Danube. In addition, just as the Danube acted as a conduit for the nation's economy, so too did it represent a strategic highway into Romania and a potential means of rapid advancement by an enemy. An invasion could be well-supplied, while creating a stranglehold on Romania's own economy. Therefore, the geographical importance of the Danube contributed to a virtual siege mentality within the Romanian government, that is, that Romanian interests on the river must be safeguarded.

This concern was exacerbated by the fact that after 1856 a European Commission, dominated by the great powers,[8] administered the river between the Black Sea and Galaţi, an area surrounded by Romanian territory. The Commission's status "in complete independence of territorial authorities" and its control by the European powers created a perception within influential circles in Romania that the agency's existence threatened the nation's independence and sovereignty. Romania's diplomatic position concerning any conference designed to create an administrative body for the river reflects, therefore, not only the objectives of a particular conferee and riparian state but also provides an insight into the conflict between the concepts of internationality and territorial sovereignty, the clash between great power interests and the Romanian ideal of *Dunărea noastră* ("our Danube").[9]

As mentioned above, the Danube Question was not merely a phenomenon of the post-1918 era; it was rooted deeply in the preceding century both as a diplomatic issue of importance and as one facet of the Eastern Question. In order to analyze the role of the Danube prior to World War I it is first necessary to define that larger diplomatic issue. Although it is neither the intention nor purpose of this study to examine the Eastern Question or the diplomatic, political, and economic events of the nineteenth century in detail it is essential to make a few generalizations in order to present the historical context of the Danube Question. Together, these events and the various statutes adopted for the Danube, which comprised part of nineteenth-century public law, form a necessary background to postwar negotiations, the diplomatic positions of the conferees, and the adoption of the *Statut Définitif.*

The Danube and the Eastern Question

Although the Danube Question was but a secondary issue in the nineteenth-century diplomatic quagmire known as the Eastern Question, it was nevertheless a factor considered vital by the interested parties. Throughout this period, the tottering Ottoman Empire was of primary concern for the major European powers.

On the surface, the Eastern Question primarily involved relations among Russia, Austria, and the Ottoman Empire. As the Turkish presence in the Balkans receded, both Russia and the Habsburg Empire sought to expand their respective interests in the area. Although their motives varied, the two eastern autocracies saw strategic and political advantages to be gained in the region.

Their own economic concerns, as well as the determination to maintain the balance of power in the Balkans also guided the other European states. The Porte, in turn, attempted to balance the interests of the powers and, more importantly, to use them, at times, as bulwarks against foreign or internal enemies. The Porte also granted economic concessions to the West, an act that only brought further European involvement in Ottoman affairs by increasing the vested interests of the powers in the preservation of the Ottoman state. Even when the various Balkan nations gained independence, the treatment they received from the powerful European states did not substantially differ from that given them by their former rulers in Istanbul. Like the Ottoman Empire, the Balkan countries were "subjected to the same policies and treatment that the powers employed in their own imperial adventures."[10]

Foremost among the European states interested in the Eastern Question was Great Britain. London considered the maintenance of the Ottoman Empire important to its interests in the Eastern Mediterranean and made this belief a cornerstone of British foreign policy throughout most of the nineteenth century. Although Britain gained only marginal economic benefit from the Ottoman Empire and the Lower Danube, it nevertheless considered the region (including the Danubian market) of sufficient economic importance to base a substantial portion of its foreign policy on stabilizing the Balkans. This attitude derived, in large part, from Britain's support of free trade, a predominant theme of nineteenth-century British economic policy. It created a belief among British statesmen that the area represented an existing, and potentially greater, economic importance; only firm diplomatic action, it was felt, could guarantee the market's accessibility.

The Danube, therefore, became an integral part of the larger consideration, the Eastern Question. It held a geographical significance for any

possible Austrian or Russian designs for expanding their influence in the
Balkans in the wake of the disintegration of Ottoman control. More importantly, in the rising age of the entrepreneur and global trade, the river
was a vital artery (actual and potential) for European commercial activities.
The absence of any suitable road or rail networks in the lower Danube
Basin exaggerated the importance of the river for the transportation of
goods. The Danube's accessibility was essential for the development of
commerce in southeastern Europe. Should any one state acquire a preponderant influence over the river and its operations, that country would
control an area that was rich in primary products and that existed as a
promising market for manufactured goods. Thus, ensuring freedom of
navigation on the Danube became a matter of European concern and a consideration that grew in importance during the latter half of the century.

During the period between the conclusion of the Crimean War (when
the first statutes for the Danube were enacted) and the depression of
1872-1879, an era of free trade marked European commercial relations,
during which international agreements were concluded in an effort to facilitate commerce. These treaties included provisions regulating railroads,
rivers, canals, and postal systems. Although the motives for establishing
international codes for the Danube were far from altruistic and failed except in the delta, the international movement to foster trade was a consideration for the regulation of the river and, in economic terms, did
achieve a measure of success. Even after trade restrictions returned
throughout Europe in the 1880s, commerce through the Danube's maritime ports continually increased.

During the thirty years before Sarajevo, an epoch often characterized
as the Age of Imperialism, the Danube remained a conduit for the export
of needed raw materials to Europe. Unlike other areas subjected to imperial adventures, however, no one nation gained control or even a dominant influence on the river south of Habsburg territory. The desire to
maintain the balance of power precluded any chance that one state
could act unilaterally. Measures advantageous to one nation (as will be
seen in the next chapter) were blocked by the powers.

The concept of balance of power for the Danube Question thus required the maintenance of stability on the river. Internationality implied
no more than a simple equilibrium of interests. Potential instability and
uncertainty portended crisis for all the European states, either politically

(due to the threat of possible armed conflict in the area) or economically. Whether interested directly (as in the cases of Russia, Austria, Great Britain, or the Ottoman Empire) or indirectly (the remaining powers, by virtue of the need to avoid confrontations that might widen into larger conflagrations), all had a vested interest in ensuring stability on the river through the establishment of an international regime designed to regulate commerce and act as a medium for resolving commercial disputes.

Their efforts attained only partial success, however. Just as the number of conflicting interests among the powers and the internal dry-rot within the Ottoman Empire precluded any solution to the Eastern Question, the attempts to internationalize the Danube failed except in the delta. The river's internationality was espoused but played a secondary role to the more important consideration of maintaining the balance of power. Internationalizing the Danube could succeed only in the delta, an area of such considerable economic importance that it mandated an accommodation of interests. But similar rules of navigation could not be extended beyond Romanian territory to German, Habsburg or Russian lands. Those nations opposed such a move, and any effort to press the issue would have upset the balance of power. Thus, internationalization worked only where interests did not seriously clash with the desires of an individual great power. By internationalizing the waterway solely within Romanian territory and maintaining constant great power control over the delta, a confrontation with Romania became inevitable, despite the latter's admission after 1878 to the European Commission. Romanian outrage at the agency's prerogatives was of little concern to the West, however. Preserving stability in the region was a great power policy; the Danube, its internationalization, and the maintenance of an equilibrium were strictly great power concerns. The position and interests of Romania (as well as the other small Balkan riverine states, Serbia and Bulgaria) were of little consequence to the West. The broader implications of the Eastern Question demanded no less than that control of the river remain firmly in the hands of the major European states.

World War I and the resulting destruction of the German, Habsburg, Russian, and Ottoman Empires effectively ended the Eastern Question but not the matter of the Danube's internationality. In the wake of the war, the Danubian Basin underwent enormous geopolitical changes that created uncertainty about river operations. Therefore, just as the framers of the peace treaties were called upon to deal with issues far removed from the mere ratification of the Central Powers' surrender, so too were they confronted with the need and opportunity to finally devise an international administration for the entire river.

The question was whether the end of the war would result in a new era for the Danube. It was obvious that the entire river would be internationalized; what was still to be determined was the regime that would be chosen to govern the Danube's internationality and whether the European Commission, a product of an era in which maintenance of the balance of power in the Balkans was an issue of utmost importance, would be disbanded.

The war did not end the questions surrounding the Danube and its administration therefore. Instead, it produced new controversies and perpetuated old ones. The responsibility for resolving the Danube Question ultimately fell upon the peace conference in Paris in 1920, a convention at which Romania would play a central role. For Romania, the strategic and economic importance of the river and the concept of *Dunărea noastră* ("our Danube"), an unfulfilled aspiration to control the course of the river that flowed through the country's territory, demanded its attention. The nation did not wish to see the history of the river during the previous half-century repeated. That situation was anathema to Romania's interests and national pride. It is those events to which we must first turn.

CHAPTER II

"IN COMPLETE INDEPENDENCE OF TERRITORIAL AUTHORITIES"

International river law remained an undeveloped concept as late as the French Revolution. Not until the Congress of Vienna in 1815 did representatives of the European states attempt tó formulate general rules for the regulation and administration of international bodies of water, specifically the Rhine River. The codes devised were designed to supersede laws that dated from the emergence of the nation-state and that sought to exclude foreign economic penetration from the state's domain through discriminatory laws favorable to native merchants.[1] The first legislation governing the Danube, enacted in 1856, adhered to precedents for the Rhine established earlier in the century at Vienna. But efforts to ensure the Danube's internationality soon clashed with special interests. The great powers were unable to devise an administrative regime acceptable to all parties and were able to reach agreement only in regard to the regulation of the Danube delta. Thus, the European Commission of the Danube, originally chartered for two years to clear the delta of debris, became a permanent, autonomous bureaucratic agency operating exclusively in Romanian territory and the sole regulatory organization on the river. The authority of the powers on the Lower Danube, in turn, led to a serious clash with the Bucharest government, which naturally viewed the independent status of the European Commission as a violation of its territorial sovereignty. This chapter will trace the dual nature of the Danube Question during the century preceding World War I and will stress the development of the issue after 1856 and Romania's policy toward the European Commission. Because of the nature of the Eastern Question and because of Romania's absence from active participation in the Danube issue before its independence in 1878, the chapter must center on the activities of the great powers. Their control

10

of the Danube Question, which left Romania with few options in regard to the European agency, forms the necessary background to the issues after 1914.

The first practical application of the principles of internationality, as defined in chapter one, came in 1792. The French Convention of that year declared it unjust for any nation to assert a right of exclusive jurisdiction on any river.[2] In the years before Waterloo, the Scheldt, Maas, Rhine, Elbe, Vistula, and Oder Rivers were given "international" status after falling under French hegemony. The concepts espoused, however, guaranteed liberty of navigation only to states bordering the river, not to all nations.[3] These rivers, in fact, became an integral part of Napoleon's ill-fated Continental System; as such, a single authority dictated the rules regarding the rivers' dispositions in the conquered territories. These decisions possessed no international sanction and were never recognized by the anti-Napoleon coalitions. It remained for the Congress of Vienna to apply the ideas of freer navigation rights on a wider scale.

This generalization does not imply that the Congress desired to further the principles of the National Convention or Napoleon. The delegates sought instead to lay down general rules as a basis of navigation on the Rhine and its tributaries. Such an action was considered vital, for in 1815 the only means of inland international communication and trade other than roads were waterways.

The *Actes du Congrès* incorporated a code of laws (articles CVIII-CXVI) for the Rhine, Main, Neckar, Mosel, Meuse, and Scheldt. The provisions, it must be noted, did not pertain to the Danube, because of the absence of the Ottoman Empire from the proceedings. The statutes stipulated that a commission, composed of delegates from the riparian states, should regulate the rivers by common consent.

Furthermore, navigation

> of the rivers, along their whole course, . . . shall be entirely free and shall not, in respect to Commerce, be prohibited to any one: it being understood that the Regulations established with regard to the police of this navigation shall be respected, as they will be framed alike for all, and as favorable as possible to the commerce of all nations.[4]

Each state

bordering on the rivers is to be at the expense of keeping in good
repair the Towing Paths which pass through its territory, and of
maintaining the necessary works through the same extent in the
channels of the river, in order that no obstacle may be experienced
to navigation.[5]

Tolls would be uniform and could be raised only with the consent of all
members of the commission. Any alteration in the agreements would be
made only upon the "consent of all the Riverine States."[6] Finally, the
signators (France, Great Britain, Austria, Russia, Prussia, Portugal, and
Sweden) agreed to act as "guarantors" of the rivers' internationality, an imprecise role important for the future regulation of the Danube.

The decisions reached at Vienna became the essential framework for
all treaties governing international rivers. After Vienna, the various riverine
commissions, the number of which grew in later years, operated in relative
harmony and resolved disputes internally. After World War I the "guarantee" of the great powers devolved upon the League of Nations and
after 1945 upon the United Nations. Nevertheless, effective power remained with the riparian states themselves. For a century, the Danube was
the glaring exception to the Vienna system.

Running from the Black Forest to the Black Sea, the Danube is Europe's
longest river. Formed by the confluence of two streams near Donaue-
schingen in the German province of Baden, it does not become navigable
until Ulm, in Bavaria. From that point, until it reaches the sea, a distance
of approximately 1,700 miles, the river flows through or borders West
Germany, Austria, Czechoslovakia, Hungary, Yugoslavia, Bulgaria, Romania, and the Soviet Union. The physical limitations of the river restrict
ocean-going vessels to the Lower Danube, that is, the area from the Romanian port of Brăila to the sea; only smaller ships are able to service the
Upper Danube. Goods must be transshipped in the Romanian maritime
ports either for passage upstream or to sea.

Because of the number of riparian countries and their often disparate
political and economic interests, the Danube was for centuries a geographical pawn in the affairs of Europe. As Ottoman power in southeastern
Europe receded during the seventeenth century, the Danube became part
of a larger battlefield. While the Turkish presence ebbed, Austrian and
Russian interests in the area grew. The possibility of a clash between the
two powers became an important facet in both the Danube and Eastern
Questions.

By 1718 Austrian hegemony reached the Iron Gates, the section of the river near the town of Orșova where passage is slowed by a narrow, natural channel formed by high cliffs. Maria Theresa and Joseph II encouraged the development of Danubian commerce through a series of favorable subsidies and laws. In 1784 a treaty with the Ottoman Empire permitted the Austrians to trade freely in river ports under Turkish jurisdiction. Austrian interests south of the Iron Gates developed slowly, however. Of greater immediate importance to the history of the river was the expanding Russian presence on the maritime Danube.

Russian influence on the river also grew slowly. During the reign of Catherine the Great, Russian troops reached the Kilia channel, the northern tributary of the Danube. Although the Ottoman Empire regained the Kilia with the 1774 Treaty of Kutchuk Kainarji, Russia received commercial privileges in the delta. Russia did not formally become a riparian state until after the signing of the Treaty of Bucharest in 1812; seventeen years later it secured the entire delta as a result of the Treaty of Adrianople. In turn, the Ottoman Empire lost the economic monopoly it maintained over the principal Danube ports of Galați and Brăila.

The Treaty of Adrianople also opened the maritime Danube to all international trade by ending Ottoman control over the river within the Danubian Principalities. Russia held a commanding position over the river's commercial traffic by its physical presence at the mouth of the Danube. More importantly, it now dominated the area that was in direct competition with the Russian port of Odessa for the expanding European grain trade. It became commercially expedient, therefore, for Russia to practice a policy of arbitrarily quarantining ships on the Danube and allowing the river's treacherous arms, the Kilia, Sulina, and St. George channels, to fall into a state of disrepair.[7] By the 1850s the depth of the Sulina, the principal delta artery, had fallen to 6½ feet. Ships unable to reach the ports were forced to transship their cargoes offshore into barges. Only vessels with narrow keels could reach port safely. Such obstructionism increased the price of wheat shipped from Galați in relation to grains exported from Odessa.[8]

The Russian policy of neglect collided with growing Austrian and British interests favoring open commerce. Expanding industrially, Britain needed to import greater quantities of grains from Eastern Europe, while the Habsburgs were developing state-supported shipping concerns. Although trading privileges and the right of free navigation had been for decades a minor concern, by the 1840s merchants in the Habsburg Empire began to seek new markets, especially to the southeast. At the same time, the export of maize, barley, and wheat to Britain from the Danubian Principalities rose 255 percent between 1838-1842 and 1843-1848.[9] Following the repeal of the Corn Laws in 1846, these totals continued to rise despite Russian obstructionism. By 1847 nearly 5 percent of all British grain purchases came from Moldavia and Wallachia.[10] Although Russia did sign a treaty in 1840 guaranteeing freedom of navigation in the delta for ten years, there was no appreciable change in Russian policy.[11] British and Austrian protests and appeals on the basis of the Vienna principles were frequent, yet futile.[12] Russia never deliberately opposed legal access to the river save for the aforementioned policy of arbitrary quarantines; but its failure to keep the tributaries free of silt disrupted navigation.[13] The Crimean War, however, altered this situation.

Russia's defeat in the war, its displacement as a riparian power through the loss of southern Bessarabia, and the inclusion of the Ottoman Empire in the peace negotiations removed all obstacles to the enactment of legislation governing the Danube. As early as August 8, 1854, the plenipotentiaries of Austria, France, and Great Britain declared that among the provisions of any settlement between Russia and the Ottoman Empire should be measures for internationalizing the Danube. The matter of the river's internationality, discussed during the preliminary peace negotiations held in Vienna from March through June 1855, was incorporated into the Treaty of Paris on March 29, 1856. The principal obstacle to the agreements disappeared when Franz Josef yielded on his prior position that only the Danube south of Habsburg territory be internationalized.[14] This action enabled the signators to incorporate five articles addressed to the question of the Danube within the text of the treaty.

Article XV of the Treaty of Paris stipulated that:

> The Act of the Congress of Vienna, having established the principles intended to regulate the Navigation of Rivers which separate or traverse different States, the Contracting Powers stipulate that those principles shall in future be equally applied to the Danube and its Mouths. They declare that its arrangement henceforth forms a part of the Public Law of Europe, and take it under their Guarantee. The

navigation of the Danube cannot be subjected to any impediment
or charge not expressly provided for by the Stipulations contained
in the following articles; in consequence, there shall not be levied
any Toll founded solely upon the fact of the navigation of the River,
nor any Duty upon the Goods which may be on board of vessels.[15]

With the exception of quarantine and police regulations, no hindrance
could be placed in the path of free navigation. The supervision of all operations would fall solely on a River State Commission, composed of the
riparian states. This organization

> in which Great Britain, Austria, France, Prussia, Russia, Sardinia and
> Turkey, shall be represented by one delegate, shall be charged to
> designate and to cause to be executed the necessary Works below
> Isaktcha, to clear the mouths of the Danube, as well as the neigh-
> boring parts of the Sea, from the sands and other impediments
> which obstruct them, in order to put that part of the River and the
> said parts of the Sea in the best possible state for Navigation.
>
> In order to cover the Expenses of such Works, as well as of the
> establishments intended to secure and to facilitate the Navigation
> at the Mouths of the Danube, fixed Duties, settled by the Commis-
> sion by a majority of votes, may be levied, on the express condition
> that, in this respect as in every other, the Flags of all nations shall be
> treated on the footing of perfect equality.[16]

At the same time, the Paris conferees agreed to create a special body, the
European Commission of the Danube. This agency was charged with clearing from the delta's channels all physical obstacles to traffic that resulted
from years of neglect and the destruction caused by the Crimean War.[17]
The treaty provided that the European Commission

> shall have completed its task . . . within the period of two years. The
> signatory powers assembled in conference, having been informed of
> the fact, shall, after having placed it on record, pronounce the dissolu-
> tion of the European Commission, and from that time the perman-
> ent river commission shall enjoy the same powers as those with which
> the European Commission shall have until then been invested.[18]

Upon dissolution of the European Commission of the Danube, all operations in the delta would revert to the River State Commission. The latter

> which shall be permanent shall: 1. prepare regulations of Navigation and River Police; 2. remove the impediments, of whatever nature they might be, which still prevent the application to the Danube of the Arrangements of the Treaty of Vienna; 3. order and cause to be executed the necessary works throughout the whole course of the River; and 4. after the dissolution of the European Commission, see to maintaining the Mouths of the Danube and the neighboring parts of the Sea in a navigable state.[19]

The River State Commission would thus take sole jurisdiction over the administration of the entire Danube, including operations in the delta. By supporting the creation of a River State Commission, the delegates recognized the belief expressed in the Treaty of Vienna "that the administration of an international river, so far as joint administration is necessary, should be left in the hands of the riparian states."[20] The *Actes du Congrès* clearly placed the Danube within the guidelines established at Vienna; like the Rhine, the Danube would be governed by a single regime.

The River State Commission, however, maintained only a short-lived existence with little practical authority. Its charter, the Act of Navigation of November 7, 1857, drawn up by Austria and signed by all the riparian states except the Danubian Principalities, clearly served Habsburg interests to the benefit of the "Danube Steam Navigation Company" (*Donau Dampfschiffahrts Gesellschaft*). The latter was an Austrian shipping concern that was granted a monopoly by Vienna in 1846 over Austrian Danube commerce. The Act of Navigation would have extended that power south of Hungary by limiting cabotage operations of nonriparian companies. This action and the ambiguity of the Treaty of Paris concerning the equality of all ships and possible preference to riparian fleets produced a rift in 1857 between Austrian and British representatives to the committee created by the signators at Paris to supervise the formation of the River State Commission. The British minister, Lord Cowley, asserted that the privileges accorded the riparian countries violated the Final Act of Vienna, which stipulated that rules be made "alike for all, and as favorable as possible to the commerce of all nations." Furthermore, he argued,

Article XXXIV of the Act of Navigation permitted the individual riverine states to take measures not previously specified under the Paris charter.[21] The Austrian representative to the committee, Baron Hübner, countered that the Vienna agreements only sought to grant freer access to waterways and did not support the concept of equal rights of navigation for non-riparian nations.[22] No compromise could be reached between the two positions, and the Act of Navigation was never ratified. Thus, while the Paris provisions were in a sense superior to the Vienna articles, by calling for a single agency with specific functions, the plenipotentiaries failed to devise a settlement satisfactory to all interests. Instead of drawing up uniform codes on a centralized administrative regime, each riparian country now formulated its own set of laws designed to operate within its own territory. The European Commission of the Danube remained the only functioning international agency on the river.

The acute condition of the Danube in 1856 mandated the creation of the European Commission. Not only had the river's three channels fallen into a serious state of disrepair due to neglect, but also during the course of the war rock-laden ships were sunk at the entrances to the Black Sea to hinder naval operations in the delta. The nature of the river itself further aggravated this situation. The swiftly moving current annually carries enormous deposits of sediment downstream, which, if left untended, quickly create sandbars and narrows the shipping lanes. The task faced by the European Commission was not insignificant therefore, either in the work required or the potential benefits to European commerce.

Preoccupied by events surrounding the River State Commission, the members of the European Commission did not begin operations until April 1858. In August, with the paralysis of the River State Commission already obvious and their own efforts barely begun, the envoys voted to continue work clearing the delta until completion. The technical committee, led by Sir Charles Hartley, initiated a program of improvements shortly thereafter. Instead of trying to clear the entire mouth of obstacles, Hartley chose the Sulina as the principal channel. His plan called for narrowing the Sulina in order that the artery "might be deepened by the concentrated action of the river current."[23] By using the Danube's own natural force, Hartley's corps of engineers succeeded in deepening the channel so that by 1860 river traffic regained the pre-1854 levels.[24] Although more work was needed for the Sulina to be able to accommodate

larger vessels, the immediate physical hazards to shipping resulting from
the war had been removed.

With the completion of the first stage of Hartley's project, the Commission fulfilled its *raison d'être*. However, without an agency for the entire
river, the European Commission grew in importance as a guarantor of the
Danube's internationality. The states represented in the organization
agreed, therefore, to extend its life and continue the physical improve-
ment of the channels and port facilities until an agency came into existence with jurisdiction from Ulm to the sea. Toward that end, the commissioners began to draft rules of navigation for the Lower Danube. In
addition, after Istanbul failed to deliver promised funds needed to carry
out the rest of Hartley's program, the Commission voted to raise revenues
through the enactment of a system of loans and tolls on shipping. The re-
payment of any loan contracted by the European Commission was later
guaranteed by all the powers with the exception of Russia.

Through these actions the commissioners removed the agency from
financial dependency on the governments of the member-states and
thus gave the organization an autonomous status. Revenues from taxes
collected in the maritime ports of Sulina, Tulcea and Galaţi,[25] provided
for agency salaries, maintenance of port facilities, and dredging operations
on the Sulina channel. For major capital projects such as the straightening
of the Sulina's curving passageways, the commissioners looked to government-sponsored loans. Usually the agency could use private banks as a
source for the supplementary funds; loans to the organization, guaranteed
by the respective governments, were sound investments for commercial
banks. On a few occasions, the commission was forced to ask particular
member-nations for support, but those instances were rare. Loans from
private institutions were generally adequate and easily repaid from tax
revenues received by the commission. This situation left the organization
virtually self-sufficient economically.

With the finances of the Commission in order, the members then codi-
fied the previous temporary arrangements regarding the agency's powers.
Through the Public Act of 1865 the representatives designated the body to
be an administrative, judicial, engineering, and planning commission
"under the guaranty of international law."[26] The European Commission
would administer regulations, fines, and inspections; civil and criminal
jurisdiction for serious infractions such as smuggling or forged cargo rosters

remained with the local authorities. The Public Act of 1865 called for regular sessions to be held twice a year with provisions added for additional meetings. Major changes in policy required a unanimous vote of all members. Powers of appointment formerly held by the Ottoman government, most notably the Inspector-General of the Lower Danube and the Captain of the Port of Sulina, reverted to the Commission.[27] Only the British request to extend jurisdiction from Galați to Brăila, "the highest Romanian port on the river to which sea-going ships resort,"[28] failed to gain approval; Ottoman authorities, seeing their control over the delta quickly slipping, opposed any further extension of the Commission's territoriality. Nevertheless, despite Britain's failure to include the port of Brăila under the organization's umbrella, the European Commission of the Danube within five years had become a recognized institution.

The London Conference of 1871 prolonged the life of the Commission until 1883. In response to Russia's denunciation of the 1856 provisions neutralizing the Black Sea, the congress internationalized all works, establishments, and employees of the European Commission. This action extended the idea of internationality beyond simple geography to the representatives and facilities of the agency. In the event of future war, the entire body would have a neutral status. At the same time, over the vigorous objections of the Porte, the delegates recognized Austria's power to tax vessels entering the Iron Gates in order to defray costs of improvements to the region.[29] This became the first successful effort by a riparian nation to achieve a greater share of control than that stipulated in the Paris agreements.

The Treaty of Berlin following the Russo-Turkish War of 1877-78 radically altered the status of the Danube for a second time, even though the question of the river's position was a secondary issue for the delegates. Whereas the Treaty of Paris created the European Commission, Berlin gave it an extralegal and extraterritorial status. The Paris accords professed fealty to the ideal of a single riparian commission; at Berlin this was no longer considered.

A number of actions taken by the framers of the Berlin treaty had an important effect upon the future course of the Danube Question. Romania received official recognition as an independent state.[30] In turn, that country was granted a seat on the European Commission in recognition of the agency's operations within Romanian territory. Russia reacquired southern Bessarabia; this measure placed Russia's border on the Kilia, thereby making it a riparian state again. In return for the cession of Bessarabia, Romania received the Dobrudja. With this territorial exchange, the entire delta, except for the northern bank of the Kilia, now fell exclusively within Romania.

At the same time, the Treaty of Berlin contained six articles addressed specifically to the Danube and the European Commission. Under Article LIII, the delegates granted the Commission a status "in complete independence of territorial authorities" thus leaving the agency completely self-sufficient on Romanian territory.[31] They reconfirmed the prior treaties and decisions concerning the privileges of the body, including exclusive control of all tax revenues. The statutes prohibited Romania from charging transit duties on any goods passing through the Sulina.[32] The framers of the Treaty of Berlin thus recognized Romania's possession of the delta by granting the country a seat on the European Commission, yet they removed all jurisdiction in the delta that Romania might, as an independent state, otherwise possess. This grant of "complete independence" from Romanian authority forms a central issue throughout the remainder of this study.

No question regarding the Danube was of greater significance than demilitarization. The war had proven the inadequacy of neutrality guarantees and navigation ceased as the river became a front during the hostilities. The treaty decreed, therefore, that all fortresses be destroyed and all warships, save policing vessels of the individual riparian states and the European Commission, be prohibited from the Iron Gates to the delta. This provision was never extended north of the Gates, that is, into Habsburg or German territory.

The most difficult negotiations centered around the creation of a unified regulatory agency for the Middle Danube. No longer did the delegates consider the formation of a single agency to govern navigation on the entire course of the river, as they had in 1856. Instead, Article LV of the treaty attempted to revive the defunct River State Commission by authorizing "an European Commission, assisted by Delegates of the Riverain States, and placed in harmony with those which have been or may be issued for the portion of the river below Galatz."[33]

The project, proposed by a subcommission of delegates from Germany, Italy, and Austria-Hungary, called for a mixed-commission to supervise the area. This body, to be composed of representatives from Serbia, Romania, Bulgaria, and the Habsburg Empire, would have given the latter virtual control over that section of the river. Although decisions were to be settled by a majority of its members, Austria, through its position as presiding officer, held the deciding vote in the event of a tie.[34] By securing the vote of one of the others, Vienna could control the activities of the commission.[35] The plan also provided for the eventual dissolution of the European Commission. This proposal looked to the unification of the river's administration therefore, but only south of the Iron Gates. Although the plan upheld the general rules established at Vienna and Paris, it would have left the Habsburg Empire in a dominant position both strategically and economically on the river south of Germany.

The Austrian proposal conformed to the general Habsburg foreign policy, which viewed the development of Danubian trade as an economic necessity. Domination of the Danube, the region's principal artery, would strengthen Austria's economic position throughout the area served by the river. In addition, the Austrian Foreign Ministry could also hope for the newly independent states of the Balkans to develop a greater reliance on Vienna. This could, in turn, avert a similar movement by those nations toward greater dependence upon St. Petersburg.

The remaining members of the European Commission viewed the Austrian plan with disfavor. Led by the British, strong protests centered on the exclusion of any nonriparian country from the agency. By 1880, British shipping accounted for 49 percent of all commercial traffic in the delta.[36] Britain was wary therefore of any controls that might curtail trade. It not only adamantly refused to consent to the dissolution of the European Commission but also refused to yield to Austria any position of leadership on the river.

Opposition to the Austrian project led to a counter-proposal in May 1882 by the French Minister Barrere. Through the addition of a rotating nonriverine representative, this project sought to end Austrian preponderance on the new organization by removing the casting vote from Vienna's control. This was the only substantial difference between Barrere's plan and the Austrian project of 1878-79. The regulatory powers of the mixed-commission remained unchanged, as did the European Commission's complete authority over the maritime Danube.

Both the Austrian and Barrere plans would have given the Habsburg Empire a disproportionate influence over an area beyond its borders, that

is, the section of the river contained either exclusively in Romania or form-
ing the Romanian-Serbian and Romanian-Bulgarian borders. Therefore,
Romania rejected both proposals.

Romania's refusal to permit the creation of a commission for the Middle Danube marks the formal entrance of that country into the Danube
Question. No longer was the issue simply a matter of the great powers trying to stabilize an area of southeastern Europe that was under the jurisdiction, albeit nominal, of the Ottoman Empire. The Danube Question
now involved the operations of an international administration within the
sovereign territory of an independent nation.

A vassal state of the Ottoman Empire before 1878, Romania had held
little practical authority in the Danube Question. In 1856, the Danubian
Principalities of Moldavia and Wallachia, the name by which the country
was known before 1878, were granted representation on the River State
Commission, but that agency never came into being. Without a seat on the
European Commission, the only functioning body on the river, the Principalities had few options regarding the Danube and its delta. Not until
the Treaty of Berlin could the country actively pursue a Danube policy as
a fully independent state with membership on the European Commission.

From the beginning, Romania opposed any extension of foreign influence within its territory. Now, in the face of the two proposals for the
Middle Danube, Romania moved to block the creation of any regime
limited to the area south of Habsburg lands. Its opposition to both the
Austrian and Barrere proposals stemmed from numerous underlying causes.
First, the Congress of Berlin did not authorize the formation of a regulatory commission. If an agency for the Middle Danube was created, the
Romanian delegation to the Commission argued, it should hold no more
than supervisory powers. Second, Romania feared Austrian economic
penetration and domination of the region. Potential Habsburg hegemony
over the Middle Danube could deny Romania (as well as Serbia and Bulgaria) the opportunity to devise a protective customs policy similar to
that "applied against them by incomparably stronger European powers
and by their neighbors."[37] Third, the government in Bucharest did not
wish to see Austria dominate Romania's economic lifeline. The under-
developed Romanian railroad network could not handle increasing grain
exports, which had doubled between 1831 and 1877.[38] The lack of an alternative means of shipping its primary products exaggerated the importance

of the river for Romania. Fourth, Romanian public opinion, the nature of which will be examined in a later chapter, was already enraged by the loss of Bessarabia and opposed the formation of any agency in which Romania would play a secondary role. The Romanian delegation proposed, therefore, that the mixed-commission be composed of the three riparian nations and two rotating members of the European Commission; the agency would also hold only supervisory authority. Until the others agreed to this measure, Romania vowed "to use our veto and wait."[39] Negotiations thus continued through 1882 with little hope for a satisfactory resolution.

The failure of the Congress of Berlin to establish a unitary international body for the entire length of the Danube was the last serious attempt to reach a definitive settlement before World War I. Protestations of allegiance to international ideals clashed dramatically with strong evidence of particularism, exemplified by Austrian designs upon the Middle Danube (through the Act of Navigation of 1857 and the proposals of 1878-79) and growing Romanian opposition to expansion of the European Commission's prerogatives. Overriding concerns of foreign policy and growing nationalism blurred the issue of internationality. Whereas Vienna looked upon the river as a vehicle for economic expansion, Bucharest sought to prevent foreign economic penetration. Rising Romanian nationalism, buoyed by events culminating in independence and the proclamation of a kingdom in 1881, opposed the powers of the European Commission. The principal grievance against the agency was the provision granting it powers "in complete independence of territorial authorities." Curiously, this clause did not pertain to Russia after the latter was granted virtual control over the Kilia by the powers; the statute was directed solely at Romania.

In response to the control of the delta by the powers, Romanian political tracts began to speak of the river in national terms. Liberty of the Danube and defense of the homeland were seen as synonymous ideals. Peter Carp, one of the leaders of the Conservative Party, believed that "the Liberty of the Danube has for us a politically grave importance [and] attaches itself to the existence of our state."[40] In the years following the Congress of Berlin, the Commission increasingly became a symbol of apparent foreign domination. The Commission's privileges, from free access to telegraph facilities to the use of a separate flag and special armbands, became irritations magnified by nationalist zeal. Accordingly, the eventual destruction of the agency became a central focus of a foreign policy designed to limit outside influence in Romania.

At the same time, the European Commission represented, paradoxically, a barrier against possible Russian or Austrian expansion. The constant presence of the great powers would prevent either Vienna or St. Petersburg from establishing control over the mouth of the river. Despite the loss of port revenues, which went into the Commission's treasury rather than Romania's, the benefits of assured channel operations to a nation dependent upon agricultural exports were obvious. Thus, whereas Romania vocally opposed the regulatory nature of the Commission, it quietly approved the supervisory function.

Examples of Romanian praise for the Commission abound. Vasile Boerescu, the Foreign Minister, wrote that only under the European Commission could Romania "be assured that the Danube will be truly free, when this freedom shall be guaranteed and watched by all the great European powers."[41] King Carol I in 1894 applauded "the great service performed by the Commission for the work of commerce and navigation in the Danube delta," adding that Romania received "the advantages."[42] Dimitrie Sturdza, a leader of the National Liberal Party, called the European Commission "one of the greatest institutions created by the civilization of the nineteenth century."[43] Such words of praise were notably absent in 1883, however.

The London Conference of 1883 proved to be the last major diplomatic meeting before 1914 regarding the duties of the Commission. The congress was called to extend the life of the organization and to seek a solution to the impasse over the Middle Danube. Although Britain and France sought the admission of Romania to the conference with complete voting privileges, Germany objected on the grounds that only the original Paris signatory powers could renew the authority of the European Commission. This diplomatic technicality left Romania without full representation at the meeting. Angered by an invitation to attend in only an advisory capacity, Bucharest refused to send a delegation.

Romania's absence from the London Conference permitted the other members not only to prolong the agency's existence but also to settle that portion of the Berlin agenda left unresolved. With relatively little debate, the delegates adopted the Barrere plan for the Middle Danube. In addition, they approved a British proposal to extend the European Commission's dominion to Brăila. The distance from Galați to Brăila represented an extension of only 7 miles, but it was an area that, with proper physical maintenance, could accommodate maritime shipping. Britian was less successful in its attempt to make the European Commission a permanent organ; both Austria-Hungary and Russia refused to consent to such a move. The representatives denied Serbia admission as a voting member of the Commission and Russia received the authority to levy tolls on the section of the Kilia channel that passed through its territory. Although the European Commission continued to remain technically responsible for the Kilia, in fact, the administration fell to a joint Russian-Romanian Commission, dominated by the former.

Romania never accepted the decisions of this final prewar Danube conference, basing its opposition on its exclusion from the work of the meeting despite its status as a full voting member of the European Commission. Ioan Ghica, the country's minister to London, presented Romania's reply to the British invitation to attend the conference, stating that "the government of His Majesty [Carol I] cannot accept a situation whereby it would be accorded only a consultative vote and which therefore would not permit it to take part in the decisions of the Conference."[44] Instead, Romania held to a principle established in 1818 at the Congress of Aix-la-Chapelle that a decision reached by a conference was not binding upon a state that did not take part in the proceedings.[45] Romania reiterated its objections to any plan for the Middle Danube that included the presence of Austria-Hungary. The latter, in the eyes of the Romanian statesman Mihail Kogălniceanu, was "against the complete liberty of navigation on the Danube."[46] Carol I accepted the concept of "the strictest regulations. . . designed to assure the liberty of all ships [on the Middle Danube]," but these rules must "be applied by Romanian authorities."[47]

On the surface, Romania's position regarding the Danube appears self-contradictory. On the one hand, government officials praised the work of the European Commission. On the other hand, they attacked the special prerogatives of the agency and the attempts by the great powers to grant similar privileges to another commission for the Middle Danube. But, this apparent contradiction was based upon the pragmatic recognition that the country was powerless in dealing with a bureaucracy that was already entrenched and had the blessings of the powers.

Although no one source pinpoints Romania's overall Danube policy, a few generalizations may be made. Bucharest actively supported the concept of internationality of the river but believed that internationalization of the Danube should not violate the sovereign rights of the individual riparian state. Bucharest viewed the European Commission as an agency that, by its limitation to Romanian territory and its broad powers "in complete independence of territorial authorities," threatened Romanian sovereignty. Despite general praise for the activities of the Commission, the Romanian government continually sought to replace the agency with a single administrative unit for the entire river. The Romanian authorities responsible for matters of foreign policy also realized that they could do little in the face of the powers' support of the body. Thus, the immediate program became one in which Romania would oppose any extension of the agency's prerogatives. Concurrently, the government tried to remove foreign influence on the European Commission by supporting the nominations of Romanian nationals to key positions within the organization. Both in an attempt to build its import/export trade and to prove its reliability in aiding the smooth flow of commerce, Romania constructed or expanded port facilities on the fluvial Danube and kept that portion of the river under its own jurisdiction free of debris. Bucharest also subsidized the development of a native merchant fleet. Through these general policies, Romania hoped to demonstrate that the country could provide the necessary services for navigation. In the future, this program might convince the powers that the European Commission was not indispensable.

The decision of the powers in 1883 to expand the jurisdiction of the Commission to Brăila and create a mixed-commission for the Middle Danube thus directly clashed with Romania's policy for the river. Romania's only option was to refuse to recognize the work of the London Conference. Through this policy of intransigence, Romania used the discord that often plagued relations between the powers to its own advantage. In this case, the powers were lukewarm, at best, about the plans for the Middle Danube. Without Romania's tacit approval or the use of force to compel Romanian compliance, the great powers could not carry out the aims of the conference. Romania's policy of maintaining the *status quo* thus succeeded.

The failure to found an international regime north of Galați meant that for the next three decades a lack of cooperation among the riparian countries and the interested nonriverine powers marked the administration of the Danube. Instead of the unity sought by the Congress of Vienna and the Treaty of Paris, a plurality of regimes governed the river. North of Galați the river "remained subject to the territorial jurisdiction of the bordering states."[48] Each riparian nation was responsible for collecting customs, policing the river, administrating tariffs, and constructing ports. In reality, nine regimes (and thus nine sets of laws) governed the river: Germany; Austria-Hungary; Serbia; the Iron Gates (regulated exclusively by Austria-Hungary); Romania; Bulgaria; the nonfunctioning mixed-commission for the Middle Danube; the Kilia channel and the Otchakof mouth (controlled by Russia); and the European Commission.

Within the European Commission, the representatives exhibited a remarkable degree of harmony, considering the differences in the foreign policies of their respective nations. Meetings were held twice a year at regular intervals, dredging operations permitted an easy flow of river traffic, and trade increased in volume. Regulations were revised and duties were lowered as loans contracted by the Commission were repaid. Although attacks by Romanian polemicists continued, they had no practical effect. Romanian policymakers recognized the futility of trying to disband an organization that the great powers believed to be both in the best interests of trade and necessary to maintain the balance of power in southeastern Europe. Only open warfare between the European powers could present Romania with the opportunity to bring about the end of the European Commission.

CHAPTER III

WORLD WAR I AND THE DANUBE

The war years represented a unique epoch in the history of the European Commission, the relationship of Romania with the agency, and the river itself. It was an era that threatened the very concept of the Danube's internationality and left in its wake an administrative vacuum that Romania hoped to fill. This chapter will examine the Danube Question during the war and trace the events that led to the virtual destruction of the European Commission of the Danube as an effective organization. The lessons and effects of the war left an indelible imprint upon the postwar Danube Conference. Each conferee would work to ensure that the chaotic history of the war years would never be repeated. For the Western powers, this meant the internationalization of the entire river under their direction. The riparian nations, on the other hand, would attempt to gain greater control of the Danube in order to prevent the great powers from ever again dominating the river. Finally, the epoch marked the first time that Romania alone regulated the Lower Danube. The previous chapter, of necessity, focused upon the great powers because control of the river's international status lay clearly in their hands. By 1915 the center shifted to Romania. As the war increasingly diverted the interest of the powers from the delta, Romania obtained a greater share of responsibility for river operations within its own territory, a mastery it was reluctant to relinquish after the war.

The War and the Danube's International Status: 1914-1916

On the eve of the war, the representatives of the European Commission found themselves confronted by the usual questions of taxation and

28

service. As the number of ships using the Sulina increased, the problem
of revising tax rates and carrying out the agency's construction projects
persisted. The larger capacities of newer vessels forced the commissioners
to adjust the tax table periodically. In July 1914 this problem again sur-
faced.[1] No reference, however was made to the approaching conflagration
in Europe, save for the reaffirmation of the body's neutral status in the
event of war.[2]

By October 1914 and the convocation of the regularly scheduled
autumn session, the issues of taxation, rate structure, and regulation
were no longer important. What mattered was the question of the maritime Danube's·internationality in the face of a widening war and the
maintenance of river operations despite the crisis to shipping brought
about by the hostilities. The delegates had pledged to uphold the river's
internationality in the special July session; the task now was to put into
concrete form their promises to preserve the internationality of the Lower
Danube and to guarantee continued freedom of navigation in the delta.

Although the European Commission was composed of representatives
of the major belligerents, its members demonstrated a remarkable degree
of harmony. Only the French plenipotentiary, Guillemin, was absent
from the October meeting, the first since the war began. A conciliatory
atmosphere marked the sessions and no overt instances of hostility mar-
red their deliberations. The president of the meeting, the delegate from
Austria-Hungary, Alfons von der Felner, opened the conference by prais-
ing Romania's King Ferdinand for the neutrality of the host country.[3]
He then called upon the members of the European Commission to preserve "their traditional courtesy and co-operation."[4] This simple statement was the only allusion contained in the official records of the meeting
to the rift that split the various member-nations. It must be noted that
most of the accounts and minutes of the Commission's deliberations were
destroyed when the building which served as the organization's headquarters in Galați was shelled in October 1917.[5] Despite the destruction
of most of the agency's records, no evidence can be found to contradict
the impression that, considering the war's severity and the mounting passions on both sides, the bi-annual sessions of the European Commission
were conducted in any atmosphere other than one of cordiality. It was as
if the members lived and worked in a vacuum and turned their backs on
the war engulfing the continent. Friendships and professional courtesies

continued but such was not the case with the Commission's navigational
duties.

In summarizing the effect of the war's first weeks on the Commission
and its activities, the Secretary General of the organization, Francis Rey,
wrote that:

> The beginning of the war had as an immediate consequence the
> [almost complete] suspension of the Commission's activities [taxa-
> tion, unloading ships, etc.] although the theater of hostilities for the
> moment was far away from Romania.[6]

General mobilization

> throughout [many of] the countries of Europe, . . . led to a con-
> siderable reduction in the personnel of all services and the halting
> of navigation, resulting from the closing of the Straits, [thus] sup-
> pressing all receipts.[7]

Although the autumn session, as well as the next meeting held in the spring
of 1915, was conducted in a manner unchanged from prewar gatherings,
the business of the Commission was on paper only. Not only did the war
create hazards for maritime shipping, but also the entrance of the Ottoman
Empire into the conflict on the side of the Central Powers resulted in the
closure of the Straits to virtually all outside traffic. This action, in turn,
blocked the access of the principal Western shippers to the Lower Danube.
With ships unable to reach the agency's ports, the decisions taken by the
commissioners had little effect. Their *raison d'être* was reduced from the
responsibility for assisting the flow of commercial traffic to one of merely
paying salaries and dredging the now little-used Sulina channel. The closure
of the Straits effectively blockaded the Lower Danube; as a result, the
European Commission of the Danube became a body isolated from its
primary duty of aiding commerce.

Shipping statistics compiled by the Commission graphically illustrate
the almost complete cessation of activities in the delta. In December 1913
a total of 155 ships, representing the interests of 15 nations, used the
Sulina. An aggregate of 329,492 tons passed through the artery. In December 1914 only 8 ships used the channel: 4 Italian, 2 Romanian and

1 each of Greek and Russian registry. The total tonnage of only 5,034 represented a net decline of 98.5 percent from the previous December. On the surface, the difference between the yearly figures from 1913 and 1914 was not substantial. In 1913, 936 vessels totalling 1,742,907 tons passed through the Sulina, while during 1914 statistics show totals of 718 ships and 1,356,090 tons. But, only 85 ships, carrying 127,726 tons, used the Commission's facilities after July 31, 1914.[8]

By themselves even these figures are deceiving. The immediate prewar years had witnessed a decline in the use of the river due to the Balkan Wars and the Italian-Turkish conflict of 1911-1912. The Commission's treasury was already depleted by the eve of the war, therefore. By 1915 it was almost empty.

The Secretary General of the European Commission observed that as early as late 1914 the loss of revenue was sorely felt. He stated that:

> By abruptly suppressing receipts, the war gravely affected the finances of the commission, after sharply suffering during the successive wars in Eastern Europe. . . . Receipts in 1914 reached a level of 2,664,000 francs. . . while expenses were 2,290,000 francs.[9]

To maintain an equilibrium, the Commission was forced to contract a loan with the National Bank of Romania for 480,000 francs.[10] This proved to be a temporary measure; with the continued closure of the Straits, the difficulties could only grow worse.

The Commission and its members did not feel the impact of the financial crisis confronting them until the following year. In 1915 only 95 ships used the port facilities of the Lower Danube to load or discharge goods. The total tonnage of 102,647 represented a net loss of 1,640,230 tons compared to the aforementioned levels of 1913.[11] The deteriorating situation resulted in huge financial deficits that required emergency funding.

The burden of the Commission's operations, both physical and financial, increasingly fell upon Romania as the other members of the agency directed their resources toward their own war efforts. In addition, as the fighting intensified, most of the non-Romanian functionaries returned home. The only nonbelligerent state represented on the body after Italy entered in the war in 1915, Romania had to perform greater services to the

Commission. Without Romania "coming spontaneously to the aid of the Commission,"[12] the now limited dredging and maintenance operations would have ceased entirely.

In an extraordinary session of December 29, 1914, called to deal with the financial crisis, the Romanian government offered the Commission "monthly advances at five percent interest, placing at its [the agency's] disposal, on demand, the sums necessary to carry out its current affairs."[13] During the course of the next nine months (January through September) the total sum lent by the National Bank reached 960,000 francs.[14]

As mentioned in the previous chapter, this method of government-sponsored loans was the Commission's principal source of revenue, apart from general tax receipts. These loans were necessary in the event of unusual expenses due to the demands of additional construction or physical deterioration of the channels brought on by natural resources. Before 1914, the Commission rarely had reason to float such loans because its income was steady. This, in turn, made its credit sound. When needed, bonds were easy to float. Not until 1916 would this ability to contract foreign loans be tested.

The ease with which the Commission raised capital for its expenditures, even in a time of crisis such as 1914-1916, not only saved the work of the agency during the first years of the war, but also provides one of the basic arguments, presented by Romanian scholars,[15] that Romania was capable of administering the Lower Danube alone. River operations, they argue, actually paid for themselves through taxation, without requiring contributions from the member-states; on the rare occasions when additional funding was necessary, banks readily provided the capital. What such an argument overlooks, however, is the fact that most bonds were sold to Western banks. It is questionable whether a single guarantee by Romania would have provided a similar inducement to the financial community. On the whole, however, the Romanian argument has merit. Loans based upon the taxes received from commercial users of the Danube's maritime ports were attractive, and there were sufficient alternative sources of income, even through Romanian banks alone. Even during a period of crisis, such as the suspension of receipts in 1914, Romania was able to provide the necessary capital. Only during a prolonged state of emergency did Romanian funding prove insufficient.

By the spring of 1915, the Commission required contributions from the members in order to remain solvent. The delegates asked their respective

governments to contribute the sum of 400,000 francs each. Only Romania
was granted an exemption from such payments. Provided over the course
of two years on a flexible, revolving basis, these contributions enabled the
Commission, albeit barely, to continue paying salaries and renovating facilities (see Appendix 1). Despite this measure, however, expenses rapidly
depleted reserves in the treasury. In 1915 alone, expenditures exceeded
income by over 3,000,000 francs. The budget strained the available resources of the organization.

Administration	1,024,916 francs
Technical service	962,229
Special expenditures	395,663
Diverse expenses	332,292
Debt payments	328,767[16]

It was evident that loans and government grants were only stop-gap measures clearly insufficient for the agency's needs.

The spring 1915 session proved to be the last formal meeting of the full
European Commission for four years. The exigencies of the war in areas
of Europe far removed from the delta increasingly diverted the attention
of the individual representatives. More importantly, the closing of the
Straits and the resulting cessation of maritime shipping on the Danube
left the organization, if not without purpose and direction, at least in a
state of limbo. The members provided for a means of financing their limited activities through loans and grants from the Romanian government;
beyond that they could do very little. The problems that confronted the
plenipotentiaries proved beyond their capacity to solve. As the war continued, the Western members delegated greater individual responsibility to
Romania. As long as that nation remained neutral, a measure of stability
was maintained; it could act in the name of the entire Commission and continue the upkeep of the river. Through Romania, the interests and ideals
that formed the basis of the agency's *raison d'être* were preserved.

Romania Enters the War: August 1916—February 1918

Secretary General Rey's brief summary of Romania's entrance into the
war symbolized the abrupt change in the affairs of the Commission caused
by the Romanian action. On August 27, 1916

Romania entered the war on the side of the Allies. The delegates of the enemies [note: no longer co-members] Germany, Austria-Hungary, and Turkey, MM. Markeinecke, [von] der Felner, and Haider-Bey were asked to leave the country . . . as for those enemy employees not already mobilized by their home countries, they were interned in concentration camps [*camps des concentrations*].[17]

Just as the first two years of the war had shown that the Commission could function during a period of emergency, Romania's declaration of war demonstrated the fragility of the organization's international status; the Commission, which had stood since 1856, in effect, dissolved, being replaced by an agency of the Allies. "Enemy" functionaries were either expelled or imprisoned. In one stroke, Romania's move transformed the Lower Danube into a theater of wartime operations.

For the purposes of this study, the motives behind Romania's decision to enter the war are unimportant. Only those military aspects that affected the river and ultimately led to the signing of the Treaty of Bucharest in 1918 and the imposition of a new German-Austrian administration for the river are significant.

From the beginning, Romania's military venture was a failure. The timing of the initial attacks against Austrian positions in Transylvania was poor, the strategy ill-conceived, the troops unprepared, and supplies non-existent. Military supplies, for example, were sufficient for only six weeks. These ingredients combined to produce swift defeat. The concentration of the country's forces in the north did bring some initial victories, but these proved to be Pyrrhic successes because the strategy exposed the southern flank to a German-led counterattack from Bulgaria.

In early September 1916 German Field Marshal August von Mackensen seized the redoubt of Turtucaia, capturing 28,000 Romanian prisoners and creating a bridgehead across the Danube.[18] This operation opened a path to the Dobrudja and initiated a rapid chain of events that brought the evacuation of Silistria and the port of Constanța. The German invasion cut the Cernavoda-Constanța railroad line, forcing the Romanians to destroy an important bridge over the Danube to prevent it from falling into enemy hands. The German counter-offensive in the north, commanded by General Erich von Falkenhayn, formed a pincer with Mackensen's troops from Bulgaria and forced the Romanian government to flee Bucharest in late November. The city fell on December 6.[19] Brăila capitulated a month later. For all practical purposes, in less than five months Romania was defeated, although it formally remained in the war for another year.

In early 1917 the fighting stabilized along a front running from Moldavia to the Lower Danube east of Brăila. The military advance of the Central Powers was halted in large part by the arrival of the long-awaited Russian "Army of the Danube" in mid-December as well as by the siphoning away of Mackensen's crack troops for use on other fronts.[20] For the Central Powers, the Romanian entrance into the war, brought about by leaders Falkenhayn contemptuously dismissed as being "little capable of judging [the real situation] themselves,"[21] was but a minor irritant. To only a slight degree did the Romanian theater prove to be the thorn in the German rear that would relieve pressure on other, beleaguered Allied fronts. Instead, Romania's defeat afforded the Central Powers the opportunity to use the country as a source of badly needed supplies and foodstuffs. This allowed Germany, in fact, to continue the war until 1918.[22] It also opened more of the Danube to their unobstructed military use and shortened vital supply lines to Bulgaria and the Ottoman Empire; only the delta arteries remained outside German control. The Allies continued to hold the area, but the formal authority of the European Commission had disappeared.

For the Allied members of the Commission who stayed in Romania after August 1916 (John Baldwin, Commander Leoni, P. de Kartamyshew, and Duiliu Zamfirescu) the events unfolded quickly. On August 19, Romania's Foreign Ministry instructed Zamfirescu to request that the other delegates grant him the power to place all Commission materials and facilities in Galați and Sulina at the disposal of the Romanian High Command upon demand.[23] On September 21, two weeks after the capitulation of Turtucaia, most Commission functions fell to the Romanian military leadership, headed by the Minister of War, Vintilă Brătianu.[24] Russia, Italy, and Britain had all but conceded this change in authority in a private meeting of August 29, the same day as the original Romanian request.[25] For the first time since the founding of the European Commission, the organization ceased operations in all but name. Although the Commission continued to exist and decisions were made by its remaining delegates in its name (that is, the Allies) and the internationality of the river, in reality, its duties were controlled by military authorities, either Romanian, Russian, or German, for the duration of the war. The Commission retained only the responsibility for paying its employees. With the fate of the European Commission, as well as the entire maritime portion of the river, in the hands of the military, events on the battlefield would dictate the future.

After the fall of Turtucaia, the Commission formulated contingency plans for moving to the Russian city of Odessa. On October 27, Zamfirescu requested that the Foreign Ministry provide ships to transport records and personnel of the organization either to Russia or to Moldavia, citing the growing "urgency" of the situation in Galaţi due to the German advance in the Dobrudja.[26] Five days later Bucharest informed the Romanian minister to St. Petersburg, C. Diamondy, of the possible move.[27] He was also apprised of the military situation in Romania, which was contributing to "talk of panic" among the population between Brăila and the Black Sea.[28] On December 21, the Italian delegation in Galaţi informed Romanian Foreign Minister Emanoil Porumbaru that the "noose" was tightening around the city.[29] With the fall of Brăila and Galaţi apparently only a matter of days away, on December 22, 1916, the remaining members of the European Commission either boarded the yacht "Carol I" bound for Odessa or retreated to parts of Moldavia more removed from the front.[30] This dispersal included all nonessential employees and their families; they took along as many records as possible and all remaining funds in the organization's accounts, a total of 100,000 francs, as well as 500,000 lei from banks in the city.[31] Baldwin returned to Great Britain, and the Italian legation went to Jassy, the new site of the Romanian government after it fled Bucharest. Thus, the center of the European Commission no longer could be found in Galaţi; instead, the official headquarters became the "Carol I", anchored in Odessa harbor.

As the front stabilized west of Galaţi, defense of the city, as well as the entire delta, fell to a joint Romanian-Russian command established in the port of Sulina, located at the junction of the Black Sea and the Sulina channel. With the aid of a small contingent of technical personnel left behind by the European Commission, a group essential in running the agency's equipment, the military authorities succeeded in keeping the arms of the river open; this, in turn, provided a vital access for supplies sent to and from the Moldavian front. Russian troops occupied the Commission's facilities. Only the agency's properties in Sulina remained under direct Romanian jurisdiction, through the office of the Captain of the Port, headed by Eugene Botez.[32] All agency personnel, although ostensibly responsible to the central organization in Odessa, were paid by Romanian military authorities and were under the direct supervision of Romania's Engineer-resident, Magnussen.[33]

Friction quickly arose between the Russian and Romanian military contingents over strategy in the delta, as well as the program needed to keep the channels open. As they argued, conditions along the Sulina progressively deteriorated. By February 1917 the artery had fallen to a depth of only 19 feet. Further silting of the channel threatened the delivery of badly needed supplies to the Romanian army. Equally important, Romania feared Russian machinations in the delta, especially agitation among the country's Lipovenian population, a group with a Russian ancestry.[34] Behind Romania's mistrust of its ally was the precedent of Russian actions during the 1877-1878 war with the Ottoman Empire; in that conflict Russia promised, in return for permission for Russian troops to pass through Romanian territory, that St. Petersburg would not seize any Romanian lands. But, at the Congress of Berlin, Russia retook southern Bessarabia. A similar fear that Russia might seek other gains in the future at Romanian expense again arose within the governing circles in Jassy. Thus, the attempts by the government to limit Russian activities in the delta to ones of military necessity only reflected those fears.

Romania's concern was not limited to possible Russian designs in the delta; by 1917 the condition of the Sulina channel demanded prompt attention. In a communique in March to Zamfirescu, Vintilă Brătianu stressed the urgency of the situation and demanded that immediate steps be taken to dredge the passageway.[35] But, the Minister of War wanted the measures carried out under the auspices of the European Commission, citing the delicacy of the matter, a veiled reference to the necessity of working separately from the Russians.[36] Since the flight of the European Commission, Russia had appropriated the dominant position in the delta by virtue of its military presence. The Russian army command began to take a greater share of responsibility for decisions involving defense of the river and priority repairs to the delta's channels. Since Romania had received a mandate in 1916 to represent all of Europe's concerns in the area, Jassy viewed Russian actions in the region as interference and an infringement detrimental to the best interests of Romania and its allies.[37] Brătianu also indicated that it would be to Romania's best advantage if strictly native personnel were used to perform the work, rather than allowing the Russians to continue to control river operations. Brătianu thus sought to revive interest in the European Commission as a buffer against any possible designs by Russia in the region.

The situation did not change. By April, the depth of the channels had fallen another two feet. Although this worried the policymakers in Jassy, the Russian problem caused even greater concern. Romanian apprehensions increased with reports that the Russians, commanded by Admiral Fabrizki, were using 200 Romanian deserters as employees in the delta, although the motive for this was unclear.[38] Russia also began to finance a greater share of the desperately needed dredging operations and payment of salaries, thereby taking on the primary duties of the European Commission. Furthermore, St. Petersburg had been engaged, since March, in negotiations aimed at leasing all Commission property, including the fleet. As for Brătianu's hope to use the Commission as a bulwark against the Russians, the observations of Zamfirescu and the Sulina command quickly dispelled any illusions. The organization no longer had the necessary funds for either work projects or salaries;[39] to raise such capital required the negotiation of the lease.

A note sent to Prime Minister Ioan I. C. Brătianu in May underscored Zamfirescu's anxiety over Russian activities. According to Zamfirescu, Russia would be Romania's greatest opponent in any future Danube negotiations. As evidence, he cited the examples of Bessarabia in 1878 and the 1883 usurpation of the responsibility for the Kilia.[40] St. Petersburg, he believed, had clear designs in the area, exemplified by its current actions. These fears notwithstanding, Zamfirescu, along with the other members of the European Commission with whom he was in contact, supported the accord with Russia regarding the lease of the organization's materials. Conditions in the delta demanded attention that only Russia appeared capable of providing.

Under the terms of the agreement, Russia rented the Commission's properties for a fixed sum and agreed to provide materials necessary for the river's upkeep. The Commission, in turn, promised to pay all salaries.[41] In summarizing the effect of this pact, Captain Botez observed that the European Commission of the Danube was, "in fact, abolished because of complete dislocation, [and] no longer having material or personnel."[42] Botez believed that the future of the agency and the entire delta now belonged to Russia, as the latter would enter any peace negotiations in full

control of the area. The only question remaining, Botez stated, was the
survival of Russia itself in the face of the deteriorating internal situation
brought on by the war and the revolution of February 1917. If Russia
emerged from the war as a victorious ally, it would be in a commanding
position to dictate future terms for the Lower Danube.[43]

On July 14, 1917, Zamfirescu signed the treaty with Russia "in the
name of Italy, Britain, and France." Russia leased all ships and facilities
at 16½ percent of value (approximately 25,000,000 francs).[44] Despite his
apprehensions about his Russian partners, Zamfirescu had little choice but
to defend the pact. The accord, he argued, referred only to dredging activities and ships, not Romanian territory; the latter was beyond Zamfirescu's jurisdiction and the Commission's competency. He permitted the
Russians to undertake work where military needs were present because
"it would be extraordinary not to accord Russia this right when we are
allies."[45] Responsibility for directing operations remained with the Romanian Engineer-resident, Magnussen, who was the highest-ranking functionary of the European Commission still in the delta. It was necessary to
add Russian personnel, but this was essential if the work was to be accomplished.[46]

Romanian fears that the July accord would lead to Russian control
of the delta were never well-founded. In fact, the overall effects of the
lease were minimal. Few payments exchanged hands and any possible Russian intentions aimed at expanding their influence in the region, even if
considered, had no chance to succeed. Events in Russia and Romania
were proceeding too fast.

In early October 1917 German artillery heavily shelled Galați. The
hotel that served as the headquarters of the European Commission burned
on October 10 with the loss of virtually the entire library and archives.
The destruction of the building symbolically reflected the military situation in Romania; for both the European Commission and Romania everything appeared hopeless.

In spite of the fact that Romania repulsed the German summer offen-
sive of 1917, the nation could no longer continue fighting. The Russian
Revolution of November 1917, and Russian withdrawal from the war,
left Romania without an ally in the east and created a new enemy, Bolshevism, which loomed as large a threat as Germany. The army was exhausted physically and materially and there were devastating shortages

throughout Moldavia. Thus, on December 10, Romania concluded a provisional armistice with the Central Powers. On February 11, 1918, the Brătianu cabinet, which had sought the declaration of war in 1916, gave way to a government headed by General Averescu, the country's ablest field commander. Although Romania hoped this move might enable the nation to gain additional time for aid to arrive from the West, Field Marshal von Mackensen would brook no delays. On March 18, Romania and the Central Powers signed a preliminary treaty at Buftea, a small village north of Bucharest. The formal surrender by the new Prime Minsiter, Alexander Marghiloman, came two months later, on May 7, with the Treaty of Bucharest, a pact which ended the fighting in Romania.[48]

Since the Russian Revolution of November 1917, Romania had been solely responsible for the maritime Danube; now its capitulation left the river entirely under the control of the Central Powers. Although this situation was short-lived, it meant that, for the first time since 1856, the Danube was subject to the sole jurisdiction of the riparian states, save for the limited voice of the Ottoman Empire. In fact, the Danube from February to November 1918 was an artery under the complete domination of the German and Austro-Hungarian Empires.

Under German and Austrian Domination

. The terms of the Treaty of Bucharest were harsh. Among its provisions, Bulgaria received the southern Dobrudja, and the rest of the region became a protectorate of the Central Powers. The treaty placed all Romanian food exports under the direction of a joint German-Austro-Hungarian commission, which was responsible for sales and prices. Romanian oil production was to be controlled by the German *Öllandereien-Pacht-Gesellschaft m.b.H.* for a period of thirty years.[49] Germany and Austria thus took stewardship of Romania's economy.

The treaty granted the Central Powers hegemony over the maritime Danube. Under Articles XXIV-XXVI, Romania agreed to sign, "together with Germany, Austria-Hungary, Bulgaria, and Turkey, a new act of navigation on the Danube."[50] The treaty set no date for the commencement of these negotiations, which were to be held in Munich. Until the formalization of a new body of laws, the Act of Navigation of 1857 (see chapter 2) would be applied to the Romanian sector of the river. From Brăila to the sea, a new "Commission of the Mouth of the Danube" composed of riparian delegates, as well as a representative from the Ottoman Empire, would form the sole administration for the river. Its competence would cover all branches of the waterway. Romania pledged to guarantee the contracting parties free lines of communication along the length of the Danube within its territory. It also promised to safeguard freedom of navigation in its ports. Taxes could be levied strictly on the basis of use, that is, no discriminatory duties against the ships of the Central Powers could be imposed. All previous rights granted to Austria-Hungary in the region of the Iron Gates, through the Treaty of London of 1871 and the Congress of Berlin, remained in effect. No agreement could be made with a nonmember (hence nonriparian) without the consent of a majority of the other representatives.[51] These general provisions pertained to all members of the new organization. Romania and the individual states of the Central Powers then signed separate agreements.[52]

These pacts included special privileges for Austria, Hungary, and Germany to construct facilities along the river; they were to be permitted the right to build and use rail lines for a period of thirty years. After ratification of the Treaty of Bucharest, two delegates, representing Germany and Romania, would meet with a neutral plenipotentiary in Bucharest to execute the provisions of the accord.[53] On July 4, 1918, the Romanian legislature in Jassy accepted the treaty by a unanimous 86-0 vote.[54] Thus, the Danube fell under the direct control of the dominant riparian states, Germany and Austria-Hungary, for the remainder of the war.

In April 1918, after the preliminary peace at Buftea, the Captain of the Port of Sulina before 1916, Franjo Vilfan, returned to his former residence at the mouth of the river. Now the representative of Austria in the delta and the chief agent of the Central Powers, Vilfan immediately demanded that the Romanian engineers transfer all material to his disposition in order to reorganize navigation between Sulina and Brăila, the latter officially the terminus of the new maritime organization.[55] As for any intransigence on the part of Romania or the European Commission, Vilfan warned that Vienna would tolerate no interference or delays. His country would, in such cases, not hesitate to use force to guarantee compliance with his orders.[56] Zamfirescu cautioned Vilfan to refrain from any arbitrary acts against the European Commission. He reminded the Austrian delegate that the decrees of that body comprised part of the "public law of Europe," and those statutes were recognized by all nations.[57]

There was little substance to Zamfirescu's admonitions. He was warning the Central Powers not to take actions similar to those that Romania and its allies had taken against German, Austrian, and Turkish members of the Commission. Neither Romania nor the Western Allies could oppose Vilfan; he held the military trump. Thus, the new Romanian Foreign Minister, C. C. Arion, had no choice but to comply with Vilfan's demands. Arion replaced Zamfirescu with M. Burghele and instructed Admiral Bălescu to conform immediately with the new order.[58]

On June 27, the first meeting of Austrian, German, and Romanian delegates to establish new rules of navigation for the use of the Danube took place in Bucharest. Unrealistically, Romania maintained a strictly legalistic attitude throughout the sessions, in sharp contrast to the previous three months of compliance. Constantly referring to past precedent, as if the European Commission was still a viable entity, the Romanian representative, Burghele, argued that the three nations could not take any action as an executive committee without the unanimous consent of all members of the European Commission, that is, Britain, France, Russia, and Italy.[59] Romania lodged an official protest against the actions of the Central Powers toward the Russian delegate, de Kartamyshew, who had fled the new Bolshevik regime in Russia only to be arrested by the Central Powers.[60] The imprisonment of de Kartamyshew, Burghele asserted, violated the internationally recognized position of a Commission member. Despite these legalistic pretensions by Burghele and Arion, the outcome of the June meeting was preordained. Germany and Austria intended to act as executive agents, in much the same manner as the Allies had acted in 1916, until the creation of the Commission of the Mouth of the Danube. A report by the German representative, Anderheiden, reconfirmed this intention a month later;[61] for the present, Germany and Austria decided not to alter the basic codes of the European Commission but rather only to eliminate the roles and privileges of the Allies, thereby gaining themselves exclusive power.

During the eight months following the preliminary peace at Buftea, therefore

> the Central Powers made certain that the river was in a good state of navigation, to assure lines of communication with the Ottoman Empire and with the Caucusus from which they were receiving indispensable materials.[62]

For the moment the administrative apparatus of the old European Commission, with minor alterations in personnel and authority, was sufficient for the new masters of the Danube. Plans were already being formulated to implement the provisions of the Treaty of Bucharest; however, for the present, requisitions and the war effort took precedence. The Germans and Habsburg governments furnished their agents with the sums necessary for the continuation of services, and their military authorities provided the materials needed to clear the channels.[63] The Danube became a German river and a vital economic artery for continuing the war effort. Only the collapse of the Central Powers in October/November 1918 prevented the formal installation of the new regime.

Thus, World War I represented a glorious and inglorious period for the European Commission of the Danube. For Romania, despite pretensions to the contrary, after 1916 it was a catastrophic era. The first two years of hostilities had shown that an international institution could indeed function during a time of crisis. In this instance, the members of the European Commission recognized the importance of preserving the Danube's internationality. Despite differences that separated their nations, they continued to meet and work together during the war's first years. The willingness of all parties to act as a unit was admirable, even though their efforts were in practical terms futile. Employees were paid and the Sulina channel was maintained at a sufficient operating depth, although at great cost and financial loss. The plenipotentiaries recognized the tenuous threads that joined them together and thus granted Romania the principal position among them, a post that it upheld admirably. The latter guaranteed the agency enough revenue to maintain limited operations and acted as a cohesive, stabilizing force among the members. Yet, in spite of these positive aspects, everything ultimately failed.

In the final analysis, the internationality of the Danube proved to be too fragile. Romania's entrance into the war and its rapid defeat brought dramatic change to the Lower Danube. Romania's ill-advised actions and Bucharest's expulsion of the representatives of the Central Powers to the agency placed the European Commission's status of neutrality in jeopardy. Just as Romania was defeated, so too was the Commission, being forced to flee Galați for the safety of Russia. By 1917 the organization existed in name only. As the only remaining member of the Commission present in the delta in 1918, Romania had no recourse but to watch the Central Powers make greater military use of the river. The Treaty of

Bucharest enabled Germany and Austria to take complete control and attempt to create a new regime for the waterway. In the deliberations that followed, Romania's protestations regarding the actions of the Central Powers were only a minor irritation to the new masters of the Danube. It is of little consequence that the "Commission of the Mouth of the Danube" never formally came into existence; the war shook the foundations of the European Commission. As the German and Austrian troops in the delta retreated, they left an administrative vacuum in their wake that the old European Commission seemed incapable of filling. As Europe began to recreate a semblance of order, efforts had to be made to do the same for the Danube. The disorder appeared to present Romania with an excellent opportunity to take firm control over commercial activities in the delta; but, appearances would prove to be deceiving.

CHAPTER IV

THE DANUBE AND POSTWAR ROMANIA

Before turning to the events surrounding the Danube Question after World War I, it is first necessary to pause and reflect upon a factor long ignored in considering the issue—the political and economic situation in Romania between 1918 and 1921. It is the contention of this study that the time seemed ideal for replacing the European Commission with a single international regime for the entire river. With the defeat of Germany, Austria-Hungary, and the Ottoman Empire, and the isolation of Russia after the Bolshevik Revolution, the importance of the agency as a means of maintaining the balance of power was no longer a viable argument. Romania could now devote full attention to the long-standing policy of removing the organization's authority from Romanian territory. At the same time, however, the internal situation in Romania was sufficiently grave to place the entire matter of the Danube, including the issue of the European Commission, in a position of secondary importance.

In the wake of the war, Romania's leaders were confronted by enormous problems both domestic and external in nature. The foreign policy objectives of unification demanded a forceful presentation of Romania's claims at Versailles. Concurrently, the war aggravated an already serious internal situation, which by 1919 contributed to inflation, food shortages, and land hunger. The war also overturned the country's political structure, leaving Romania without steady leadership. These three factors, foreign, political, and economic, distracted the nation's attention.

A paradoxical situation emerged, therefore, in which the Romanian government outwardly sought the end of the Commission but within diplomatic circles could not press the issue due to other weighty factors.

Whereas in 1919 foreign policy considerations preoccupied the country, by 1920 the success in external affairs, both at Versailles and in the war against Hungary in 1919, combined with increasing internal turmoil to lessen the importance of the Danube Question. The more vital foreign policy objectives, notably the acquisitions of Transylvania, Bessarabia, and Bukovina, had already been won. These successes contributed to a general feeling of satiation within Romanian govenmental circles. Instead of concentrating on the few remaining diplomatic issues, such as the Danube Question, the government turned to the more immediate problems facing the nation: land reform, a monetary crisis, an unstable political situation, and economic dislocation. These issues, it was felt, were of greater importance to the future of the state than was the matter of the Danube.[1] The latter now became the concern of only the Foreign Ministry, which was the single organ of the Romanian government relatively untouched by political upheaval within the country. Whereas before the war all branches of the government took an active interest in the Danube Question, other problems now preoccupied Parliament and the prime ministers. In simplest terms, more important issues than the existence of the European Commission troubled the nation. As will be seen in chapter eight, Bucharest devoted little attention to the Question before and during the Danube Conference, a fact that belies the traditional view that the delegation had the enthusiastic support of the entire Romanian government. In truth, the matter created hardly a ripple within the ruling circles of the capital. Thus, it is essential to survey briefly the immediate postwar situation in order to place the negotiations in Paris within the framework of the other issues facing the country. Although these events may, at times, appear to have little relationship to the Danube Question, their impact upon the issue was enormous. The intensity of the problems facing Romania lessened the importance of the Danube issue and in that light the Conference must be examined.

Of all the states in Eastern Europe, Romania emerged from the postwar conferences with the greatest gains. Doubling in size from 130,177 square kilometers in 1913 to 295,049 in 1920,[2] Romania obtained all it sought at Versailles. If an Irredentism was present on a large scale in Romania before the war, it certainly was assuaged, if not satiated, by the country's successes after the armistice.[3] Furthermore, Romania's hated neighbors, primarily Hungary, which lost approximately 40 percent of its territory to Romania, and the Soviet Union, from which Romania regained Bessarabia, were in a weakened state and in little position to contest Romania's acquisitions. Despite these gains, however, hostile countries still bordered Romania on three sides: Russia, Bulgaria, and Hungary. To counter these potential adversaries, Bucharest could play two diplomatic trump cards by raising fears among its allies of both Russian Bolshevism and a resurgent Hungary led by a restored Habsburg monarchy. The West's alarm over the former enabled Romania to gain significant victories at Versailles and force the recognition of the union with Bessarabia in 1920; concern over the Hungarian situation led to the formation of the Little Entente with Czechoslovakia and Yugoslavia in 1920-21. Negotiations with Belgrade and Prague, which took place concurrently with the Danube Conference received principal attention within the Foreign Ministry.

Romania presented itself as a bulwark against communism and Habsburg counter-revolution. The danger of *revanchism* remained nevertheless. To combat this threat, the country needed the assurance of great power interest and support. Despite actions by its wartime allies that it considered to be against rightful Romanian claims, it could not afford to alienate its western support. In that regard, it is interesting to note that the continuation of the European Commission meant physical great power presence in the delta. This could be viewed as added insurance should Romania find itself at war, especially with the Soviet Union with whom it had been skirmishing over possession of Bessarabia since early 1918.

These problems, however, loomed as only potential ones. Although far from ideal, in 1920, Romania's geographic and diplomatic positions were sufficiently advantageous to create a general feeling of satisfaction among its citizens. The country had achieved the territorial objectives sought in 1916 when it entered the war, and the annexation of Bessarabia was an added windfall. Issues such as the Danube Conference and the Romanian share of war reparations, finally set at 1 percent by the Spa Conference of 1920, remained open, but these suddenly held a lesser importance in light of Romania's overall diplomatic situation. This picture of relative external security and success in obtaining its major objectives contrasted markedly with the country's internal situation and contributed to an exaggerated feeling of self-importance within the country.

The euphoria generated by Romania's diplomatic victories at Versailles colored its self-perception. An illusion of power, based, in large measure, on territorial gains resulting from the war, blinded the country to many of its internal problems and the need for inter-Balkan cooperation. On the one hand, Romania sought recognition as a great power in European affairs. On the other hand, it turned inward and economically isolated itself from the rest of the continent. The population viewed the war as a Romanian victory, a vindication of the country's rights and salvation from the foreign "yoke."[4] Victory exaggerated this myopia and heightened nationalist sentiment. By 1922, the policy of the National Liberal Party, "By Ourselves Alone," not only would dominate the nation's economic and political policies, but would also symbolize, in a sense, Romania's general position in Europe.[5] Professor I. N. Angelescu, one of the country's leading economic theorists, exemplified this attitude by stating that:

> Those who know the economic forces of Romania about the time of the war, understand that we are not a country destined to be subservient to a constellation of powers which dominate the world's political economy.[6]

Nationalist histories, best characterized by the works of the politician and prolific historian, Nicolae Iorga, flourished and schools preached chauvinistic, xenophobic ideals.

Of course, Romania was not unique in this regard. Similar attitudes helped contribute to the appeal of radical-right movements throughout Europe during the interwar years. Rather, the atmosphere created an attitude within the country that precluded all chances for regional cooperation and fostered a mood that was wary of anything non-Romanian. Any policy not conforming to Romanian desires was viewed as an attack upon the foundations of the state itself. The idea arose that the small state was being prevented by the powerful Western nations from attaining its rightful place in the sun.[7] Problems were often seen as stemming from outside forces rather than being inherent in the nation itself. Leaders of Romanian society argued that Romania alone should be the captain of its own destiny. Yet, as the nation turned inward by the 1920s in an attempt to deal with its internal difficulties, results failed to live up to expectations.

The internal problems confronting Romania may be divided into four major categories: the land reform question, the incorporation of new territories with the resulting introduction of a large non-Romanian population, political turmoil, and serious economic dislocation. Each problem was of vital concern to the future of the nation, just as similar questions were important to the other European states. In Romania, the difficulties were not solved, partly due to their scope and the lack of available resources (primarily financial) and to their neglect by the government. The latter "failed to evaluate realistically the staggering difficulty of modernizing their backward economy and truly integrating a society rent by long historical separations, class divisions, and ethnic tensions."[8] After the war, Romanian leaders held great faith in the nation's economic potential. Their measures failed, however, to tap and harness the resources, were short-sighted, and were often counterproductive. By 1922, the problems were in most cases as persistent as they had been five years earlier. Beset by internal matters, Romania focused its attention on problems that remained unresolved. Nowhere was this internal confusion more apparent than in the postwar political structure.

During the period 1918-1922 Romania's political situation lacked stability. Governments continually rose and fell, and offices constantly changed hands. All semblance of order ceased to exist (see Appendix 2). Not until January 1922, with the ascendancy of the National Liberals (who ruled until 1928), did one political faction obtain firm control over the reins of government.

The geographical unification of Romania in 1918-1920 meant more than the mere incorporation of new lands and the inclusion of a large minority population, which grew to be approximately 28 percent of the country's overall population, according to the census of 1930.[9] Within the Romanian community itself, this act led to the introduction of new political parties composed of functionaries schooled in different traditions. This, in turn, fomented a clash between the new political factions, foremost among these being the National Peasantists, based in Transylvania, and the prewar National Liberal Party.[10] This conflict was exacerbated by the fact that many Transylvanian Romanians viewed their fellow nationals in the Regat as "orientals." Officials from Moldavia and Wallachia, appointed by Bucharest, took over local offices and created an antagonism that reached its nadir in 1922 with the refusal of many Transylvanian politicians to attend the coronation of the King in Alba Iulia. The political problems in Romania went far beyond mere regional friction however, and the nation foundered in a state of political chaos caused by governmental instability.

Prior to 1916, there were essentially two political parties in the country: the Conservatives and the National Liberals. The prewar position of the former, favoring the Central Powers (and honoring the Secret Treaty of 1883 with Austria) and their signature of the ignominious Treaty of Bucharest, effectively destroyed them as a viable entity in Romania. A small core of Conservatives remained, led by Alexander Marghiloman, but their power base was clearly minimal. Another Conservative splinter group, headed by Take Ionescu, did not prove to be a sufficient counter-weight to the National Liberals. Thus, the latter appeared to hold an advantageous position due to the vacuum left by the Conservative Party and the identification of the Liberals with victory in the war and the resulting territorial gains. They failed to hold their incumbency, however, and foundered until 1922. The inability of the Liberals to consolidate this favorable position derived from numerous factors, including general dissatisfaction within the country over internal problems and the creation of new political parties. This led to a situation in which cabinets constantly reshuffled in a futile attempt to obtain new alignments and some measure of stability. Political chaos, in turn, had consequences for the pursuit of the Danube Question; internal confusion in the state precluded continuity save within the bureaucratic apparatus of the Foreign Ministry.

The upheaval began in 1919 with the surprising outcome of the November elections, conceded by many to be the only free elections held in Romania during the interwar years.[11] Instead of maintaining their post-war dominance, the National Liberals obtained only 22 percent of the vote and 103 out of a possible 568 seats in the Chamber, losing to the National Peasantists of Iuliu Maniu and Alexander Vaida-Voievod.[12] The following year, the Parliamentary structure radically changed again with the electoral success of the People's Party (224 out of 369 seats); the Liberals fell to a representation of only 9 (see Appendix 3).[13] Characterized by corruption and ballot-stuffing, elections changed little in practical terms, however, despite these wide fluctuations in results. Effective rule stemmed from internal arrangements and manipulation. Thus, although the elections of 1919 did produce a government led by Vaida-Voievod, a cabinet headed by General Averescu soon replaced it; King Ferdinand disliked Vaida and actively sought his dismissal. Averescu remained head of the Council of Ministers until December 1921. In spite of his comparatively long tenure in office, Averescu could not devise solutions for the country's problems. Instead, the measures taken, most notably the land reform of 1921, were merely political in scope and failed, therefore, to address the real economic afflictions.

Romania's political instability simply reflected the nation's economic difficulties, which became all-pervasive and which the government never fully confronted. The elections mirrored the unrest and dissatisfaction of the population. The government represented only itself with no practical accountability and little success.

For the Romanian government, no issue was of greater significance at the end of the war than that of land reform. The threat of Bolshevism, used so shrewdly as a diplomatic weapon at Versailles, was, at the same time, a volatile domestic problem. By 1917, close contacts along the Moldavian front with Bolshevik elements in the Russian army, and the military debacle that saw over one-half of the country occupied by foreign troops, forced Romanian authorities to awaken from their inertia on the land question. "The state of mind in the country in 1917," according to Professor N. Basilescu, was one of "disbelief in the government, disbelief in the speeches in the Parliament, disbelief in the constituted authority. . . . Today, as yesterday, revolution appears to the Rumanian peasant the only possible means for him to resolve the great case between him and the proprietors of the estates."[14] In order to stem the tide of discontent that threatened the state, in April 1917, King Ferdinand pledged to make changes and to give the peasantry land and the vote "without delay." He reaffirmed this promise on November 12, 1918, and, a month later, signed a law granting the peasants the right to own property, along with a redistribution of land based on need.[15] The Averescu government promulgated a second reform in July 1921, bringing a total expropriation of 6,000,000 hectares. Of this amount, 3,900,000 hectares were distributed to 1,393,000 peasants.[16] Although these measures succeeded in halting the spread of Bolshevism and revolution, the land reforms were economic failures. They had been formulated not with the positive goal of improving the bleak economic situation, but rather were enacted with the negative intention of preserving the old system with minimal loss. Although the reforms altered the land distribution pattern in the countryside, the power structure remained the same. The peasants, comprising the overwhelming majority of the population (72.3 percent according to the 1930 census),[17] were effectively shut off from the centers of power, their needs and views ignored. The reforms were hastily enacted without reaping any positive benefit save the prevention of revolution. Nor were the peasants entirely satisfied; the expected economic gains did not materialize. Furthermore, the state's attention turned to industry once the reforms were made. In his study of the laws, David Mitrany cites a peasant's evaluation of his government's actions as indicative of general dissatisfaction: "He's [the government] pushed the bowl nearer, but he's given me a shorter spoon."[18] The errors of the reforms serve as but one example of the government's failures in the economic sphere; half-measures could not bring satisfactory results. The land reforms failed to address the problem directly and the mistakes had repercussions for the rest of the economy.

Losses resulting from the war created upheaval throughout the economy. The cost in monetary terms was staggering for a nation with a backward economic structure, a problem compounded by the Soviet seizure of Romania's gold reserves sent to Russia during the war for protection. By 1921 the public debt reached 20,000,000 lei and an import/export imbalance in cereals totalled 302,799 tons as the country, an agricultural nation, was actually forced to import grains.[19] Bread shortages plagued the state throughout the winter of 1919. The harvest that year attained only 50 percent of prewar levels partly due to the dislocation created by casualties during the war of nearly 1,000,000 (approximately 20 percent of the country's active work force). Industrial production likewise fell between 15 and 50 percent, depending upon the industry in question.[20] Due to both physical destruction and German (and later Allied) requisitions, transportation was in a shambles and impeded the delivery of foodstuffs to many areas of the country.

Furthermore, inflation during the war rose 450 percent, and the incorporation of new territories meant the introduction into the Romanian economy of two new currencies: the Austro-Hungarian corona and the Russian ruble. This left the country with three forms of money. By 1921, compared to 1914 levels, prices had risen 922.2 percent for beef, 1,032 percent for pork, 2,000 percent for sugar, and 797 percent for milk, among others, according to the *Romanian Statistical Annual* of 1923.[21] This resulted in a decrease in purchasing power of 70 percent compared to 1914.[22] Inflation hit all countries after the war, but in Romania it ran eight times greater than in France and nineteen times greater than in Great Britain.[23] This caused the leu to plummet in relation to Western currencies.

By the end of 1921, 100 lei equaled 9 French francs, whereas in 1916 one leu was equivalent to 9.2 francs.[24] Loans were difficult to procure.[25] The aforementioned Spa Conference failed to provide the expected income from reparations. Cereal exports fell as Western governments turned to policies of economic autarky in an effort to bolster their own sagging economies. Except for oil, Romania sold no nonagricultural product in appreciable quantities on foreign markets, thus deepening the economic malaise.

It is within this framework that Romania entered the Paris Conference, and the events there must be considered in the light of this situation. In comparison with the other problems facing Romania in 1920-21, the Danube Question was of secondary importance. Internal matters, both political and economic, held the attention of the country. The Danube issue did not. In the diplomatic sphere, the nation already gained significantly, thus reducing the importance of pursuing the dissolution of the European Commission. At the same time, due to its geographical position, Romania could not risk fraying relations with the Western powers over the question of the Commission.

Before 1914, the weight of the Danube Question attracted the attention of the entire government. The issue was one that involved the economic future of the country and that implied a threat to its territorial sovereignty. Now the politicians were silent on the matter and concentrated instead on other, more immediate problems than the presence of a commission, dominated by Romania's allies, in Galați. The general policy of seeking the end of the agency and its replacement by an administration for the entire river remained; the authorities in Bucharest never pressed the issue, however. Instead, the resolution of the Danube Question became the concern and responsibility of the delegates to the Paris Conference and the European Commission.

CHAPTER V

DUNĂREA NOASTRĂ

The era immediately following the war brought a period of retrench-
ment to the administration of the Danube, as well as to all of Europe.
Neither the declaration of an armistice nor the signing of the subsequent
peace treaties could ensure stability or the revival of prewar systems and
conditions. New forces, nations, and demands had to be reckoned with.
Furthermore, the effects of the conflagration could not be forgotten. Its
lessons were painfully evident throughout the continent, and the Danube
was no exception. Commercial patterns and activities that developed over
decades came to an abrupt halt during the course of the war and revived
only slowly thereafter. Administration of the river was uncertain and
chaotic. Whereas once there were five riparian states, there were now
seven. After the armistice, providing for the supplies for Allied troops required the establishment of a military authority along the river. The fluvial portion of the Danube was subjected, therefore, to two administrations: a military one established by the Supreme Allied Command and
national ones responsible for services within territorial waters. In theory,
these two forms of supervision could not clash as each held separate spheres
of authority. The reality was far different, however. The military sought to
extend powers similar to those maintained by the European Commission
to a second agency responsible for the fluvial Danube. Riparian civil
authorities represented national interests and demanded greater control
of the river within their boundaries. The conflict between the two remained unresolved until the close of the Paris Conference in 1921. For
the Lower Danube, the enormous physical dislocation wrought by the
fighting and the attempts to deal with the resulting economic problems

54

underscored the epoch. What emerged in the immediate aftermath of the war, therefore, was a period of flux, as river officials faced both the need to rebuild, and an uncertainty (characterized by the tug-of-war between civil and military bodies) regarding the Danube's future.

This chapter will trace events from the close of the war in November 1918 until the opening of the Danube Conference in August 1920. Its scope is threefold. It will analyze the conflict between the Supreme High Command, represented by the so-called Inter-Allied Commission headed by British Admiral Ernest Trowbridge, and Romania. It will also examine the Danube issue as it emerged at Versailles. Instead of addressing themselves directly to the question of the river's future status, the peacemakers chose to defer all decisions to the special Paris congress. This decision virtually assured the perpetuation of the European Commission by leaving the fate of the organization in the hands of its members rather than the broader representation at Versailles. Finally, the chapter will study Romania's actions regarding the river throughout the period. Unlike its dismal record of the previous two years, Romania, represented by Constantin Conţescu, performed an admirable service for maritime commerce by reopening the Sulina channel and restoring a measure of stability to navigation in the face of formidable obstacles.

Before one can begin to examine these events, it is necessary to describe the state of the Danube in 1918. As chapter three has shown, the outbreak of hostilities had a catastrophic impact upon the European Commission as early as December 1914: revenues ceased, reserves evaporated, and maritime shipping on the river came to virtual standstill. Circumstances beyond its capabilities and jurisdiction paralyzed the organization. Finally, the entrance of Romania into the conflict brought the war physically to the delta. Although these conditions have already been surveyed, it is essential that the overall effects of the fighting after 1916 be examined as well because the legacy of the conflict dictated the actions of the various parties during the course of the next two years.

By 1919, the total dislocation of river commerce demanded immediate attention. For almost four years traffic on the Lower Danube had ceased. Commercial relations could not resume immediately after the cessation of hostilities; it was a slow process that demanded time. This situation forced the national economies to provide more essential goods and services than in the prewar years. Three reasons stand out. First, the enormous physical and economic destruction caused each country to turn inward for recovery. Individual industries and economic sectors required reinforcement, thus forcing governments to resort to subsidies that, by nature, impede free trade. The national economies of the European belligerents were exhausted and, in many cases, required years to rebuild. Second, in the Danubian Basin the dismemberment of the Habsburg Empire destroyed a principal trader. The successor states were incapable of economically filling the void. Third, the Danube shipping industries suffered incalculable damage between 1914 and 1918. The effects of the war lingered long after the advent of peace. In fact, river traffic never again attained the levels of the prewar era; the move toward internal stabilization and autarky cut sharply into any possible resumption in the flow of trade.

By the 1920s, in terms of total ships (and the corresponding tonnage) that used the maritime Danube, river traffic was almost 60 percent lower than it had been a decade earlier (see Appendices 4 and 5). Even in 1921, the year the Danube Conference concluded, river traffic showed only a negligible increase over 1918. The total number of ships using the Sulina in 1921 surpassed 1914 levels by 32 (753 versus 721), but tonnage figures were still less by 207,976. Although there was no real difference in the manner of transportation, that is, the size of vessels using the channel, an alteration in the registry of the principal users of the river stands out (see Appendix 5). The sharp decline in the number of vessels using the Sulina, in comparison with prewar levels, may be partly attributable to the destruction of the German and Austro-Hungarian fleets. The two nations together had accounted for an aggregate of 221,307 tons through Sulina (via 103 freighters) in 1914. No vessels of German or Austrian registry used the maritime ports between 1919 and 1921.[1] Ships of Russian origin using the river diminished. Other patterns are noticeable as well. Belgian shipping dropped from an annual average of 27 cargo vessels between 1912 and 1914 to just 1 in 1919 and 5 in 1920.[2] Only French, Italian, and Romanian totals exceeded pre-1914 levels. The increase in French and Italian shipping and the consequent rise in the economic importance of the Danube for those countries may have reinforced the belief in Rome and Paris in the necessity of the European Commission. The disappearance of the organization might threaten their commercial activities if Romania could not perform the necessary physical maintenance of the artery.

For the entire river, the total commerce in 1911 was 6,802,639 tons; in 1924, the date conceded by many historians as marking the return of a tenuous prosperity to Europe,[3] the level was only 3,757,010, a drop of 47 percent.[4] Imports through Sulina fell by 50 percent.[5] At the same time, cabotage figures, reflecting the transfer of goods between internal ports of one nation, increased. This meant that the Basin states traded domestically in greater volume while importing and exporting less. Thus, even the aforementioned decline of 47 percent in river traffic is a deceiving statistic. The economies of Eastern Europe were dependent on the export of primary products; sales of these goods declined drastically.

TABLE 1

EXPORTS BY CLASS OF GOODS (IN TONS) THROUGH SULINA

	1911[6]	1924[7]
Wheat	1,412,183	98,585
Rye	232,119	6,005
Maize	1,766,036	642,563
Millet	17,161	9,676
Wood	775,225	1,090,804
Bran	18,234	6,038
Barley	521,035	217,228
Oats	126,114	16,512
Beans	75,088	50,564

The implications of this decline in trade are obvious.

For the European Commission itself the war was disastrous. Losses reached 23 percent of the agency's total assets of 12,532,630 francs. Moreover, the following statistics measure only the loss of property. They fail to assess the conflict's enormous toll in less tangible, yet equally important terms, that is, the toll in lives and morale. These nonmaterial (and thus unmeasurable) losses[8] were as damaging as the physical destruction and, like the previous statistics, must be kept in mind when considering the Danube Question after 1918.

On November 9, 1918, the Romanian army re-entered the fighting and began the re-occupation of Wallachia, the Dobrudja, and the delta in the

TABLE 2

DAMAGE TO COMMISSION PROPERTY[9]

	in Francs d'or
A. Immovables	
1. Galați Hotel (HQ)	620,000
2. Tulcea port	68,000
3. Sulina channel	10,000
4. Sulina	
a. Hotel	135,000
b. Hospital	114,000
c. Stores	10,000
d. Others	33,460
TOTAL	991,060
B. Lighthouses	
1. Isle d'Serpents	177,000
2. Others	81,000
TOTAL	258,000
C. Material "flottant"	194,250
D. Miscellaneous	16,547
TOTAL	1,459,857
Multiplied by a coefficient of 2 to reflect present costs	2,919,714

wake of the retreating German forces. On the following day, an Allied army, led by French General Bertholet, crossed the Danube at the town of Giurgiu. With the signing of the armistice on November 11, the delegates of the Central Powers "left Romania for the second time since the start of the war."[10] After the displacement of the representatives of Germany, the Ottoman Empire,[11] and Austria-Hungary, Romania became the only Commission member remaining in the region. The Western delegates had fled after the Romanian military debacle of 1916, leaving Romania as the only responsible authority on the Lower Danube.

Due to the complete absence of Commission records, the four months following the cease-fire in November 1918 remain clouded. Secretary General of the European Commission Rey, in his report on the organization's activities during the war, stated only that operations in the delta were "in a state of lethargy."[12] Order and stability no longer existed. Ships using the Sulina artery and Commission port facilities simply ignored all tax assessments. A lack of personnel meant that there could be only sporadic enforcement of maritime regulations. Funds continued to be insufficient for any major work, thus greatly reducing services. Romania could give only limited support and the absent members forwarded no contributions. Chief Engineer Magnussen, the highest ranking operative in the region until the arrival of Constantin Conțescu in February, summed up the complete breakdown in the agency's functions in a telegram to the Foreign Ministry. In it he stated that:

> It is impossible to commence dredging operations without the necessary funds, equipment. . . [and] money [even] for the unloading of coal [used as fuel by the Commission].[13]

Magnussen appealed to Bucharest to demand support from the other members of the Commission. The desperate situation in the delta led to a momentary softening of the long-standing Romanian hostility toward the organization. As in 1856 and 1878, the resources of the agency's Western representatives took on renewed importance.

Efforts to correct the difficult situation in the delta, by reviving interest in the work of the Commission among the other governments represented on the body, failed. On November 24, 1918, the Romanian Foreign Ministry transmitted invitations to the envoys of France, Britain, and Italy requesting a meeting "as soon as possible" as "it has been three years . . . since the discussion of numerous and important questions in the international institution."[14] Nothing came of the effort. This meant that until the appointment of Conțescu the only real authority on the river was of a military nature.

Following the surrender of the Central Powers, the Allies established a military commission, centered in Istanbul and commanded by General Franchet d'Esperey, to oversee the provisioning of troops in Eastern Europe and to control the flow of traffic on the Danube. Acting under the overall authority of the Supreme Economic Council in Paris, a body composed of Britain, Italy, France, and the United States, the military commission had the task of facilitating the transportation of food and commerce "without interfering directly with the internal operation" of the riparian states.[15] Toward this end, the Council divided the river into three sectors. The course of the waterway north of the Iron Gates at Orşova fell under the supervision of British Admiral Trowbridge. France's Admiral Belloy was granted jurisdiction between Brăila and Orşova. The delta remained the responsibility of the European Commission.

From the beginning, this new military agency, the Inter-Allied Commission, had difficulties. The powers of the organization, especially the authority of its commanders to redirect traffic and establish priorities regarding the use of shipping lanes and ports, were never clearly spelled out. In addition, the two military delegations, headed by Trowbridge and Belloy, did not operate in harmony.[16] Lacking both direction and cooperation, the Inter-Allied Commission foundered.

The ambiguous nature of the commission's jurisdiction and the squabbles with the French angered Trowbridge. He began to lobby with the Supreme Council and the High Command for greater centralized authority in order to overcome difficulties "prejudicial to the function of services."[17] Admiral Belloy, in contrast, opposed any extension of the military body's prerogatives. Upon the advice of Premier Clemenceau, the Supreme Council on May 19 decided in favor of the British admiral and empowered him with regulatory authority over the entire fluvial Danube.[18] D'Esperey, the head of all Allied military forces in Eastern Europe, relayed the decision of the Council to his naval commanders on the river on June 21.[19] Henceforth, all vessels, including ships of the lesser Allies, Serbia and Romania, came under the jurisdiction of Trowbridge and the Inter-Allied Commission. Again, however, no exact list of the organization's powers was set forth. This ambiguity regarding the authority of the military agency within Romanian waters produced a clash with Bucharest that lasted long after the peace treaties were signed.

While the Supreme Council debated the issue of the fluvial Danube, at the Paris Peace Conference itself the entire Danube Question was placed under the overall competency of the Ports, Waterways, and Railways Commission. Established on January 25, 1919, the organization was originally composed of 15 members, 2 each from France, Britain, the United States, Italy, and Japan, and 5 from countries "with special interests": Serbia, Greece, China, Belgium, and Uruguay. This body reflected, in microcosm, the dominant position of the great powers at Versailles and the more limited "consultative" vote permitted other nations that had "sacrificed heavily for the Allied cause."[20]

Already at odds with the Big Four over its status at the conference as a "minor ally," the Romanian delegation, headed by Prime Minister Ioan I. C. Brătianu, vigorously protested its exclusion from the waterways commission. As a result, on February 3 Georges Clemenceau recommeded admitting Romania, along with Poland, Czechoslovakia, and Portugal, in a move designed to pacify opposition to the commission's limited membership. Over the objections of Woodrow Wilson, who felt that an increase in membership would give the smaller states a vote "almost equal" to the great powers, the Council approved the measure two days later.[21]

The position of the Romanian delegation to the waterways commission was summed up in the address to the body in March by N. Stefănescu, the former director of navigation in Romania. A mixture of history, moralizing, warnings, and histrionics, the speech symbolized Romania's opposition to any increase in the powers of other nations within his country's territorial waters. He centered his attack on the European Commission, a body that, he argued, held "rights and privileges [dating] from the Turkish epoch, a state which at the mouth of the Danube was incapable of executing, by itself, the work of amelioration of navigation and the affairs of policing the river."[22] The situation now "has changed." Romania possessed the ability, ports, and personnel, and had shown at Galați, Brăila, and Constanța its "capabilities" in executing needed work. His nation also embodied the "attributes" of the organization, that is, the firm belief in the concept of internationality. Thus:

> In view of this situation, Romania intends to maintain its rights of territorial sovereignty [against the] ancient rights and privileges of the European Commission of the Danube.[23]

There "must" be a revision by 1922 in the prerogatives of the agency. Romania believed that the body

> . . . has the competency [only] on the condition that the right of territorial sovereignty is respected and that the riverine states have the right to execute the work of navigation approved by the Commission toward the application of police regulation, collecting taxes. . . .[24]

As a last word, Stefănescu warned that if these demands were not met Romania held the "right of reservation" over any Danube regulations.[25]

Thus, an apparent incongruity emerged regarding Romania's policy toward the Danube and the European Commission. On the one hand, recognizing the chaotic conditions between Galați and the Sea, Bucharest attempted to revive and use the Commission temporarily. On the other hand, Romanian delegates argued openly for a change in the structure of the agency. Versailles became a forum for attacks on the Commission, therefore, while, at the same time, the appropriate authorities in Galați and at the Foreign Ministry attempted to work with the Commission's representatives to obtain aid. In that sense, the policies pursued by Bucharest had a degree of continuity. The attempt to mobilize the resources of the agency's members was a short-term measure, while the long-range policy remained its eventual elimination.

The work of the Ports and Waterways Commission, most of which is beyond the scope of this study,[26] required, by its very nature, the discussion of general articles governing trade and transportation as well as numerous specific cases such as the statutes regarding the internationality of the Rhine and Vistula, the Kiel canal, and so forth. The plenipotentiaries devoted little attention to the Danube, however, even though several articles pertaining to the river were written into the individual treaties with Germany, Austria, Hungary, and Bulgaria. Unlike the Rhine, the Danube received no definitive settlement.

The treaties provided for a congress to be called within twelve months from the signing of the accords to establish exact regulations for the river (article 349 of Versailles). The framers revived the European Commission with a "provisional" membership of Britain, France, Romania, and Italy (article 346). They also created a second organization, the International Commission of the Danube, for the rest of the navigable portion of the river (347 and 348). Thus, the entire river was, for the first time, completely international in character. Neither organization had precise duties, however, save the guarantee of equal treatment for "all nationals, property, and flags of all Powers."[27] Riparian countries on the International Commission did obtain the authority to maintain territorial facilities and execute work, but these were provisional powers subject to revision.

By incorporating only four general articles devoted to the Danube into the treaties, the Versailles peacemakers left the river's future administration in limbo for another year. Their failure to provide for the immediate establishment of the International Commission created a situation wherein the Inter-Allied Commission, under Trowbridge, remained the only functioning agency on the fluvial Danube. At the same time, as will be seen in chapter six, the very fact that the peacemakers extended the life of the European Commission without a time limitation eliminated any real chance for Romania to obtain the agency's abolition and the substitution of a single administrative body for the entire river.

While the framers of the Versailles agreements were engaged in the reestablishment of the international status and composition of the sixty-three-year-old body, in point of fact, it had been since November 1918 an exclusively Romanian organization, not by design but rather by circumstances. By ignoring all invitations to return, the Allied members left Romania, by default, in charge of the maritime Danube. On February 1, 1919, Constantin Conțescu, a functionary in the Commission during the war,[28] replaced Burghele as his country's delegate. Conțescu therefore became de facto head of the European Commission and, in turn, of the Lower Danube. His leadership revitalized the Commission, and river operations began a slow recovery process. The provisions of the Versailles agreements provided moral support for the organization; Conțescu, months previously, was already making it work.

Again, these efforts to use the Commission's offices did not mean that Conțescu, and therefore Romania, sought to strengthen the agency. Rather it indicated the importance placed on the revival of commercial activities in the delta; on this, Bucharest believed, the entire economy depended. The government, however, could not take unilateral action in the name of Romania. This would have been an abridgement of international agreements dating to 1856 and would have opened a breach with its allies. Instead, it had to operate through the facilities of the European Commission despite the fact that, in reality, Romania was acting unilaterally due to the prolonged absence of the other representatives. This put the country in the paradoxical and, for it, undesirable position of supporting the European Commission at seemingly the agency's weakest moment. In that sense, Conțescu's actions could be viewed as self-defeating, for they aided an organization Romania sought to eliminate. In truth, however, the end of the Commission would have to be a matter of negotiation. The recognition of this fact is evident in the content of Stefănescu's speech to the Ports and Waterways Commission. Thus, Conțescu's actions did not prolong the life of the organization, this being the prerogative of the diplomats at Versailles and later at Paris. Instead, his work benefited commerce in general and the economies of the Basin and his own country specifically.

To a great extent, Conțescu acted on his own initiative. Other issues, primarily the peace treaties, the country's territorial demands, and increasing tension with Hungary that led to war in July 1919, held the attention of the Romanian Foreign Ministry. Nevertheless, Conțescu's program corresponded to the general policy for the Danube that Romania had pursued since 1878. First, the smooth flow of commerce was considered essential. Any objection to the existence of the European Commission was secondary in importance to ensuring continuous commercial operations. Second, the resources of the other members should be marshaled in times of crisis. Third, within the Commission itself, Romania should try to exert a leading position by expanding its influence and presence through the appointment of its citizens to key agency positions. Fourth, by his actions on behalf of commerce, Conțescu would be demonstrating the value Romania placed on facilitating Danubian trade. The hope was that this policy would lead to concessions by the powers and, ultimately, the elimination of the entire organization and its replacement with a unitary administrative regime for the entire Danube.

Three weeks after taking office, Conțescu issued his first report on the situation in the delta; his views were not encouraging. In Galați, the destruction of the headquarters was complete; nothing remained but "a shell of walls." The "new" archives sat on chairs. Books, records, and registers had been left in Odessa after the Bolshevik Revolution. The head of bookkeeping resigned in December, leaving no successor and chaotic records. Budgetary personnel now comprised "a legion of cooks, cooks' helpers, stewards, watchmen, on land and water, who can do no more than receive money and cry daily when they don't come up with it." All *esprit de corps* disappeared. The organization suffered from "a loss of effective functionaries." Cargoes were improperly reported and duties evaded. As for receipts, there was a "page totally white between 1916 and 1918."[29]

In Sulina, the shortages of personnel and needed materials were worse. The river depth of 17 feet was impeding traffic. The lighthouse on the Isle of Serpents (off the coast of the Sulina channel) had been destroyed. Ships entering Sulina were not using channel pilots, thus jeopardizing the safety of operations. The Commission had no means of enforcing its regulations. The hospital was in ruins, a victim of German shelling. Typhus raged throughout the city. Lower functionaries suffered from long hours, low pay, little food, and disease, causing Conțescu to draw an analogy between Sulina and a penal colony.[30] Technical personnel were badly needed as were funds from the other members of the organization who had not contributed to the upkeep of the river since 1916. Technicians from the West had also not returned to the delta. Among those absent was E. Ward, the British first engineer, who left Romania before the war. Therefore, Conțescu advised the Foreign Ministry to request Britain, France, and Italy to send delegates immediately, as the situation demanded "quick action" for which they "must have the courage to take singular positions."[31] The Ministry transmitted this address on March 15 but again received no response.[32]

Acting on his own initiative, but always in the name of the Commission, Conțescu took a number of steps to alleviate the constantly deteriorating situation confronting commercial operations in general and the organization in particular. By March 27, dredging had increased the depth of the Sulina to 20 feet;[33] two months later it reached 22 feet. Conțescu stopped French military ships under the command of Vice-Admiral Eclamans from using port facilities reserved exclusively for the Commission's vessels.[34] He established rules classifying ships for the purposes of taxation as well as regulations for the collection of duties. Up to now the evasion of payments perpetuated a state of "anarchy;"[35] the Commission's role as sole authority over traffic in the delta was simply being ignored and the resulting loss of revenue further decreased the agency's ability to undertake badly needed work. Conțescu successfully lobbied with the Foreign Ministry for the use of a tugboat (the "Dragos") to replace one lost during the war; this vessel was obtained over the objections of the Minister of Public Works, "in order that service can continue without interruption."[36] The prolonged absence of Ward, which left the engineering corps without direction, forced Conțescu to appoint N. Georgescu to the post of Engineer-in-Chief. Recognizing the opposition of the other members to the appointment of Romanians to key positions in the agency, Conțescu assured Rey that Georgescu would enforce regulations "strictly" without regard to national registry.[37] Food shortages eased after a successful appeal to the French military command in Romania for assistance of 18,000 rations per month, one-half the needs of minor personnel.[38] The American Red Cross distributed another 1,600 meals daily.[39] In addition, d'Esperey agreed to furnish the coal necessary for running the agency's equipment.[40] Conțescu instructed the Bank of Sulina to aid in the collection of all authorized taxes. Romania advanced the Commission a total of 1,200,000 lei between February and July which, although barely sufficient to meet the agency's needs, enabled Conțescu to maintain its solvency.[41]

Beyond these immediate actions, Conțescu took several long-range measures designed to alleviate many of the "inconsistencies and old ways" that caused stagnation within the Commission's administrative apparatus.[42] He tried to cut the "cumbersome" bureaucracy and payroll padding. One example of this was the continued use of guards, an office begun in 1877-1878 to protect munitions that no longer existed.[43] The top echelons absorbed a disproportionate share of the Commission's budget, he argued, while dockworkers, who provided an essential service, earned as little as 50 lei a day (plus bread).[44] He therefore initiated a graduated system of wages based upon service and size of family.[45] Functionless administrators were either dismissed or received salary cuts of 50 percent. Conțescu also created a *Service de ravitaillement* to distribute funds and services to needy workers. As head of this central regulatory body, Gheorghe Mihailescu had sole discretionary use of the money provided, which included a grant of 50,000 lei from the Romanian government.[46] Conțescu's efforts inaugurated the period of recovery for the European Commission, but his actions required the approval of the other members, a vote of confidence that was not forthcoming.

In July, Secretary General Rey visited the delta to meet with Conțescu and observe the state of the Commission. Rey reported to his Western colleagues that the situation was "precarious" despite "the grand activities of the Delegate of Romania, his agents and his government;" the resources at the disposal of the agency were "clearly insufficient."[47] After returning to France, Rey called for a session of the European Commission to deal with the situation. It would be held in lieu of the "ordinary autumn meeting." As its site he chose Paris because of the city's proximity to "rapid lines of communication," rather than the legal seat of the organization at Galați.[48] N. Docan, the Foreign Ministry officer in charge of Danube policy, sent Rey a sarcastic reply that Romania was pleased to see such concern for the river "after so many years," a pointed reference to the Western delegates' long absence and Rey's use of the term "ordinary autumn meeting." The convocation in Paris, despite its advantages, Docan said, would perpetuate "a lack of comprehension" regarding conditions in the delta; the delegates would be "completely ignorant of the actual state [of affairs]."[49] Therefore, Docan ordered Conțescu not to attend. Rey's rejoinder that, if necessary, they would hold the sessions without Romania did not change his stance. Instead, Conțescu asked whether Rey meant this as "a simple suggestion or a disguised threat."[50] Conțescu continued to oversee the Commission's operations in the delta, therefore, while other delegates, absent from the area for over three years, undertook organizational and financial measures based on Rey's brief observations.

The *session extraordinaire* opened on October 15, 1919. In his opening remarks, French Minister Albert Legrand, acting as host and therefore president of the meeting, praised Romania's activities since the end of the war and stated regrets at its absence. Rey's oral report on the state of the Commission since 1914, cited extensively in the previous chapter, comprised the rest of the first session. He ended his summary by calling for immediate measures to deal with finances and personnel. The European Commission, in his view, was "responsible for the revitalization of a region." Up to now the Allies had been "pre-occupied" with other questions, he argued, but now the "restoration" of the agency was a "necessity."[51]

During the course of the next two days the plenipotentiaries made sweeping changes in the Commission's tax structure based on Rey's recommendations. Many of these moves overrode the actions of their Romanian colleague and angered both Conțescu and the Foreign Ministry. Foremost among these was the passage of British delegate John Baldwin's request for a 700 percent increase in taxes (200 percent higher than the original proposal put forward by Rey). The delegates also reinstated the franc as the sole monetary unit, even though such rigid currency rules could have an adverse effect on commerce during periods in which supplies of hard currencies were stretched thin.[52] The representatives approved additional loans, the traditional means of raising capital, although the sum of the bond issue was left open.[53] Finally, they overturned the appointments made by Conţescu because having Romanians hold the posts of Captain of the Port (Botez) and Engineer-in-Chief (Georgescu) was "not in keeping with the international character of the commission."[54] Among the changes in personnel, the Commission's members reinstated Ward as Engineer-in-Chief replacing Georgescu,[55] and chose a representative from Hungary for the post of Aide-Engineer. These actions greatly angered Bucharest, especially the appointment of a Hungarian to a position usually reserved for Romanians.[56]

Upon learning of the decisions of the *session extraordinaire* Conţescu informed Legrand that the implementation of the new taxes by the inaugural date of December 1 was impossible.[57] Article V of the 1856 charter, he argued, guaranteed a six month delay between establishing a new tax scale and putting it into effect.[58] Furthermore, the higher duties would drive up the cost of Romanian cereals in a world market in which grain prices were stable. This situation would make Romanian products less competitive. The other members took that action without fully examining its implications for Romania and the economies of all the Basin states.[59]

The measures taken at Paris were, Conţescu admitted to Prime Minister Vaida-Voievod, "perfectly legal" but "regrettable." According to his calculations, the use of French francs, computed at face value, resulted in a per ton charge of 45-48 lei. At minimum valuation, depending upon the value of the franc, the change in assessment would mean an average per ton levy of 30-35 lei, an increase that was 1,000 percent higher than the current 3-4 lei per ton duty. This "exaggerated increase in taxes would contribute to lower traffic." Conţescu therefore refused to implement the new rates.[60]

As for the motives behind the Paris measures, Conţescu stated that "everything, absolutely everything is vague, confused."[61] Historically, Britain had opposed any increase that would be detrimental to trade.[62] Yet, in this case, Baldwin not only supported an increase but fought for a proposal that was 300 percent higher than the original one made by Legrand and 200 percent higher than Rey's.[63] Later, Conţescu would argue that the British move was "not an imprudent gesture" but rather one "designed to strike at our principal products." It was an action that violated the charter of 1856 (which called for "fixed, suitable taxes").[64]

This change in attitude toward the British stemmed from the order by Rey and Legrand that Admiral Trowbridge use all available means to enforce the collection of the duties after Conțescu failed to do so on December 1.[65]

Conțescu's hostility toward the actions taken at Paris was not limited to taxation; on other matters, he believed, the delegates had taken equally ill-advised measures. The loans called for in Paris were poorly conceived and inflationary, being designed, in large part, to raise the salaries of upper personnel that Conțescu had been attempting to limit. The hikes "were exorbitant" with departmental heads getting the equivalent of 200,000 lei annually according to his calculations.[66] Fourteen people would thus receive almost 2,500,000 lei.[67] The work of the *session extraordinaire* thus was dangerous to Romania's economy specifically and navigation in general.[68] These objections were duly transmitted to Legrand along with a request to suspend the tax increase until after the March session of the Commission.[69] Legrand answered only that the delegates had acted to "stabilize the situation . . . with unanimity;" beyond that he did not address any of the points raised by Conțescu nor did he explain the reasons for the decisions reached at Paris.[70]

Conțescu did not concede the issue. In his first formal speech to his colleagues after they returned to Galați in May 1920, Conțescu appealed to a "spirit of conciliation" and reminded them of Romania's activities during their prolonged absence. The tax increase, which Conțescu wanted reduced to 400 percent, directly affected the Romanian economy. Although he admitted that inflation *did* warrant an increase, the cost of Romanian grains under the adopted plan would be higher in price than cereals from its competitors, thus reducing demand.[71] His appeals fell upon deaf ears. Balwin dismissed Conțescu's objections; he (and his colleagues) had "no hostile intentions toward Romania." Legrand likewise believed that public opinion in Romania had greatly exaggerated the consequences of their actions.[72] Therefore, lines were clearly drawn months prior to the Paris Conference regarding the power of the Western states to impose regulations Bucharest believed to be detrimental to Romania. Furthermore, the breach between Conțescu and his Western counterparts had re-opened. The only solution appeared to lie in Paris.

Concomitant with these events, Romania was engaged in active opposition to the activities of the Inter-Allied Commission. Its head, Admiral

Trowbridge, had become, by mid-1919, the most important figure on the river, having consolidated the two sectors under his command and being the nominal British representative to the European Commission, in Baldwin's absence. In addition, on June 21, a week before the signature of the Versailles agreement, the Supreme Council expanded his powers by placing all captured vessels (including those originally seized by the Central Powers from Serbia and Romania) under his jurisdiction.

Romania viewed any broadening of Trowbridge's powers as ominous. Already Romania saw him "taking in hand the exploitation of the Danube above Orşova, in the name of the allies; that is, the part of the Danube situated in hostile [that is, Austrian, German, and Hungarian] territories."[73] The regime now being applied south of the Iron Gates, however, had "a tendency [to put] more and more [of the river] in a state of occupation." Civil and commercial revitalization, Romania felt, should not be subjected to "the control...of a commission...which they [the Big Four] themselves establish."[77]

Transmitted by the Foreign Ministry to its delegation at Versailles, these fears were brought before the Supreme Council on June 29. After again recounting the past history of the Danube and the nation's "sacrifices" for commerce, Romania restated its objections: Trowbridge was using Hungarians as technicians in the Gates, an issue that was extremely sensitive to Bucharest in light of the open warfare between Romania and Hungary; the commission had been granted excessive powers over the use of captured vessels, rights of provisioning, and use of lines of communication. These privileges, Bucharest charged, violated the prinicples of internationality that were clear not only from past precedent but also from the articles contained in the peace treaties themselves. Therefore, Romania demanded that all riparian ships be returned, the powers of the military organization be limited, and a Romanian intermediary be appointed to the commission.[75]

On August 25, d'Esperey accepted the last demand and invited delegates from Romania, Czechoslovakia, and the Kingdom of the Serbs, Croats, and Slovenes to join the agency.[76] However, this was the only request to which the Allies agreed. D'Esperey did not answer the charges regarding the disposition of the ships claimed by Bucharest and Belgrade. In response to the ultimatum that control of the Iron Gates be given to a joint Romanian-Yugoslav Commission, the Council continually reported that the area was to remain under the complete control of the military body for an unspecified period of time.

Despite only partial success in its efforts, the Romanian Foreign Ministry continued to seek the restitution of the disputed ships as well as the division among allied riparian states of "all [other] ships pertaining to the former Austro-Hungarian Monarchy."[77] In addition, the Ministry asked for the immediate inauguration of the International Commission of the Danube in accordance with article 347 of the Versailles treaty. In so doing, they hoped to circumvent the authority of Trowbridge and his organization.

While Romania worked to end the influence of the Inter-Allied Commission, relations between Trowbridge and Bucharest became increasingly strained and, at times, openly hostile. The verbal warfare between the two need not be pursued in detail; for the purposes of this study, three examples will suffice.

In July 1919 fighting erupted between Romania and Hungary. As Romanian troops advanced into Budapest in August, Trowbridge put a squadron of monitors on alert to keep all ships in the harbor under close surveillance. Prior to the Romanian-Hungarian clash, Trowbridge had consistently ignored Bucharest's demand that the ships seized by the Central Powers, and presently located in Budapest's port, be returned Now Trowbridge was putting his naval forces on alert to prevent Romanian General Cinoski from taking the ships that Bucharest claimed as lawful Romanian property.[78] Tension increased between Romanian and British military authorities. To Bucharest, it seemed as if the British admiral openly supported Romania's enemy. Bucharest therefore viewed Trowbridge as a foe of Romania.

The matter of the disputed ships remained unresolved until an American arbitration commission decided the issue years later. Although Trowbridge was in fact acting under the orders of the Supreme Council not to surrender any vessels, Romanian officials never ceased believing that he personally stood in the path of the country's just claims.

The second confrontation involved taxation. On December 9, 1919, Trowbridge advised the members of his organization that a 2,000 percent hike in duties for vessels using the Iron Gates would begin January 1.[79] At the same time, in his capacity as British representative to the European Commission in the area, he ordered the monitor "Lady Bird" to Sulina

to force the immediate implementation of the taxes ordered at the *session
extraordinaire*. Conțescu had no power to stop Trowbridge,[80] although
the Foreign Ministry did protest this use of a British military vessel within
Romanian waters and demanded the immediate replacement of the officer
by Baldwin.[81]

The incident most characteristic of the unfriendly relations between
Trowbridge and Romania was the "Sofia" episode. Romanian historiography portrays this affair as a brazen affront to the country's pride. While
certainly not as blatant as that, it was not an event that could be easily
forgotten, and it bred distrust in Bucharest for the nation's river "partners."

The issue concerned the November/December meeting of the Inter-
Allied Commissin, a conference to which Romania, either due to a cleri
cal error or poor communication, never received an invitation or notification of its date or location. At the time of the sessions, Romania, in
effect, had no full-time representative to the commission; because of
animosity toward Hungary, Romania did not send a permanent representative to the agency's seat in Budapest until March 1920. The Foreign
Ministry sent its delegates to Budapest only for the regularly scheduled
meetings of the agency. In November 1919 Bucharest believed that the
conference would again be held at the commission's headquarters in the
Hungarian capital and ordered the Romanian envoy, M. Carp, to attend.[82]
The three-day meeting was not held in Budapest, however. Instead members of the Inter-Allied Commission met aboard Trowbridge's yacht
"Sofia" anchored near Belgrade.

Romania's problem was compounded by the fact that its representative could not be reached by the Foreign Ministry until December 2, the
date the conference ended. The Ministry did not even know Carp's exact
whereabouts, as the Romanian was home attending to family problems.[83]
Carp did not receive his orders to travel to Budapest until after the conclusion of the "Sofia" discussions. Although its delegate could not have
attended a conference in either Budapest or Belgrade, Bucharest seized
upon the failure of Trowbridge to notify the Foreign Ministry of the change
in location in order to claim that the British admiral snubbed Romania
purposely.

It is questionable whether, as Romanian historians contend, Trowbridge intentionally failed to invite Romania. Trowbridge later claimed
that the information was transmitted simultaneously on November 10 to

the Navy Departments of all the member-states that the meeting would open on November 27.[84] He "regretted" Romania's failure to arrive. He and the other plenipotentiaries attributed the choice not to attend as being "voluntary and independent. . .based upon a governmental decision and one in which they [the other delegates] had no influence."[85] Whatever the reason for the confusion, Romania's absence did enable Trowbridge to oversee the work of the conference with greater ease as the nonriparian outnumbered riparian states.[86] The work of the sessions however quickly faded from view. The diplomatic repercussions of Romania's absence remained.

Bucharest again protested Trowbridge's actions to the Supreme Council.[87] Previous diplomatic niceties disappeared. Attacks on the admiral's character included a charge that he favored Hungarian interests because he was "favorable to the idea of a re-establishment of the monarchy with a British prince."[88] As in October, however, with the work of the *session extraordinaire*, Romania was caught in a defenseless position. Despite the matter of the undelivered invitation, actions nevertheless had been taken by a legally constituted body, and Romania's absence could not prevent the measures from being binding upon all members. Bucharest, in effect, tried to use the diplomatic strategy employed in 1883 when it refused to recognize the work of the London Conference because the country had not been invited with full voting privileges. However, such a tactic of nonrecognition was not viable in this case. Romania's insistence that the results be annulled had no legal basis, nor did the country have the power to block the implementation of the provisions as it had in 1883. Its only real resource was to demand the immediate institution of the International Commission and the limitation of the Inter-Allied agency's powers to those originally set aside for the organization, that is, military provisioning. Like their previous protests, these demands had little impact.

In May 1920 the Inter-Allied Commission dissolved, its *raison d'être* as a military organization at an end. Its official replacement by the International Commission did not substantially alter the basic structure of the agency: Trowbridge became the head of the new organization; its headquarters remained at the Hotel Hungaria in Budapest; it continued to regulate all navigation along the length of the fluvial Danube in a manner similar to that conducted by its predecessor, even though such powers, according to the peace treaties, could be granted only after the adoption of the *Statut Définitif*. The creation of the International Commission came from the top. Until the clarification of its exact prerogatives, which would occur at Paris, it was an agency that was "new" in name only. Thus, for both the European and International Commissions, the convocation of the Paris Conference provided the only chance to settle the controversies between Romania and the organizations.

Thus, the period between November 1918 and August 1920 was one of frustration for Romania in regard to the Danube. Left in charge of river operations, the authorities were confronted by severe physical and economic dislocation. Not until the appointment of Constantin Conțescu to the position of Romanian delegate to the European Commission did substantive results take place. Conțescu diligently pursued his tasks and showed great foresight into many of the agency's deficiencies. He therefore deserves credit for the enormous strides made after the war toward recovery along the maritime Danube. Yet, despite his activities, real power lay elsewhere, in the hands of two groups: his colleagues, who for so long had failed to take an active interest in the river, and the military, specifically Admiral Trowbridge. Both had the blessings of the Supreme Allied Council and thus had ultimate authority. The Council itself chose to leave the Danube Question, for the moment, to these two groups and the river's future to a special conference. This situation, on the one hand, ensured the continuation of the European Commission and great power interest along the river and, on the other hand, set the stage for the conflict between the riparian and nonriverine states, a clash that would need to be resolved in Paris.

CHAPTER VI

THE INTERNATIONAL CONFERENCE OF THE DANUBE

The *Conférence Internationale du Danube* opened in Paris on August 2, 1920. During the course of the next eleven months 68 meetings would be held before the delegates finally agreed upon the *Statut Définitif*, which was the most important single piece of legislation governing the Danube since the signing of the Treaty of Paris in 1856. The work of the conference was divided into two parts: the first ended with adjournment after reaching preliminary agreement on the text in November 1920, and the second began when the conference reconvened five months later. The first session addressed the theoretical aspects of internationality and their application to the Danube. The second involved discussions of a more concrete nature directed toward exact wording of the *Statut* that would balance national self-interests with the theories expressed at the previous gathering.

Despite the duration of the congress, which exceeded all expectations, the general tenor of the final product was readily discernible after the first meeting. The opening project put forward by the French delegate and president of the conference, Albert Legrand, left little doubt that the great powers would seek to preserve their strong influence over the affairs of the river. As such, the powers often forced the riparian states that had full voting privileges—Romania, Czechoslovakia, and the Kingdom of Serbs, Croats, and Slovenes—into a defensive position from which they could only try to limit the prerogatives of their Western allies within their waters.

Standard accounts of the convention emphasize the importance of these two blocs, the first composed of the delegates from Britain, France,

Italy, Greece, and Belgium, and the second representing the riparian allies
mentioned above. This generalization has some merit, primarily in relation
to the consensus that prevailed among the nonriparians. But, in the final
analysis, it presents an unrealistically simplistic picture that overlooks the
numerous disagreements between particular delegations. Neither group acted as a unit. In fact, diplomatic stances taken at Paris were not based on
the existence of two camps but rather on the much simpler and more
traditional concept of national self-interests as distinguished from regional
or political considerations.[1]

In large part, perceptions stemmed from the inner workings of the
European and International Commissions, both of which were fully
operative before the conference opened. With the congress designed to
legalize the powers of each, an individual nation's delegation acted in
response to the current attributes of the two agencies, either to maintain
present conditions or alter them. At times this resulted in the formation
of "blocs," but these groups held together only on particular issues and
lacked any close bonds. Bucharest's program at Paris, therefore, was not
based on any united action with Belgrade and Prague. Instead, Romania's
stance, in large measure, derived from four decades of trying to limit the
activities of the powers on the Danube.

As the opening date of the conference drew near, strained relations
continued between Conţescu and his French and British counterparts
over the operations of the European and International Commissions.
This discord not only affected the internal affairs of the organizations
but also helped contribute to a hardening of positions at Paris.

In February 1920 tension arose again between Conţescu and Secretary
General Rey. During the special Paris session of 1919, the Western members of the European Commission raised taxes and removed a few Romanian nationals from key agency positions on the basis of Rey's recommendations. Conţescu, it will be recalled, strongly opposed these actions
as against the best interests of his country and the Commission. Now Rey,
at work in Paris preparing for the opening of the Danube Conference,
delegated his responsibilities in the delta to a subordinate, M. Lebre.
Friction quickly developed between Conţescu and Rey's replacement
and produced a situation that the Romanian described as "intolerable."[2]
On February 13, Conţescu suspended Lebre from his duties after Lebre
blocked his access to the Commission's archives on the assertion that only

the Secretary General should be able to use them.[3] Conțescu put much
of the blame for the incident on Rey, although he gave no reason for such
an accusation.[4] Despite the apparent insignificance of the incident, Legrand dispatched a second appointee, M. Vautier, to replace Lebre.[5] Although Conțescu believed that Legrand sent the new representative to
alleviate "the inconveniences resulting from the absence of the [other]
delegates,"[6] Vautier's job was to arrest the ill-feeling between Conțescu
and Lebre (and Rey, as well). Such animosity, Legrand correctly say, threatened the forthcoming conference.

As the tension eased with the French, relations between Conțescu and
the British deteriorated. The British minister to Bucharest, Frank Rattigan,
pressed Conțescu and Docan to collect the October taxes (see chapter five)
that, despite the intervention of Trowbridge and the monitor "Lady Bird,"
had not been fully implemented. Conțescu and the British still could not
agree either to the terms of the duties or to the necessity of their collection. Rattigan argued that the increase amounted to no more than a 13.87
lei per ton charge and the additional revenue was essential if operations
were to deepen the Sulina from its present depth of 18 feet.[7] Conțescu
countered by stating that the taxes meant a 60.38 lei per ton duty on
goods at the current rate of exchange. Furthermore, the depth of the channel was over 20 feet, thus lessening the urgency of such a sizable rate hike
(to provide funds for capital expenditures).[8] In addition, he told the British that salaries were being paid and that misleading reports to the contrary originated with Trowbridge's staff. The fault for the conditions in
the delta, according to Conțescu, lay not with Romania but rather with
its allies who sent promises of assistance but neither money nor materials.[9]
With continued poor relations between Conțescu and his British counterparts (and also, to a lesser degree, the French), it appeared logical that
Romania would have to seek allies for the conference in the Basin.

Cooperation among the riparian allies was less than solid, however. Historians traditionally describe the formation of a riparian bloc as being a product of the Little Entente, which formed at the same time the Paris Conference was being held. This was an alliance based upon but a single purpose, however: fears of Hungarian *revanchism* and the possible restoration
of a Habsburg monarchy. Apart from that, the Little Entente did not
create substantially closer relationships between Romania, Czechoslovakia,
and the Kingdom of the Serbs, Croats, and Slovenes. At the Paris Conference

assurances of loyalty to a central position[10] were often no more than hollow promises; internal Romanian dispatches reflect the failure to establish any real measure of solidarity among the delegations. The interests of the riparian nations were too dissimilar, in spite of the efforts by Prague, Belgrade, and Bucharest to prove that their respective programs for the river were moderate and in the best interests of all.[11] The Yugoslav representatives, for example, joined with Romania in arguing for a reduction in the powers of the international bodies (especially the Inter-Allied Commission) within its territorial waters and in the region of the Iron Gates. But, Belgrade and Bucharest could not agree on a coordinated diplomatic stance aimed at obtaining either end. Beyond professions of homage to the concept of internationality and the idea of a joint Romanian-Yugoslav Commission, the two parties disagreed on the future administration of the Gates. At the "Sofia" Conference, the members of the Inter-Allied Commission consented to the Yugoslav demand that the "co-riverines" alone govern the river below the Gates, if an agreement with Bucharest could be reached.[12] When this too failed, Romania chose to wait until the conference decided the matter.[13] At the same time, there is no evidence that Bucharest made any real effort to seek Czech assistance either in regard to the disputes with Trowbridge or in coordinating a Paris strategy during the months prior to the conference. No accord was reached among the Little Entente states, therefore, despite the fact that such a move would "sanction that [the riverine] point of view."[15]

In the absence of regional cooperation, Romanian authorities felt that they were providing a great service to navigation by "doing the necessary work because Serbia is today not in a state of collaboration."[16] As the conference opened, it appeared to some as if the riparian "allies" would act in unison. In reality, however, the Romanians admitted that "pretensions of our amiability with Serbia and Czechoslovakia have no foundation."[17] Thus, Romania entered the Paris negotiations with a heightened sense of self-importance that combined with a long-standing self-perception of being a martyr in river affairs, that is, the injured partner on the European Commission and the true champion of internationality in active struggle against Western interference.

The delegates assembled in the home of M. Paleologue, France's Secretary General of Foreign Affairs. Ironically, this was the same site as the

first meeting of the European Commission in 1856. Of the conferees delegated by the framers of Versailles, only the United States did not send a
representative. Paleologue greeted the plenipotentiaries (see Appendix 7)
with a charge to "rehabilitate the economic life of Central Europe," an
object in which the French government placed "great interest."[18] After
his opening remarks Paleologue retired, and the delegates chose the conference's officers—Albert Legrand as President and Toma Stelian, the
Romanian representative, as Vice-President.[19]

The reasons why Stelian, and not Conţescu, headed the Romanian delegation are unclear. As early as January 1920 the Minister of Public Works,
I. Popovici, lobbied for Stelian's nomination, stating that the country
could not afford to have anything less than the finest representative
available.[20] Popovici believed that only a "juridical" person familiar with
diplomacy "will have the strength necessary to sustain our cause." Stelian,
he argued, knew the Danube situation, having had long discussions with
Gheorghe Popescu, one of Romania's delegates at Versailles and a prolific
writer on the subject of the river's administration.[21] After this intercession by Popovici, no other word on the matter was forthcoming until the
Foreign Ministry formally approved the nomination in May. The King
signed the measure, including the appointments of Conţescu and Popescu
as alternates, on July 3.[22]

The absence of discussion concerning Stelian's designation (as reflected
in Romanian archives), and the late date of final action, support the hypothesis presented in chapter four that the Danube Question seemed less
important in 1920 than other matters confronting the government. Despite the demands by Popovici and others that someone be named early
in order to present a well-defined position,[23] no internal Foreign Ministry discussions took place concerning the composition of the delegation;
the recommendations of Popovici were simply accepted. The matter was
treated as if it was a formality that could be postponed until the last
minute without damaging the nation's position at Paris. Stelian did not
receive notification of his appointment, therefore, until only four weeks
remained before the conference opened and months after the French
and British had chosen their representatives.[24]

Regardless of the delay in formalizing the nomination, the appointment of Stelian was, in retrospect, a clever move. Stelian was not only
a former Minister of Justice and one of the country's leading jurists, he

was also a neutral party among the principal antagonists: Baldwin, Legrand, Rey, and Conţescu. Despite his overbearing ego, he would be better able to present the theoretical and legal arguments upon which Romania based its claims than would the more volatile Conţescu. The latter's relationships with Legrand and Baldwin were at such a low point that it appeared as if another individual, in this case Stelian, would be more likely to wring concessions from the Western representatives. The choice of Stelian was thus a tactical move designed, in part, to disarm any personal animosity toward the Romanian position (through the person of Conţescu) and to push a legalistic stance. Conţescu and Popescu could engage in the hard, technical negotiations, but Stelian was sent to Paris to confront Legrand and Baldwin.

As president, Legrand began the work of the conference by calling upon his fellow conferees to "sacrifice . . . national interests for the good of all" and demonstrate "a spirit of European solidarity" during the course of the "vast" work ahead.[25] To assist them toward that end, he presented a proposed text (see Appendix 8) upon which he hoped they would base their discussions. Among its provisions, the text devoted the first section to a general statement internationalizing the entire river through the creation of two commissions: the International Commission between Ulm and Brăila, and the European Commission from the latter to the Sea. In section two, he discussed the character of the European agency, which was unchanged except for the admission of Greece as a full member[26] (upon the consent of the other four representatives). Legrand formalized the extension of the body's jurisdiction to Brăila. All previous rights and prerogatives of the organization remained intact.[27]

The establishment of the International Commission comprised the bulk of the document. Located in Budapest and composed of all the riverine states plus the members of the European Commission, the new agency would have full regulatory powers over the fluvial Danube.[28] Subject to the approval of the body's entire membership, the riparian nations held the right to perform all tasks necessary to maintain river traffic. A subcommission made up of the co-riverine countries would control the Iron Gates under the direct supervision of the International Commission.[29] The European and International Commissions would exchange necessary information and coordinate activities as conditions warranted.[30] (This last, imprecise provision portended a possible extension of the stronger powers

held by the European agency to the river north of Brăila.) The League of
Nations would arbitrate all unresolved disputes. Finally, "all treaties, conventions, acts, and other arrangements relative to international rivers in
general and the Danube and its mouths in particular" would remain in
force.[31] (This measure thereby invalidated Romania's nonrecognition of
the 1883 Treaty of London.)

   These proposals were subject to revision, as Legrand reiterated at the
opening of the next session on August 4. He hoped, however, that they
would serve as the foundation of their discussions and provide the framework for the final accord.[32] But, his expectations were dashed quickly
as most of the delegates presented a series of counter-proposals during the
next two meetings.

   Mihailo Ristić, representing the Kingdom of the Serbs, Croats, and
Slovenes, began the chorus of denunciations. Although he agreed with
Legrand's sentiments supporting the principle of internationality, as expressed in article I, he claimed that the rest of the text was based on
arguments used in 1856; Europe was still discussing the Danube Question in identical terms sixty years later.[33] This was a new Europe, however, and the Paris Conference and the *Statut* must recognize that fact.
Therefore, he argued, the *Statut* should reflect the views of the general
convention of the League of Nations (which echoed the technical opinions expressed at Versailles by the Ports and Waterways Commission)
rather than the mere repetition of old ideas. According to Ristić, the
League measure, the *Projet de convention sur le regime international
des voies navigables* (see Appendix 9), that Stelian introduced into the
record, should be the framework for their discussions.[34]

   Stelian expanded Ristić's arguments against the French proposal and
seconded a call for adjournment in order to study "the enormous differences" between the two projects. In terms of work, police, the right
to declare free ports and zones, the nomination of agents, and the existence of the European Commission, Legrand's measure was "diametrically
opposed" to the League's rules, as well as the principles established at
Vienna in 1815. The League's rules were not "inutile," as Baldwin and
others argued, but rather reflected the work of an "international body"
composed of "highly competent legal and technical minds." Furthermore,
these statutes made up a document to which all the nations represented
at the present congress had granted approval.[35] This fact, Stelian asserted,
must be kept in mind, for no Danube settlement could violate laws accepted

by the League of Nations. Prerogatives of the Danube commission(s) must correspond to the general rules established by the League, and which would also be the subject of the upcoming conference in Barcelona in 1921.[36]

This difference of opinion regarding the powers and composition of the river agencies remained the major stumbling-block for the next eleven months. Every word change and discussion revolved, in some manner, around this central problem of balancing national interests with generally accepted definitions of internationality. Therefore, blocs formed not out of prior arrangements among the various governmental ministries but rather came together depending upon the particular article in question. The content of the article and the possible effect upon national interests brought voting groups together, in sharp contrast to the traditional view that the conference was characterized by a riparian versus nonriparian struggle. This pattern was clearly evident as debate began.

The questions raised by the introduction of two dissimilar documents split the convention and forced its adjournment until September 6. This break allowed the members to formulate their own positions via formal counter-proposals. More importantly, it allowed the representatives and their respective governments to conduct inter-ministry negotiations aimed at gaining adherents to those positions.

Stelian's report on the initial meetings reflects an uncertainty regarding Romania's hopes at the conference, as he expressed both satisfaction and disappointment with the proceedings. On the one hand, he introduced the League's regulations, which supported Romania's fundamental principles and which gave the delegation a legal basis for its position On the whole, however, "the Conference began in a painful condition for us."[37] The Legrand project, which Stelian incorrectly believed was supported by a pre-conference alliance of Britain, France, Greece, Hungary, and "probably Italy as well,"[38] was a "grave attack on the sovereign rights of riverines" and "an absolute violation" of League doctrine.[39] At first he thought that the conferees "would follow the rules constituted by the League of Nations," but the French proposals "changed" that "system." Therefore, Romania's best hope lay in direct negotiations by the Foreign Ministry with the various governments represented in Paris.[40]

Taking Stelian's advice, the Romanian Foreign Minister Take Ionescu now began to coordinate the country's diplomatic activities regarding the

Danube. In return for Yugoslav support of Romania's proposals, Ionescu vowed that the country would lend to Belgrade assistance in all river operations because "Serbia does not have the necessary materials and personnel." He told the Yugoslav Foreign Ministry that the conference "is a great opportunity for the two governments [to act] in accord."[41] He promised Greek Prime Minister Venizelos that Bucharest would sustain Athens' bid for admission to the International Commission in return for assistance at the congress.[42] He also instructed the legations in London, Paris, and Rome to voice strong opposition to the Legrand project, primarily the provisions pertaining to the powers of the International Commission and the choice of Budapest as the body's seat.[43]

The response to Ionescu's activities appeared favorable. After an exchange with Venizelos, he was confident that an accord with Greece could be reached.[44] In addition, the President of the Council of Ministers in Belgrade replied that Ristić would be instructed to act in unison with Stelian. But events quickly ran counter to expectations.

Before the conference re-opened, Ionescu cabled Stelian instructions to "obtain all that is possible" but not to argue any point that would "isolate" him from his fellow delegates. He should concentrate on the question of the International Commission's seat, the designation of that agency as the sole judge of infractions, disputes, and policing the river (article XVIII of Legrand's project), and the question of designating free ports.[46]

What Ionescu failed to include in his assessment of the French proposals, however, was any reference to the European Commission. It appears highly probable, therefore, that the Foreign Minister already conceded the issue, preferring instead to direct his delegation's attention toward the question of the fluvial Danube's future rather than an issue that could not be won. Thus, when the delegates reconvened on September 6, Romania's bargaining position was directed clearly toward obtaining, if possible, any concessions regarding the European Commission, but, more importantly, toward the future of the International agency.

The work of the first meeting following the month's adjournment lasted only ninety minutes. Legrand's initial draft had clearly failed to provide a satisfactory middleground. Instead of quickly ratifying any text, the delegations presented counter-proposals to the one put before the conference by Legrand a month earlier.[47]

Romania's plan, prepared by Stelian, placed the Danube in "uniformity" with both the regime in operation on the Rhine and the principles established by the League. Composed of 26 articles, his alternative *projet* (see Appendix 10) called for a single river commission housed in Galați, that would consist of all riparian nations, present members of the European Commission, and Belgium. Despite Ionescu's pledge to Venizelos, Stelian's plan excluded Greece from representation on the organization. Stelian reserved all rights of cabotage, taxation, policing, and initiation of work exclusively to the national states in the Basin. All disputes would be arbitrated by the International Court of Justice. Warships could be stationed only within territorial waters of the vessel's state of origin.[48] Like the Rhine agency, the International Commission would hold only supervisory powers (not regulatory), thus assuring the predominance of the national state within territorial waters but, at the same time, protecting rights of navigation by tying all parties to the League's rules.[49]

As usual, Stelian believed that he put his colleagues on the defensive. In his report to the Foreign Ministry, he stated that Romania (that is, Stelian) had been able to devise the only complete counter-proposal (other than Greece's) to the Legrand project. In his opposition to Legrand he was "in complete understanding" with Ristić and Muller, (his Czech "ally"), but the Greek delegate (Coromilas) had "ignored" all requests for collaboration. Italy was also leaning toward the Romanian position.[50] What Stelian did not explain was whether the ties with the Czech, Yugoslav, and Italian delegates were firm or whether they were based on but a few general points. The fact that Ristić's own project, for example, maintained the European Commission and, in fact, increased its membership to include all the riparian states[51] certainly implies the latter.

On the question of the European Commission Stelian sketched only the barest details. In private discussions with Legrand and Baldwin he insisted on the organization's "destruction." At the same time, he tried to prevent the agency's extension to Brăila.[52] Toward that end, he arrived at a "basis of understanding" with the Western delegates to limit the Commission's supervisory powers to only the waterway between Galați and Brăila. The ports of Tulcea, Galați, and Brăila would remain beyond the body's formal jurisdiction.[53] This stance represented a significant departure from Stelian's previous statements and indicated a tacit recognition that the "anomaly" (which he termed the European Commission) would be preserved by the conference.

Stelian also informed Ionescu that he could not undertake any joint action with Coromilas.[54] The accord Ionescu made with Venizelos furthermore presented him with an "impossible situation." In order to obtain the best results for Romania, he was "obliged" to work closely with Ristić and Muller, and they did not wish to add the Greeks to either administration.[55] Thus, he asked, "what price awaits . . . for the rest of the problems . . . if I betray them [Ristić and Muller] from the beginning?"[56] If the Foreign Minister wished him to puruse the Greek alliance, Stelian felt he would have to resign or be replaced "by another delegate [who would] represent the best interests of the country."[56] On this matter he had to ignore Ionescu's assertion that close ties with Greece represented "one of the cardinal points of our foreign policy."[57]

Within four days after receiving Stelian's report, Ionescu began redirecting his policy. First, he abandoned the hoped-for alliance with Athens. Although he earlier believed that an accomodation with Coromilas would weaken any Greek-British-French bloc[58] after his own discussion with the Greek plenipotentiary he concluded that Athens' position, especially its support of free and open cabotage, was antithetical to Romania's best interests. Ionescu advised Coromilas, therefore, that the congress had no power to admit Greece to the two agencies because Versailles did not specifically authorize the conferees to take such an action.[59] By abandoning his earlier accommodation with Athens, Ionescu hoped to limit nonriparian influence on the Danube and, at the same time, not anger Belgrade and Prague. This, in turn, freed Stelian from a stance that the latter believed jeopardized his future relations with Ristić and Muller. Again, this did not contribute to any closer cooperation between the three states of the Little Entente. Stelian continued to assert that "they [Ristić and Muller] did not look with good neighborly eyes toward the Danube—I believe that this . . . stems from the foundation of our superiority."[60]

Ionescu also concluded that Romania could not hope to win the battle over the future of the European Commission. He told Stelian that "the [fate of the] European Commission of the Danube was decided at Versailles and cannot be interrupted therefore, [and] our cause cannot be reinforced . . . if we insist on abolishing the Commission."[61] After a conversation with French Foreign Minister Millerand, he saw that there "is no possibility that the European Commission of the Danube can be destroyed."[62] "The [Versailles] Treaty is precise;" the Western states would never violate its provisions.[63] The Romanian delegation should pursue the agency's limitation, therefore, and allow its extension to Brăila only if the ports were removed from its jurisdiction. Furthermore, Stelian should block any attempt to increase its membership. The idea of admitting other riverine states to the Commission "is absurd" as it removed all need for two organizations and would grant Romania's "enemies" (the former Central Powers) seats at Galați.[64]

Romania thus abandoned all hope of removing the European Commission from its position of authority on the Lower Danube and of replacing it with a single river administration. Stelian (and later Conțescu) would publicly continue to pursue the latter policy, but, in fact, the argument was futile, as Ionescu accurately observed. By maintaining the *status quo* until the *Statut* could be written and by stipulating that the river would be governed by two agencies, the Versailles framers handed Bucharest a *fait accompli*. Romania could not move against the dictates of the peace treaties. The Foreign Ministry had no alternative but to accept the Commission's existence and concentrate instead on limiting its powers. Stelian also foresaw this when he asked Ionescu whether, in the event that the other delegates refused to accede to his remonstrances, he should "withdraw from the conference."[65] However, this was not a viable option. As mentioned earlier, this tactic of withdrawal and non-recognition succeeded in 1883 but had proven to be less successful when employed against Trowbridge in 1919. At Paris it would have failed again. First, the Western Allies refused to brook any Romanian interference. Brătianu's strategy of intransigence at Paris did obtain early successes, primarily due to splits within Western ranks. At the same time, Brătianu's actions led to an anti-Romanian attitude on the part of Western leaders. Any attempt by Stelian to thwart the work of the conference would have been viewed as a continuation of Brătianu's policies and, like the protests of Trowbridge's control of the requisitioned ships, would have been ignored. Second, such a withdrawal would have been a breach of the Versailles treaties. Despite its diplomatic victories of 1919, Bucharest was in no position to act in a manner contrary to the Versailles accords and the League of Nations (under whose aegis the conferees were meeting). Third, Romania was still threatened by revanchist neighbors that, except for the narrow border with the Kingdom of the Serbs, Croats, and Slovenes, surrounded the country. In such an atmosphere, Romania

could not afford to alienate her powerful Western Allies, and perhaps
Belgrade and Prague as well, over the question of the European Commission. Any break with the West also threatened ratification of the Bes-
sarabian annexation (not confirmed until October 28, 1920), which was
a foreign policy objective considered more vital than the matter of the
Galați agency. Strained relations with the West also portended peripheral
consequences. In the fall of 1920 the Romanian monetary crisis wors-
ened and precipitated efforts by Bucharest to raise a substantial loan
in the West "paving the way for further large deals, strengthening Romania's credit and making a really large loan possible."[66] Any threat to
disrupt the Danube agreement might be viewed by European capitals as
a threat to Western commercial interests. This would damage the country's hope for better economic relations and credit. Finally, to have left
the Paris negotiations would have required marshaling Romania's internal forces, especially public opinion. With the diverse, complex problems
facing the country in 1920 and the absence of any real public sentiment
on the issue (the subject of a later chapter), the consequences of any dis-
ruption of the conference outweighed the disadvantages perceived to exist
through the continuation of the European Commission. Stelian thus
shifted his emphasis from the latter to the International Commission and
became the proponent of a fluvial agency in line with the general rules
established by the League. In so doing, Stelian portrayed Romania as the
defender of the concept of internationality as defined by the framers of
Versailles. Only in this direction lay a possibility of success.

Having failed to link the discussions of the conference to the previously
mentioned *Projet de convention sur le regime des voies navigables,* Stelian
now pressed for a *Statut* "in conformity" with the system in operation
on the Rhine, that is, a supervisory commission with full riparian rights
over the collection of taxes, work, and so forth.[67] He attempted to intro-
duce a "preamble" that called for a Rhine-Danube accord giving the
rivers similar administrative regimes. He based this measure on article
338 of Versailles, which called for general rules governing all international
rivers (the basis of the Barcelona convention of 1921), and article 353,
which envisioned the construction of a canal linking the two rivers. Stelian said that without an accommodation with these two provisions, there
would be four separate regimes after the completion of the canal: one
for the mouth of the Danube, a second for the rest of the river, a third
for the canal itself, and a fourth for the Rhine.[68]

Although Legrand dismissed these arguments as having "little importance,"[69] he correctly saw that this opposition threatened to delay or perhaps even prevent the approval of a *Statut*. Therefore, Legrand presented
a second project addressed more toward the wishes of the riparian states
than the earlier document.

Although the International Commission retained strong regulatory
powers and the European Commission was left unchanged, the new text
altered the basic tone of many of the original articles. Legrand proposed
granting the riparian states greater control over work, taxation, enforcement of regulations, the designation of free ports, and cabotage. Only a
riverine state could authorize the creation of free ports and zones. The
national states rather than the central river authority would name in-
spectors and the chief inspector would come from a nonriparian nation.
Cabotage could be reserved by the riverines for national vessels except
in the case of "continuous" (that is, regularly scheduled) service by
foreign concerns; with the exception of "noncontinuous" shipping, all
vessels would have equal access to the river's ports. Warships would be
permitted to operate on the Danube, but only in numbers necessary for
policing the river and suppressing the importation of contraband.[70] After
the completion of the Rhine-Danube canal, joint rules would be drawn
up by the signatory states of both conventions.[71] Even though these
measures did not disarm his critics, by demonstrating a conciliatory
spirit, Legrand removed many of the fears expressed by the riverines
that foreign interests would dominate the river. At the same time, Legrand began to use his authority as president to assert firmer control over
the proceedings and to open debate on the first articles.

The first formal discussion of specific articles began on September
20, seven weeks after the conference opened. Another two months would
pass before the delegates approved an initial draft. For the moment, most
of the debate centered on the scope of the various articles rather than
the exact wording. On the whole, the second Legrand project satisfied
the general tenor of the meeting. Long, often tedious debates would
take place in an effort to iron out the final form, but generally these
changes would be only cosmetic. Over a few questions, however, the
work of the conference stalled.

A delicate issue from the beginning concerned the status and powers
of the "defeated" nations. The delegations from those states argued that

the formulation of any document without their participation violated the principle of parity and equality and destroyed any pretensions of constructing a true *Statut Définitif.*[72] Article 332 of Versailles, and similar articles in other treaties, required that ships of the former Central Powers receive special permission before using the port facilities of an "allied" riparian state. The delegates from the nonvoting bloc saw this as only a temporary provision and thus should not be included in the Danube agreements.[73] Stelian, Ristić, and Muller countered by demanding "absolute respect" for the provisions of the Versailles pacts.[76] They viewed any liberalization of the limitations under article 332 as a potential threat to the protection of internal commerce, particularly cabotage rights, and renewed domination of fluvial shipping by the powerful riparian states of the north. This conflict threw the very definition of liberty of navigation on the river into heated debate.

As a compromise, all parties agreed to include an additional article stating that the *Statut* would not abridge the wishes of the Versailles treaties. This circumvented the question whether the framers in 1919 envisioned the anti-Central Power clauses as transitory or long-term measures. It also enabled the delegates to pass the first article, which proclaimed the internationalization of the Danube from Ulm to the Black Sea. With the definition of the river's internationality now complete, they turned to the problem of limiting the jurisdiction of the two commissions.[74]

Legrand placed into discussion a series of three articles setting up the two agencies: article II stating that such an action conformed to the dictates of the peacemakers, article III establishing the International Commission from Ulm to Brăila, and article IV maintaining the European Commission. This was the first open test of Romania's resolve to abolish the European agency.

Stelian's opening remarks in response to Legrand's proposals for the Commission portended a test of strength. He called upon his fellow representatives to "respect the dispositions of the [Versailles] treaties" but claimed the European Commission was an "anomaly" that "constitutes a servitude for Romania."[75] At this point, however, his tone changed. If the agency were to be kept, Stelian believed that only one article would be sufficient "to simply enunciate the existence of the two commissions charged to assure liberty of navigation."[76] In that regard, he proposed an alternative article consolidating the three. It would establish two

administrative bodies, one a "maritime" agency (hence an attempt by Stelian to avert the extension of the Commission to Brăila, due to the question whether the latter was actually a maritime port) and the other a
"fluvial" organization.[77] By including the two under the same heading,
Stelian also hoped to bring the powers of the European Commission more
into harmony with the future prerogatives of its companion organization.
This amendment, slightly revised by Legrand, was approved with little
further debate, thus ending the question of the European Commission,
for all practical purposes.

Romania's acquiescence to the existence of the two commissions
meant that in the ensuing discussion of the articles pertaining to the
European Commission principal opposition to the maintenance of the
body's composition and jurisdiction would come not from Stelian but
from the other delegates. Stelian became a staunch defender of the "anomaly," vigorously demanding the continuation of the *status quo* against
the protests of Greece's A. Andreades, Belgium's Brunet, and Ristić.

Andreades attacked the other delegates for ignoring the commercial
activities of Greece on the Danube and failing to include a representative
from Athens on the European Commission. Greek shipping comprised
23.5 percent of total river traffic in the years immediately preceding the
war and thus contributed a substantial portion of the organization's operating budget. Also, 130 of 193 pilots employed by the agency were Greek
nationals. Despite Greece's interests, however, the conferees "played to
Romania's demands" by limiting the Commission's membership rather
than making it a truly international body; in so doing they ignored Greece,
which Andreades characterized as "the agent of conciliation and model
of moderation in Eastern Europe."[78]

Ristić and Brunet likewise demanded admission of their countries
to the Commission. The former declared that all riverine nations must
be allowed representation on the European agency because of the importance of the delta to the commerce of the entire Basin.[79] Although admitting Belgium's modest physical maritime role, Brunet supported his
nation's claim on the basis that its ports acted as the primary transship-
ment center for East European grains and that its interests would grow
after the completion of the Rhine-Danube canal.[80] Their arguments, like
those of Andreades, were valid but futile.

Although the noncommission members could openly seek the modification of the agency, they could do little beyond verbal protestations.

In order to pass any measure altering the composition of the agency, they needed the unanimous approval of its members. This was an impossible task.[81] Any support from the Western members of the European Commission for the claims of Andreades (and the others), despite the favor Britain and France had shown toward admitting the Mediterranean state, would have been blocked by Romania. This would have forced an indefinite extension of the conference if the demands for admission continued to be pressed in the face of repeated Romanian vetoes. The disadvantages of Romanian intransigence and a possible change in Romania's policy of conceding the issue of the continuation of the Commission outweighed any diplomatic benefits that might be gained by granting Athens, Brussels, or Belgrade a seat in Galați. Thus, with the four members of the European Commission in agreement to maintain the *status quo ante bellum*, the plenipotentiaries passed Legrand's four articles pertaining to the European agency in less than an hour's time. So long opposed by Romania's diplomats, politicians, and a vocal group of writers and historians, the European Commission was thus quietly prolonged, and Romania had little choice but to accept the diplomatic defeat. Yet, by extending the Commission's jurisdiction to Brăila only in regard to the waterway and not the port itself, the Western representatives avoided a confrontation with Bucharest, seemingly ended a dispute that had existed since 1883,[82] and provided the Romanian government with a face-saving measure. Bucharest could now claim vindication of its principles by forcing the West to concede the question of using Brăila as a Commission port.[83]

The *Conférence Internationale du Danube* now became a convention designed to formulate rules for the fluvial Danube, the portion of the river that since 1856 had been subject to only national regulations. Devising a code acceptable to the conferees was not an easy task, however. It involved major concessions by the riparian countries to interests that they viewed as threatening rights belonging to the national states. At the same time, it meant that the Western nations had to balance the desire to promote their own commercial advantages with the fears of the riverine countries.

The contrasting views expressed by Baldwin and Stelian best summarize the debate over the powers to be granted the International Commission. The former believed that internationalization of a waterway conferred rights to all nonriverines within the territorial waters of the river-bordering states. These prerogatives could be granted by the convention and, as such, he (Baldwin) could decide the extent to which the riparian state's jurisdiction could be limited. Stelian, on the other hand, stressed that only powers of supervising navigation belonged to the commission; no one had the right to intercede in national ports.[84]

Beyond this fundamental theoretical difference of opinion, each state had its own particular concerns. This was evident in the discussion of each article. Often general agreement could be obtained through no more than the modification of a few words or deletion of a phrase from Legrand's second project. In some cases, however, the conflict between the various positions was resolved only after fierce debate over the interpretation of an article.

The first measure that provoked heated words was the issue of the initiation of work. Unlike the strong powers granted the European Commission, Legrand proposed allowing the riparian states to undertake all physical construction and maintenance of all facilities (articles XI and XIII) subject to the approval of the entire organization. Costs would be borne by the respective states.[85] This was approved with a minimum of discussion. At the same time, however, it created a significant problem— the question of the agency's power to act in the event that a particular state did not perform the necessary tasks. Legrand's original proposal permitted the International Commission to authorize another riparian state to undertake the work if a default should occur. This angered most of the riparians. Ristić declared that his country could never allow another state to act within its borders; this right was protected under article 351 of Versailles, which guaranteed the territories of his country, Romania, and Czechoslovakia from outside intrusion.[86] Curiously, Stelian did not join this argument in support of his nominal ally, a silence that reflected either the advanced nature of Romania's river facilities and capabilities compared to those of the other allied riparian states or a willingness to allow Ristić to carry the brunt of the attack. In spite of Stelian's passive role during this debate, riparian opposition, led by Ristić, forced Legrand to present a compromise. In the event that a state did not carry out the authorized functions, the International Commission reserved the right, subject to the stipulations of Versailles, to complete the work.[87] This satisfied the objections of the riverines, many of whom feared the possible intervention of "enemy" nations within their territorial waters, yet gave the International Commission ultimate authority, by virtue of the article's vagueness, to ensure the maintenance of the river's facilities.

The issue of taxation required a similar compromise. The more advanced commercial states, including Austria and Hungary, which, despite losses during the war, sought to reinvigorate their shipping enterprises, argued for strict regulation of taxation by the central organization. Austria asserted that the 1856 Treaty of Paris prohibited the imposition of any duties; removal of obstacles was the responsibility of the state and as such should be supported by that nation.[88] Muller said that only "grand work" could be covered by tax revenues.[89] Stelian and Ristić, on the other hand, demanded complete coverage. The Romanian stated that no one could interfere with a right that was a national rather than an international prerogative.[90] The compromise reached by the delegates again reflected the need to defer any firm commitment; the state became responsible for all payments for work, but these could be recovered in part by duties authorized by the main body.[91]

Enforcement of revenue provisions posed the related problem of the use of police vessels and warships. Unlike previous matters, this directly affected the sovereignty of each riparian state. By nature, internationality implied neutrality, but there was considerable disagreement as to whether this also meant demilitarization. Legrand proposed that only police ships be permitted to operate on the river and only in numbers restricted to actual need. Speaking in his capacity as the representative of France, he hoped that the others would not interpret this "as an act of disarmament by some powers on other powers." Instead, he saw it as a "spirit" of voluntarism that he hoped would "inspire" the world.[92] Baldwin was equally in favor of demilitarization but far less altruistic in his presentation. The Treaty of Berlin, he asserted, authorized such a measure, although he neglected to mention that this was confined to the river south of the Iron Gates. Now this could and would be implemented. If the riverines did not accept the limitation, Britian held the right to station its own warships on the Danube, a move seconded by Italy.[93]

Stelian viewed the issue from a different perspective. He acknowledged and appreciated the president's idealism but stressed that Romania could not neglect its own defense. No one in the Basin had "aggressive intentions," but without sea defense Romania would be vulnerable to attack, "especially from the East." Therefore, he could not talk about international rights and "voluntarism." Disarmament had "dangerous consequences" that threatened the "principle of sovereignty and political independence of our state." Neutrality for Romania was "a political problem that exceeds the competence of this conference."[94]

Faced by a strong opposition to the limitation of warships on the river, Legrand reluctantly withdrew his recommendation.[95] In its place the members adopted a modified article that left the question of the number of police vessels open and required only their registry with the commission.[96] They could not resolve the issue of the warships and chose to defer the matter until the next session by including three proposals in the preliminary text. The French article opened the river to all warships, subject to the guarantee of liberty of navigation. Baldwin limited the ships to those of "maritime usuage," thereby ensuring the British navy's domination. Stelian restricted military vessels to territorial waters, thus allowing only riparian ships to be stationed on the river; passage of nonnational warships could occur only with the permission of the riverine states.[97] This deferral enabled the delegates to break a substantial roadblock that threatened to delay their work. They now turned to the subject of cabotage, the issue that brought the bitterest debate.

In this controversy the principal antagonists were Coromilas and Baldwin, in support of totally free rights of navigation, and Stelian, who demanded the protection of his nation's inter-port trade. Coromilas declared that anything less than free and open cabotage would violate the spirit of the peace treaties and the Danube's internationality. The only restrictions on free commerce pertained to the defeated nations (article 293 of Saint-Germain). To abridge historic principles (that is, the spirit of Vienna, the Rhine and Congo agreements, and so forth) would mean abandoning something supported by the peacemakers. Although Baldwin admitted that this favored his own country, he argued the concept of internationality made all national interests secondary.[98]

Stelian countered that an end to cabotage restrictions threatened "the independence and dignity of the state." He also cited Versailles for support. Article 332 of the treaty with Germany guaranteed the protection of the small riparian states. Cabotage, by ships of all nations, must have the prior approval of the territorial states in order that the latter might "defend the economic institutions which assure [its] existence and

independence." Against Baldwin's charge that Romania was trying to sub-
stitute all nonriverines for the word "German" in the aforementioned
article 332, the Romanian delegation responded that the Treaty of December 20, 1919, between Romania and the Great Powers, and similar
pacts with Belgrade and Prague, also "expressly recognized the right of
cabotage in its [Romania's] ports" and, as such, did not consider it an
abridgement of the principle of freedom of navigation.[99]

In this debate, as with numerous others, the delegates used the peace
treaties to support completely opposite positions. Just as the Versailles
articles were often sufficiently vague to lead to different interpretations,
so too were the plenipotentiaries in Paris forced to write inexact articles
in order to obtain a compromise. The difficulty of their task was compounded by the fact that they were debating rights, not territorial changes,
percentage of reparations, or economic concessions. They dealt in grey
matters of theory rather than fact; all positions had equal merit, therefore. In addition, despite approval of the rest of the preliminary text,
the delegates occasionally voted for articles as a means of gaining time
to reassess a position. For the moment the conferees were more interested in formulating a first draft of the *Statut* than in obtaining exact
wording of the provisions. Diplomacy was conducted in two stages, therefore: first to elaborate theories that culminated in compromises ame-
nable to national interests; second, to gain adherents to that view so that
at the next session no retreat from that position would have to be made.
Thus, whereas long and arduous debate did result in compromises such
as the guarantee that the riparian allies could reserve cabotage for national
companies, in reality, these were no more than stepping-stones to the
renewed hard bargaining of the second session.

In two cases no compromise could be reached, and after numerous
hours of fruitless negotiations the delegates wisely decided to leave the
matters until the 1921 session. The first involved the river's "affluents,"
that is, the degree to which the tributaries of the Danube would be included under the *Statut*'s provisions. The riverine states naturally sought
to limit the extension of the powers of others on the International Commission to control additional fluvial operations within their borders. The
other issue concerned the future seat of the agency. In this case the Little
Entente states adamantly refused to accept the proposed site of Budapest
yet could not agree among themselves on a suitable alternative.

Only one remaining issue delayed the completion of the preliminary draft: the future administration of the Iron Gates. Stelian and Ristić demanded that their two countries govern the area. Both proposed creating a subcommission, composed of the co-riverines and a third member (preferably a nonriparian state), to be fully responsible for the sector. Although this did not differ substantially with the concept of the subcommission contained in Legrand's project, the three disagreed over the application of authority. Legrand gave the International Commission full power to set the prerogatives of the new agency.[100] Ristić entrusted the subcommission with complete jurisdiction, but the coordination of its activities would be supervised by an intermediary between it and the International Commission.[101] Stelian, in contrast, left less control with the latter than did Ristić. Under Stelian's amendment, the powers of the subcommission would be clearly defined by the conferees at the present congress rather than waiting for any future discussions, as Ristić and Legrand wanted. Thus, he attacked the Serb for being too vague. Stelian proposed granting the subcommission full authority under the auspices of the parent organization, but the latter could act only if the new body violated the provisions of the *Statut*. Granting the Gates' commission full jurisdiction stemmed from his belief that "internationalization of a river should not signify the expropriation of the [rights of a] riverine, but rather the harmonization of their respective interests with the general interests of navigation." Protection of the latter would stem from the inclusion of a third member. Romanian and Yugoslav acquiescence to the French proposal, on the other hand, would reduce their rights to ones of mere consent and lead to the "expropriation of the natural riches of the co-riverines," especially their right to harness the area's hydraulic potential.[102]

This debate over the Gates and the fear that Romania would lose what Stelian believed to be legitimate national rights in the region led to a threat that the delegation would cease negotiations. The "impasse," they informed Legrand, created a situation wherein "it is impossible to continue the deliberations." During the course of the conference, Stelian asserted, Romania had granted many "concessions," but "with the question of the Gates, the interests of Romania are of another nature."[103] This warning was not carried out, however, and discussions continued. Finally, on November 12, the delegates reached yet another compromise. They agreed that the subcommission, consisting of three members, would have full local authority, as Stelian demanded. They also included two additional provisions. The first approved the takeover of all former Habsburg facilities in the region, as foreseen in article 288 of the Treaty of Trianon; the second gave the International Commission the power to keep the prerogatives of the Gates' agency in conformity with its own laws,[104] thereby keeping ultimate authority in the hands of the larger body.

This proved to be the last major obstacle to the completion of the initial draft. Yet, like many of the other issues, it was only a temporary measure designed to permit the delegates to finish a rough text and adjourn for consultation with their respective foreign ministries. The future of the Iron Gates, like the other questions, therefore, remained unresolved for the present.

After the ratification of a preamble, the work of the first session ended. This, in turn, closed the portion of the Danube Conference that dealt in grey areas of theory. When the convention re-opened, negotiations revolved around specific privileges and wording. Each future meeting involved attempts by the various delegations to either consolidate or alter earlier positions. Therefore, the first draft was little more than what Legrand termed his first project. It was merely a "model." Months of difficult negotiations remained.

CHAPTER VII

THE COMPLETION OF THE *STATUT*

On April 5, 1921, the plenipotentiaries returned to Paris. With a frame-work for the *Statut Définitif* already constructed, they began the task of completing the document. Although the 1920 session witnessed a wide divergence of opinion and lasted longer than the delegates expected, there was little reason to suspect that the prolonged deliberations would continue.[1] Instead, it appeared likely that final ratifications would follow brief discussions designed to iron out the few details still unresolved.

Such was not the case, however. The text adopted at the last meeting in November proved to be no more than a guide and the various delegations now sought to modify earlier positions. In addition, during their absence a League of Nations conference on the internationality of all waterways took place in Barcelona; the outcome of that convention created difficulties for the Paris conferees by seemingly conflicting with many of the provisions approved in November. Theories had thus been put forward at both Paris and Barcelona and the time had now come to resolve the remaining questions and give those theories final, concrete form.

The change from the theoretical to the technical aspects of the conference is characterized by the substitution that took place within the Romanian delegation: the egotistical legalist, Toma Stelian resigned, giving way to the Commission functionary, Constantin Conțescu. After the close of the first session, Stelian, an older man, informed Foreign Minister Ionescu that he would not be returning to Paris,[2] although he gave no explanation for this decision. Ionescu attempted to dissuade him from resigning by appealing to his sense of patriotism:

98

> Although, Minister, you communicated to me that you can no
> longer make the sacrifice to go once again to Paris, I ask you, with
> all insistence . . . to do this sacrifice for your country. You know
> that no one would be able to do as well as yourself to sustain our
> interests there.[3]

Unsuccessful in his effort to persuade Stelian to reconsider, Ionescu turned
to Conțescu.

In retrospect, the move turned out to be fortuitous for Romania.
Conțescu had been present at the first meeting, and knew first-hand the
mood of the conference. More importantly, he was intimately aware of
the problems of the river, having guided the European Commission after
the war and having acted as Romania's minister to both international
Danube organizations. He would be better able to understand proposed
word changes that might lead to administrative operations opposed by
Bucharest. Furthermore, the past bitter exchanges between Conțescu and
the other members of the agencies made it abundantly clear that he would
strongly oppose any major alterations in the initial text. This refusal to
allow the other representatives to gain an upper hand was clearly established as the first meeting reconvened.

Conțescu's opening address was of a perfunctory nature. He hoped
that his relationship with the other delegates would be amiable, and he
recommended that the now vacant position as vice-president of the conference should go to Ristić because of the latter's seniority.[4]

Conțescu's next remarks were less conciliatory, however. Although
he applauded Baldwin's plea to speed the work of the conference, he
added that this could be facilitated only by "the abandonment of all
affectations of eloquence and rhetoric and a return to the realm of positive discussion."[5] The exact meaning behind that statement was unclear,
although it may be assumed that Conțescu meant strict adherence to
League rules rather than pre-1914 prerogatives. Toward that end, he proposed that the delegates examine the decisions of the *Conférence des
communications et du transit* still meeting in Barcelona. That convention, established by the League to formulate general rules of navigation
and "internationality," should act as their guide. In response to Baldwin's
assertion that Barcelona had no effect on their work because Versailles
stipulated that the Danube was a unique case, Conțescu charged that

although they could not scrap their previous negotiations, they had to
be certain that the *Statut* conformed to the League's regulations. The
Danube pacts, he reminded the others, could not deviate from prescribed
international law.[6]

Conțescu had no real chance to align the provisions of the Paris Conference with those of Barcelona. Legrand quickly tabled the motion,
ruling that this could be discussed later, and opened debate on the preliminary text.[7]

Conțescu was under no illusion that the attempt to tie the Paris decisions to those of Barcelona would succeed. In reality, Romania's position at the second session was one of support for the preliminary text.
Yet, by expressing the idea of uniformity with the general rules of Barcelona, Conțescu forced Baldwin, his principal opponent at the second
session, into a position of trying to alter a pact that already conflicted
in a few basic points with the rules of internationality established by
the League. This gave Conțescu greater leverage in pressing his own minor
revisions, especially when they agreed with the ideals of the Barcelona
treaty. Romania could accept a few conflicting provisions "with resignation,"[8] thereby appearing more conciliatory. Bucharest could not accept
major changes, however.

The Barcelona agreements reaffirmed the basic provisions established
for international rivers a century earlier at Vienna. Although the definition of an international river did not clash with the spirit of the *Statut*'s first article, Barcelona provided that responsibility for the administration of an artery and its navigable branches belonged to a commission composed of all riparian states. These nations individually would
be responsible for work, policing the river, taxation necessary to defray
the costs of maintenance, and so forth, capabilities subject to overall
supervision by the entire central body. The latter could hold only powers
of arbitration and the right to intervene in the event of default of needed
work.[9]

In theory, Barcelona and Paris clashed on two major points: the question of the European Commission's preservation and the ability of the
International Commission to act in a regulatory fashion. Barcelona had no
practical effect, however. It could not be applied to the European Commission because its rules could not supersede statutes already in effect.
Also, Barcelona did not officially rule out the possible existence of a second river agency. Romania had conceded the issue of the European

Commission at the first session and that act was now irreversible. Therefore, the ideas contained in the Barcelona treaty could only apply to
the International Commission, but even this was of limited value because the Versailles framers did not permit those decisions to take precedence over the work of the Danube Conference. Conţescu's use of
the Barcelona convention was thus only a tool to emphasize a particular
point. It forced the others to defend policies seemingly at odds with accepted international doctrine; beyond that it had little practical value.

With their work confined to the matter of the Danube, rather than
any theoretical application of the Barcelona provisions, the delegates
now began to complete their earlier efforts. To the surprise of many,
however, they did not perfunctorily ratify the text endorsed in November. Instead of approving that pact, pausing to make a few cosmetic
changes in the wording and quickly resolving the few outstanding issues
(notably cabotage, the Gates, and the warships), the delegations re-opened
debate on many of the articles that appeared to have been resolved in
1920.

During the interim between the sessions, Ionescu had informed the
governments of France, Italy, and Great Britain that Romania would not
retreat from that which it obtained at the first gathering. He left room
open only for "reciprocal concessions."[10] Sensing that Britain might
act as the biggest obstacle to the conclusion of the *Statut* as it stood,
he instructed his London delegation to lobby with the Foreign Office
for ratification of the text. He reminded Britain of the importance of
the Danube problem for Romania.[11] "Britain," he cautioned, "knows
well . . . [Romanian] public opinion," a veiled threat to the possibility
that an effort by London to change the text substantially might result
in a suspension of the negotiations by Romania.[12]

The initial response to Ionescu's efforts was encouraging. No significant opposition to Romania's desire for ratification appeared likely
from either Paris or Rome. More importantly, the Romanian minister
to London, M. Boerescu, believed that an accord with Britain was possible.[13] The British Secretary of State assured him that London would
make every attempt "to reach an equitable solution for the general interests of the riverine states."[14]

British actions after the conference reconvened belied Boerescu's initial
optimism. He soon informed Ionescu "that the attitude of Britain is contrary

to the project." Instead of working toward ratification of the agreements, Baldwin would be presenting "hostile" alternatives to the preliminary text.[15] Conțescu also warned Ionescu that the greatest "danger" was Britain's "nasty whim" to alter the Gates' accord by increasing the sub-commission's membership to five. Baldwin's attitude, Conțescu reported, "meddles brutally in [the] internal affairs of [the] riverines, completely ignoring their sovereign rights."[16] Conțescu's primary job thus became blocking all moves by his British counterpart to alter the text.

Despite Ionescu's admonition against attempting to change the text, Britain considered Romanian opposition "a surprise." The Foreign Office told Boerescu that it was "inconsistent with that which they were entitled to expect from the friendship of an ally." Britain envisioned a new spirit of cooperation on the river and objected to the terms "conquered" and "enemy" that Romanian delegates employed when referring to the former Central Powers; these were not conducive to peace or the "spirit" of the treaties and "might ultimately . . . be harmful."[17]

London equated strong regulatory powers with riparian cooperation. In the eyes of the Foreign Office, positions opposed to the latter were detrimental to the future of the Danube's internationality and peace in the Basin. This policy was laudable but myopic. It failed to see that intra-Basin hostilities ran deep and that Britain was not viewed as an honest broker. Instead it was seen as a party attempting to maximize its own advantages while granting hated neighbors rights within the territorial waters of the riparian allies and outlawing a line of defense by demanding the elimination of warships on the river. Romania could never have accepted such measures. In the face of Britain's attempted revisions, Conțescu joined Legrand in becoming one of the principal supporters of the preliminary treaty.

The defense of rights that Conțescu believed to be in the best interests of all the riparian nations was not easily upheld. Again, the problem involved the inability of the Little Entente states to reach a *démarche* on river policy. Any hope that the riverines would work together was, in Conțescu's words, "a major dose of optimism on my part."[18] The three "allied" riparian states continued to work at cross-purposes, although Conțescu, at first, believed that differences with Ristić could be worked out "with little difficulty."[19] But Muller remained a problem and all "our efforts . . . with the Czech delegate . . . have proved to be without result."[20] Where issues concerned the powers of the vanquished states (especially Hungary) to hold a similar status with the victors, Muller and Conțescu reached an accord. Over the questions of the Gates, warships, and the European Commission, however, Prague acted against the wishes of Conțescu and Ionescu. Furthermore, Muller supported free cabotage because of the more advanced state of Czechoslovakia's shipping industry and industrial capabilities. This created a serious breach with Conțescu since the restriction of rights of cabotage was a cornerstone of Romania's policy. The profession of amiability betweeen Conțescu and Muller was but an illusion, therefore. After the conference concluded, Conțescu would dismiss his relationship with Muller as one in which "a favorable collaboration was almost impossible."[21]

As debate re-opened on the articles pertaining to the European Commission, Conțescu adamantly refused to accept or even discuss any modification of the preliminary text. He rejected the argument of the other riparians that they deserved representation because of the delta's importance for river commerce.[22] If admission was opened to all, Conțescu argued, there would be no reason for the existence of the organization, something Romania desired but few others accepted. Since the other conferees chose to sustain the body, Romania would support it "with resignation;" but, his country could not increase "the painful obligations on its territory" by extending membership to others.[23] He could support a state's admission only if the latter joined Romania in fighting to dissolve the body.[24] This was, of course, a self-defeating proposition for the other nations; a state would be attempting to join the agency only to work for its demise. Furthermore, he argued that the conference had no right to choose the composition of the European Commission. Despite the wording of article 346 of Versailles, which set the membership on a provisional basis, the structure could be changed only with the unanimous consent of its four members. Romania could thus block the admission of any other state, a power that the German delegate described as a *liberum veto*.[25] Changing the provisional composition of an agency was a prerogative granted only to the fluvial administration. As for the question of extending the Commission's jurisdiction to Brăila, Romania agreed to concede the issue only out of a sense of "benevolence. . . rather than an obligation imposed by the treaties." Romania would never "renounce those rights" that "are indispensable to the economic life of the country."[26]

Conțescu agreed to accept the formal extension of the agency to Brăila provided that a separate protocol signed by the representatives of the Commission be included, leaving the matter of the ports between Galați and Brăila open for future negotiations. Finally, Conțescu pledged that in the event that the European Commission ever dissolved his country would voluntarily extend all rights of navigation granted by the International Commission to the maritime Danube.[27] Of course, this promise did not satisfy his riparian "allies," who wanted a formal commitment guaranteeing this.

As at the first session, the plenipotentiaries had little choice but to accept the articles as they stood; Romania, through its power of the veto, held the trump card. Conțescu thus successfully blocked all efforts by the other representatives to alter the acts adopted in 1920. Therefore, the conferees turned once again to the question of the International Commission, the only agency that they were authorized to change, according to Conțescu.[28] Just as he had opposed any alteration in the prerogatives of the European Commission, Conțescu would now seek to limit modifications to the charter of the fluvial body.

The problem of wording the articles pertaining to the International Commission became a delicate matter. Unlike the relatively brief debate on the attributes of the European agency, the remaining discussions would be long and arduous. Although Conțescu and Baldwin again played the principal roles,[29] theirs was only one of the many feuds that marked the negotiations.[30] Despite the fact that these confrontations produced no substantive changes, the intense debate created a mood of ill-will that persisted beyond the conclusion of the conference. In that sense, the British Foreign Office's reprimand to Conțescu was correct; the harsh words, by all parties, were counter-productive. The rifts extended beyond the Danubian Basin, however, and Baldwin was no less immune from the antipathy than were the Basin's victors and vanquished; the same men who fought at Paris would have to put the provisions of the *Statut* into effect.

The conference thus settled into a debating forum characterized by discussions of countless minor word changes and hypothetical situations. In the end, these next three months proved to be anticlimactic. Despite the long hours of negotiations little in the preliminary text was changed except to settle the few remaining issues purposely left unresolved in November.

A major stumbling-block again surrounded the question of work; the conferees had not addressed themselves fully to the problem of paying for projects initiated by the riparian states. Most of the delegations believed that this was an obligation that should be borne by the state itself.[31] On the other hand, Conțescu argued that his country would be unfairly burdened because one-third of the Danube's length flowed in some fashion through Romanian territory. He demanded, therefore, that some of the costs be covered by taxation, a matter strongly opposed by Baldwin, Muller, and Germany's envoy, Dr. Seeliger, the latter terming Romania's position "primitive."[32] Conțescu estimated that 40 percent of all funds spent on work directly benefited foreign shipping, that is, nonnational trade. As such, those countries must bear a responsibility for covering costs. This would also ensure the upkeep of the river by preventing a state's negligence due to a lack of available funds.[33]

Again, the delegates resolved the impasse by avoiding the issue. They decided that the cost of maintenance would be the responsibility of the individual riverine country but that the state could call upon the entire International Commission for partial reimbursement.[34] This measure did not alter the basic idea adopted in November; it continued to defer any final decision on payments to a subcommission, to be created by the fluvial agency.[35]

The debate over cabotage intensified during the second session. Greece, which had lost its bid to gain admission to the two commissions, now directed its entire strategy toward opening commerce to all ships with no restrictions. Unlike his predecessor Coromilas, Andreades was not content to approve an article that did not spell out specific uses and restrictions of cabotage privileges. He protested Conțescu's refusal to honor the pledge made by Stelian in 1920 to incorporate an "interpretive article" specifying the limitations which a riverine could place on cabotage.[36] The fervor with which Andreades pressed his claims provoked Baldwin, his ally, to remark sarcastically that he "thought until now that the Danube was only Romanian, but I didn't know it was also Greek."[37]

Conțescu continued to ignore Greek and British attacks. He opposed any extension of the privilege "on the basis that this [free and open cabotage] would only be to the advantage of the upstream states." The more advanced nations to the north, all "ex-enemies" of Romania with the exception of Czechoslovakia, would quickly gain control of fluvial commerce. To counter this threat, he argued, Romania must have the capability of protecting its economic integrity and well-being.[38]

Faced with a stalemate that jeopardized adoption of the *Statut*, the plenipotentiaries agreed to a British compromise that guaranteed cabotage rights to all vessels with two important reservations. First, the delegates approved a separate agreement between Andreades and Conțescu that opened intra-state commerce to all ships that did not jeopardize "national interests," that is, did not damage native shipping industries. Second, an additional subheading, prepared by Seeliger and Brunet, restricted cabotage privileges by the former Central Powers only as long as the stipulations under the various Versailles treaties remained in effect.[39] This measure satisfied the demands by Ristić and Conțescu that the "ex-enemies" could trade in their countries' ports only with the express permission of their governments.

These actions "abandoned absolutely nothing,"[40] as Conțescu correctly observed, even though the compromise represented one of the few deviations from an article accepted at the first session. Romania would still be able to limit the commercial activities of foreign enterprises by claiming that they interfered with the development of national shipping concerns. The ambiguous wording left full power in the hands of the riparian states, which exercised ultimate authority over the extent to which "liberty of navigation" would apply. The compromise symbolized the futility that often surrounded the labors of the various delegations. "Internationality" was espoused once again, but its application, through the wording of the text, was so inexact that it threatened to permit actions at cross-purposes with the spirit of "freedom of navigation." The future of cabotage privileges thus rested with the riparian governments.

With the matter of cabotage "resolved," the final major hurdle became the question of the administration of the Iron Gates. This debate marked the culmination of the British-Romanian feud over the extent of the International Commission's regulatory powers. During the 1920 meetings the plenipotentiaries agreed that the area between Turnu-Severin and Orșova would be governed by a three-member subcommission composed of representatives from Romania, the Kingdom of the Serbs, Croats, and Slovenes, and a nonriparian state. This body would take full authority in the area, subject to the final approval of the larger organization. But Baldwin now proposed, despite strong opposition from Belgrade and

Bucharest, to expand the size of the Gates' agency to include two additional riparian representatives.[41] For the co-riverines, adoption of the
British plan would mean the inclusion of an "enemy" state on the agency
and the reduction of their jurisdiction in the region.[42]

Baldwin asserted that the original proposal lacked a "sufficient international spirit" and was not in the best interests of the riparian countries.[43] Gheorghe Popescu, Romania's technical expert, disputed this
argument, however. Popescu stated that the existence of the International
Commission protected all interests in the region. Any additional members would be unnecessary and "in contradiction of the [peace] treaties."[44] Ristić added that before the war the territorial state (Austria-
Hungary) had been granted complete control of the Gates; now "some"
of the same states (that is, Germany, Hungary, Austria, Czechoslovakia,
and Britain) were demanding an increase in membership to five. He won-
dered what advantage these advocates of a larger subcommission thought
this might bring.[45] Conţescu joined Ristić and Popescu in denouncing
the British measure. He asked whether the others thought that Romania
or "Yugoslavia" would have sought a third member if they "wanted to
shirk their duties" or "impede navigation?" Neither co-riverine could
agree to granting other nations such an "inconceivable privilege" within
their territorial waters. The interests of the co-riverines and the other
nations would not be at odds as Baldwin hypothesized. Freedom of
navigation would be guaranteed by three checks: the *Statut*, the International Commission, and the presence of a third member on the subcommission.[46]

On this issue the lines were clearly drawn. Bucharest and Belgrade
saw the matter in simple terms: they were being denied the right to
govern the region in a manner similar to the way in which Austria-Hungary
had supervised the Iron Gates before the war. They voluntarily agreed
to add another representative to the subcommission but would make no
other concessions.[47] The other riparian nations, as well as France and
Britain, believed that a separate international regime, with a broad representation, was essential because of the physical hazards in the area. They
were unwilling to place the Gates in the hands of an agency in which
Bucharest and Belgrade would have the principal vote. The difference
between the two positions seemed irreconcilable. One side saw the very
concept of internationality threatened by a small subcommission, while

the other feared infringement by outside forces in the area, (a matter that Ionescu characterized as "the British menace").[43] On this issue rested the fate of the entire conference, and the plenipotentiaries acknowledged this by their decision to complete work on the remaining few articles, except for the issue of the warships, before re-addressing themselves to the Gates' controversy.

Conțescu privately admitted to Ionescu that he might have to accept a fourth delegate to the subcommission but that this representative could only be a Czech. In turn, he revealed this to the entire membership on June 20 as "a concession . . . for an ally and a friend."[50] Legrand dismissed this gesture as "inutile," however, and Baldwin characterized the stance of the co-riverines as "absolutely contrary to internationalization."[51] It also brought strong opposition from the representatives of the former Central Powers, as creating a perpetual "victor-vanquished" differentiation and a "permanent discrimination" against their rights.[52]

The attacks by the latter elicited perhaps the strongest Romanian response of the conference in an address that symbolized the country's view not only of the Danube issue but also of their situation in the Basin. Conțescu began by stating that when the first laws for the Danube were enacted Romania naturally had no voice. After independence its views were still ignored. Now when Romania had such representation, after it had been victorious in the war, and when the Gates were no longer in the territory of those who created "an iron barrier against its [the Gates'] liberty," these same states were trying to deny the co-riverines similar rights.[53] If the vanquished nations wished to see "inequity," he told them to re-examine the provisions of the Treaty of Bucharest (see chapter three).[54] Privately, he described as "pathetic" Seeliger's appeals on behalf of the former enemies' rights of representation; publicly, he was no less vitriolic in his tone and called his reproaches to the Germans "cruel."[55] Just as he could never permit the other conferees to injure his country, he could not let them extend privileges to those who forced the Treaty of Bucharest on Romania.

In order to alleviate the stalemate wrought by the continued opposition of Ristić and Conțescu to any increase in the membership of the Gates' subcommission, Legrand proposed placing the region under the sole control of the International Commission. The co-riverines would hold only limited jurisdiction; only the choice of personnel would be

left to regional authorities.[56] This received the strong endorsement of
Baldwin, who felt that it would prevent the development of any possible
hazards to navigation resulting from future discords between Bucharest
and Belgrade.

Conţescu again refused to accept the measure. Instead, he suggested
scrapping the idea of a subcommission, as Legrand had done, and administering the area by common agreement between the co-riverines and the
Technical Services Subcommission of the International Commission.
Employees, except pilots, would be named by Romania and the Kingdom of the Serbs, Croats, and Slovenes. The two countries would also
nominate chiefs of service, subject to final confirmation by the organization in Bratislava, the latter finally chosen as the commisssion's seat.
The entire commission would be responsible for ensuring that all authorized and required services be performed, thus granting all the riparians a voice in the region's affairs.[57]

This proposal was adopted with little debate. The co-riverine states
maintained principal control over the Gates while the overall jurisdiction
of the International Commission protected the other nations' interests.
As such, it was a significant compromise. It satisfied both groups and
was one of the few controversial articles that was worded with sufficient
precision to leave little room for future debate.

With the discussion of the Gates' issue closed, the last obstacle, the
matter of the use of warships on the Danube, was quickly settled. With
no compromise possible between the positions taken at the first session,
the delegates had no choice but to bow to Conţescu's demand that the
entire question be suppressed.[58] This decision to avoid more tedious
negotiations reflected not only the realization that no accord was possible on this issue but also indicated a weariness, caused by months of
debate, that had begun to take its toll upon the plenipotentiaries.

After a few final word changes, therefore, the conferees submitted
the document to their respective foreign ministries for final approval.
Like most of the other delegations, Romania reserved judgment on one
or two points of procedure pending this examination. But Ionescu fully
understood the victories won by his delegation over the questions of
cabotage, the Gates, and warships and immediately instructed Conţescu
to withdraw all reservations and sign the document.[59]

Thus, on July 23, 1921, the conferees, with the exceptions of the
Italian and Yugoslav delegates, signed the *Statut Définitif* (see Appendix

11).[60] Even though it would be almost four years before the Italian Parliament ratified the treaty, the last body to do so, the pact became binding after three months.[61] In October 1921, sixty-five years after the framers of the Treaty of Paris attempted to internationalize the Danube for the first time, an international administration formed to guarantee the right of navigation went into effect.

For Romania, the conference proved successful. Despite a lack of interest in the issue by government leaders, the delegation "obtained absolutely all that we asked." Conțescu saw the outcome as a "triumph" of "our rights." He believed that the *Statut* would support Romania's political situation, which he described as "an element of order and progress in the East."[62] In placing the treaty before the Romanian Parliament for approval, Ionescu called it "a triumph of the Romanian point of view without lessening the bonds between us and our Great Allies." It ensured the safe future of the river for the Romanian people, "the latin sentinel in the far corner of Europe."[63]

One should not quickly pass harsh judgment on these jingoistic statements; they reflect a xenophobic nationalism that pervaded throughout the Basin during the interwar years. The Romanian Foreign Ministry, which rightly or wrongly perceived the past history of the Danube as a threat to the sovereign rights of the nation, naturally felt that the outcome of the Paris Conference was a vindication of its interests, ending "once and for all, the unequal regime" and creating a "shelter from the vicissitudes of the past, the vexatious injustices. . . ."[64] Despite pretensions to the contrary, the Danube settlement was not won by Romanian "blood" on the battlefield; its efforts in the war deserved no more than the overhaul of its military infrastructure. Instead, the new era of *"Dunărea noastră"* was won at the bargaining table. The delegation saw the issues clearly from the beginning; no political or theoretical interests were involved in the question of the administration of the river, only national ones.[65]

The internationalization of the Danube, as established by the *Statut*, was thus no more than an accommodation of national interests with the idea of internationality as defined by the great powers. The requirements of international trade necessitated its provisions; beyond that little changed from the prewar dispensation. The great powers maintained a strong influence on the river and their presence in both river agencies meant that they would continue to exercise a powerful voice in fluvial and maritime affairs. The weight of that influence on the Upper Danube, however, was limited. All efforts toward initiating a state of neutrality failed. An administration was created, but all aspects of work, appointments, taxation, and policing remained firmly in the hands of the national, riparian countries. The European Commission continued to exist, but Romania limited its membership, thereby eliminating the voice of any other riverine state in the administration of the delta. Where questions emerged that involved possible intervention within territorial waters, the compromises reached were so vague so as to make any attempt to take action practically impossible. This is not to criticize the outcome of the conference. Considering the strong feelings of nationalism throughout the Basin, the inflamed passions after the war, the unwillingness of the great powers to create a strictly riparian regime and thus surrender their direct involvement in river affairs, and the vagueness inherent in the very concept of internationality, the document produced in Paris was a sound compromise.

The *Statut Définitif* inaugurated a new era in the Basin, one in which the entire river became subject to some guidelines, albeit general and open to broad interpretation. Its provisions would remain in effect until the eve of World War II (see Appendix 12). In hindsight, the *Statut* provided one of the few intra-Basin forums for communication. Like the legacy of the European Commission before World War I, and even during the first two years of that conflict, a significant degree of camaraderie would mark the relationships between most of the delegates. Yet, just as the war in 1914 changed not only the face of Europe but also the state of affairs on the Danube, so too would the Second World War, and the upheaval in Eastern Europe that followed in its wake, change the river's administration once again.

CHAPTER VIII

THE *STATUT DÉFINITIF* AND ROMANIAN PUBLIC OPINION

The almost singularly strident Romanian public voice against the European Commission of the Danube did not abate with the close of the conference. On the contrary, it grew in intensity. Neither the signing of the *Statut* nor its ratification by the Romanian Senate in 1922 stemmed the flow of published invective. Publicists bitterly attacked the settlement as just another link in a chain of anti-Romanian actions by the great powers that prevented the country from claiming its legitimate rights on the Danube.

To the outside observer, the apparent solidarity of Romanian public opinion toward the issue creates the impression that the Danube agreements represented the gravest of national affronts and were opposed by nearly all Romanians. It seemed as if the continued existence of the European Commission threatened the very independence of the state. In fact, the British delegation at the Paris Conference referred to this public opinion as if it was one of Romania's principal diplomatic weapons.[1] In turn, Romanian historians constantly cite the unanimity of public opinion in their nation as evidence of mass outrage at the perpetuation of the European agency.

Public opinion was considered an important factor during the time of the conference, therefore. But the nature of that opinion has never been fully examined, even though it is an essential element in assessing the impact of the Danube Question upon Romania. Rather, it is merely taken for granted that the Romanian people stood steadfastly against the organization and its members and looked upon the events in Paris

112

with great interest and anticipation. This impression stems from the numerous tracts that proliferated in those years. In truth, however, these works distorted the intensity, as well as the character, of public sentiment within Romania. In particular, it obscures the fact that they (the polemicists) *were* public opinion in the country. Apart from them, public opinion did not exist.

This does not imply that the Danube Question was a minor issue; to the present it remains a central theme in Romanian historiography. Furthermore, due to its important economic implications for the nation, it was a significant factor in Romanian foreign policy throughout the interwar years even though, as mentioned in chapter four, other, often more vital issues confronted the Foreign Ministry as well. The questions rather are threefold: did the "public," so often referred to, actually see the issue as a grave matter upon with the "future" (*viitorul*) of the country rested?; did Romanians, in fact, follow the events in Paris?; and has Romanian historiography perpetuated a myth that the outcome of the Paris Conference represented a major diplomatic defeat for Romania?

By its very nature, public opinion is an imprecise term. It implies a generalized judgment by a considerable number of people on a particular issue or idea, an integration of opinion that reflects an overall consensus.[2] This definition admittedly lacks precision because the terms "consensus" and "considerable number of persons" are ambiguous. Nevertheless, for the purposes of this study, it will suffice.

In a "democratic" environment[3] it is generally conceded that public opinion is built upon the active participation of the population, that is, it reflects a discernible general will. The populace has access to sufficient information to form opinions. This idealistic model is a fragile one, however, for it presupposes an interested and sufficiently intelligent population. It also presumes that "opinion-makers," who generally represent the views prevalent in cultural and governmental centers, reflect the ideals of the broader segment of the populace.

At the same time, public opinion often means no more than simple emotion. It is a transient element easily forgotten or displaced by other matters. This occurs in any political environment, especially during times of privation, when interest in basic human needs (food, land, and so forth) takes precedence.

In less "democratic" situations the above conditions are quickly altered. The governmental and public wills are often synonymous. Such was the case in Romania. A public will simply did not exist as a definable entity.

Public opinion in Romania was different from the more "western" models. On the one hand, as in the West, there was an emotional side to public opinion in which the population took an active role (for example, the clamor for land reform). On the other hand, "public" opinion usually meant little more than the views of an educated elite, the so-called intelligentsia. For the majority of the people, day-to-day economic concerns and local and regional loyalties prevailed.[4]

Although Romanians used the term "public opinion" in the western sense, that is, as representative of the will of the people, it actually denoted the ideas expressed by a few intellectuals and leaders of the government. The ideals of this group, labeled as *public* opinion, thus received disproportionate attention.

Of course, it is true that inflamed passions by a large segment of the population could influence policy, such as in the case of the land reforms.[5] The Danube Question was not a similar issue, however. It did not arouse the interest of the people, for it did not affect them in a tangible form, which is a prerequisite in most countries, especially less developed ones, for an active mass movement. The majority of the populace was, and remained, apolitical, concerned with issues more immediate to their everyday existence.

Again, this is not to say that the attacks on the European Commission would not have reflected a general mood in Romania. The nature of Romanian nationalism, marked by a strong sense of self-pride and xenophobia, makes it clear that most Romanians would have opposed the existence of such an independent agency on their soil. The very word *"Dunărea"* ("the Danube") evokes powerful emotions in all Romanians, who view the river as the life-blood of the nation. Like the Carpathian Mountains, it is both a geographical asset and the heart of the country. The feelings of all Romanians toward the river are undeniable; the knowledge of the population regarding the existence of the European Commission, as well as the outcome of the Paris Conference, however, is a matter of conjecture.

It is doubtful whether a substantial number of Romanians knew the agency even existed, let alone the reasons why Bucharest objected to its continuation. This was due in large measure to the problem of illiteracy that plagued interwar Romania. As late as 1930, only 57.1 percent of the population aged 7 and older could read. In Bessarabia this total reached 80 percent.[6] Although this figure showed a measurable gain compared with 1914 when 60 percent of the population in Moldavia and Wallachia, and 90 percent in Bessarabia, were illiterate,[7] it undermines any notion that the available information on the Danube Question could have reached any sizable portion of the population. For the majority of the citizenry, the only method of dissemination of ideas remained the oral tradition. Yet, considering the pressing issues of inflation, land, currency reform, and so forth, it is questionable whether anyone but a handful of Romanians would have cared about a subcommission for the Iron Gates, requisitioned ships, or the presence of a few Western Europeans, especially the nation's wartime allies, in Galați.

Only the literate segment of Romanian society would have taken any active interest in the matter. For this group, information, primarily in the form of published polemics was available. Despite the existence of numerous works, however, their circulation was minimal,[8] save perhaps for the books by C. I. Baicoianu. If news about the issue, the conference, and the European Commission were to be widely circulated, the more likely medium would have been the country's newspapers.

The latter proved to be less than informative, however. Articles usually no more than three to five column inches in length appeared in the major Romanian dailies: *Adevărul, Viitorul, Universul,* and *Dimineața.* On the whole, such articles were few in number, contained little information, and dealt primarily with repetitive accounts of past injustices. It is important to note that between January 1919 and the close of the conference in July 1921 only *Viitorul* printed more than the scanty releases provided by the other organs; but this amounted to a total of only sixteen articles.[9] *Viitorul,* a pro-Brătianu publication, in a shrill, nationalistic tone, did attack the Supreme Allied Council as "imitating the old tendency toward the domination of *Mitteleuropa.*"[10] by refusing to return Romanian ships, convoking the first reunion of the European Commission in Paris instead of Galați, raising taxes "so that our cereals will especially suffer," and replacing Romanian personnel in the delta with Allied functionaries.[11] The nation's "fate" (*soarta*),[12] the paper claimed, rested on this "life and death struggle."[13] The paper also occasionally cited foreign press reports, regarding Romania's opposition to the influence of the great powers, contained in *L'Humanite* and *L'Echo de Paris,* but dismissed them as coming from "bolshevik" publications.[14] Despite these articles, however, the coverage given to the Danube Question was minimal compared to the other important issues confronting the country. Even during the Paris Conference itself, the meeting held at Spa to determine reparation payments received greater attention. The press concentrated on economic shortages, unification, Versailles, the minorities treaty, and the political in-fighting in Bucharest. Articles on the Danube, in comparison, appeared only irregularly.

Part of the reason for this lack of attention by the newspapers lies in the nature of the Romanian press itself. Although the newspapers were subject to government censorship, they also served as mouthpieces for the country's political parties. Unconcern by the press paralleled the dearth of interest in the issue by the members of the Romanian Parliament. Save for a few speeches, as recorded in *Monitorul Oficial* (the records of the body), discussion of the issue was almost non-existent. Perhaps this was a tacit recognition that the argument against the European Commission was futile. More likely it was because other matters were more pressing and time-consuming. The Parliament simply ratified the *Statut* with no substantive debate.

With minimal attention addressed to the question by the country's newspapers and government leaders, the only media that confronted the problem were published books, pamphlets, and short monographs. As the only real forum on the subject of the Danube, these works represent Romanian public opinion as it really existed, for they reflect the views of the intellectual community. This was the unanimity seen by outside observers and the source of the illusions created within the minds of the Western delegates that the Romanian people were consciously aware of the issues.

A brief examination of the common traits contained within this abundant literature is mandatory in considering the "public" Danube Question. Contemporary Romanian historiography has changed little since the Paris Conference; it continues to portray the reaction to that convention as a genuine outpouring of public sentiment, when, in fact, the limited attention given the issue represented little more than the writings and public comments of a select few. By judging the Danube Question solely in such a myopic fashion, historians have long overlooked the true outcome of the Paris Conference, that is, a significant diplomatic victory for Romania.

The overriding theme that prevails in the histories of the Danube issue is the belief that the perpetuation of the European Commission violated Romania's sovereignty. This perception stems from strong feelings of nationalism that, in Romania as in all nations in Eastern Europe, grew in intensity after World War I. Written in a monotonous, often self-righteous style, the polemics, with few exceptions, lack individuality and are selective in their use of supporting materials. It is as if the evidence favoring the Romanian position is so self-evident that the simple recitation of past injustices will clearly establish its claims. At the same time, while not necessarily a call to arms, the works do signal a need for vigilance in pressing the nation's demands.

The authors devote almost total attention to the European Commission, which, they held, had no authority because of its inclusion of nonriparian members and its "illegal" self-perpetuation. This "sovereign state at the mouth of the Danube"[15] placed Romania in a position of vassalage.

> It is inadmissable, it is shockingly unjust, that the day when it is admitted for part of the Danube river another regime more lenient, more democratic, more in rapport with the evolution of the actual times [that is, the International Commission of the Danube] than is allowed at the mouth of the Danube, the inequitable regime now 70 years old [which continues] from the time when we were vassals of the Turks.
>
> It is inadmissable that on part of the Danube, for the other riverine states like Bulgaria, Hungary, etc., vanquished countries, there applies another regime, more equitable [than that which applies for] we Romanians on [our] part of the Danube. . . . [16]

The river takes on almost human characteristics, acting as an integral member of Romanian society. Nowhere is this more apparent than in the popular poem of Vasile Alexandri.

> The brave, mother Danube
> Since the world gave me watch

> She warms me, strengthens me
> She is devoted to me and rears me.

> Blow, pass bad wind
> Pass by my head!
> The Danube and I are one.
> Victorious is the time and the fortune.[17]

On the Danube

> —like the Carpathians—lies the entire life of our people; she [the Danube] is the part which keeps us in contact with the people of Western and Central Europe and also opens for us the large route of the ocean for the exchange of products and the work of the people with the products of countries far away.[18]

Because the mouth of the river was contained solely within Romanian territory "it is natural that Romania is the most interested of all countries in assuring the best possible traffic conditions on this grand, international waterway."[19] The entire economic future of the nation depended on the river, which was the single most important factor in the "modern history" of Romania.[20]

While many Romanian historians view the Danube Question in such an important light, Western European scholars, in contrast, have ignored the issue. Compared with other matters and events (wars, treaties, the Eastern Question, alliance systems, and so forth) the Danube Question was a relative constant. Those other issues underwent continuous fluctuations, many of which had significant repercussions for all of Europe. But the Danube controversy changed only in relation to outside events: modifications in territorial boundaries, maintenance of the balance of power, and the growth of international trade. As such, the Danube Question generally is given no more than footnote treatment by Western European historians. Only for Romanian scholars did the Danube Question hold a life-or-death importance.

Once they cease expounding the country's natural interest in the river and the necessity of safeguarding its internationality, Romanian historians turn to a chronological account of past failures by the West to create a truly international administration for the river. All evidence supports the thesis of past wrongs against "the rights of a small nation."[21] The writers portray Romania as a country too weak to counter the power of the West; its only strength lay in a moral stance intent upon upholding the tenets of internationality.

The framework for all international rivers, formulated at the Congress of Vienna, was, for all the authors, the model upon which all agencies should be based. Vienna "outlined the system" whereby riparian states became "responsible for all work" and the development of the river system.[22] Furthermore

> ...by this Act the right of all nations to the utilization of the natural course of a river traversing several countries was recognized and so far from encroaching upon the inherent right of the contiguous proprietors, enlisted them as a corporate body in the discussion of and agreement upon such measures as were necessary for the improvement of navigation generally and for the administration of the river....[23]

Despite the fact that "from a practical point of view these principles [must] suffer some special modification to suit the local conditions of certain rivers,"[24] all administrations must adhere to the basic ideas. The European Commission did not.

At first, the framers of the Treaty of Paris sought to follow these principles. With foresight the plenipotentiaries saw the economic potential of the Danube and created the European Commission as a provisional agency to speed the reopening of the blocked mouth of the river. The creation of the organization was necessitated by the fact that the Ottoman Empire "could not possibly undertake such work...while Russia, having no interest on the Danube, multiplied every obstacle [to free trade]."[25] This statement reveals not only the recognition that the body was, at first, essential to the recovery of trade[26] but also Romania's distrust of Russian interests on the river, a suspicion that resurfaced in 1878 and during World War I.

The problem did not stem from the treaty itself, but rather from the abortive creation of the River State Commission and the failure to institute the original Paris provisions. The resulting refusal of the European

agency to disband after its original charter expired, produced an issue
that could only fester "like a chronic disease."[27] The importance of the
Turks and their virtual disinterest in the matter allowed the organization
to usurp powers that rightfully belonged to local officials. Although
there does exist a tacit recognition that the Ottoman Empire was incapable, both financially and technically, of providing the necessary
maritime services, this problem, the historians would have us believe,
disappeared in 1878 with the admission of Romania to the body.[28]

Instead of concentrating on Romania's entrance at this point, the
monographs emphasize other areas: the grant given to Austria-Hungary
to supervise the Iron Gates, Vienna's "design" to control Danubian trade
and the Middle Danube, and, most importantly, the article that made
the Commission independent of territorial authorities. Thus, Romania
had to fight not only the prerogatives of the European Commission but
also the machinations of the Habsburgs. The polemicists viewed Austria
as suppressing Romanian attempts toward self-sufficiency by seeking
a "strangle hold" over its commercial activities on the river.[29] Even though
those moves were thwarted, the European Commission became a "European Syndicate," which held "a temporal grant" to make laws, oversee
judicial processes, and execute all statutes; these were the attributes of
an autonomous state, not an international agency.[30] In order to maintain
the organization's existence, the other members forced Romania "to ab-
dicate a part of its sovereignty."[31] The principle of liberty, the writers
argued, must respect both international and national rights. Small states
"not having the power, the brutal force, . . . must find support in moral
force which is no less effective."[32]

The 1883 Conference of London marked the nadir in the relationship
between Romania and the agency. At that meeting, the polemicists contend, the representatives of the great powers ignored Romania's rights by
trying to create a separate commission for the Middle Danube without
providing for its extension to Habsburg territory. This violated every
accepted definition of internationality, which allowed for free and
open access to all shipping along the entire length of such rivers. The conferees also excluded Romania from its rightful position as a full voting
member, thereby violating the Treaty of Paris which provided that decisions be subject to the approval of all members.[33] Finally, the plenipotentiaries extended the powers of the European Commission to Brăila, an

act that remained a "dead letter" (*lettre morte*) in Romania's eyes.[34]
After 1883, therefore, the country's "fate" was tied to a "great principle": the prevention of any extension of the organization's prerogatives and the nonrecognition of the decisions of the London meeting.

The London Conference was not the final indignity for these writers.
The complete internationalization of the Congo in 1887 and the creation
of a unitary regime for that river created a perception, in their minds,
that their nation held a status subservient to that of those African lands
through which the Congo flowed. This belief lasted as long as the European Commission existed.

Romanian historians usually limit discussion of the period from 1887
to the end of World War I to a recounting of the provisions of the Treaty
of Bucharest, which they view as conclusive proof of Germany's grand
design to control the river. The authors fail to mention the relatively
good relations that marked the three decades prior to 1916, or Romania's
own policies toward the representatives of the Central Powers in 1916.
Instead, the coming of peace in 1918 receives maximum attention, for it
is seen as finally eliminating all obstacles to the realization of the provisions of 1856. The war changed the rationale for the existence of the
organization by ending the Eastern Question and removing the threats
to internationality from the Central Powers and Russia. All that was
needed was simply to carry out the mandate of 1856.

The mood was one of guarded optimism, however. As always, the justice of Romania's claims appeared clear, and is again restated. Over the
past four decades Romania proved itself capable of providing services
to navigation; as evidence, the writers pointed to the construction of a
number of ports without any appreciable increase in taxation, proof,
they believed, that the country could cover the costs of upgrading the
river. A single international commission composed of the riparian states
(along with possible nonriverine representation as well) would ensure
the future of operations and be able to supervise those functions presently controlled by the European Commission. In addition, the creation of a single agency representing all riparian states would help guarantee future peace and stability in the Basin by fostering a mood of
cooperation and eliminating external influences and machinations.

The events surrounding the Inter-Allied Commission and the late ad-
mittance of the country to the Ports and Waterways Commission destroyed any optimism that its aspirations would be fulfilled. Romanian

historians portray Trowbridge as a military despot who treated his agency as a personal fief. To support this thesis, the polemicists cite the "Sofia" incident, his refusal to return commandeered Romanian ships, and the edict permitting Hungarian technicians to remain in control of the Iron Gates. Furthermore, they viewed the failure of the Allies to act in regard to Romania's remonstrances against Trowbridge as a signal that the Western powers sought continued domination of the river.[36]

Having examined the Danube Question prior to the opening of the Paris Conference in this manner, the historians and polemicists could not help but see the *Statut Définitif* as an anti-Romanian document. Nothing short of the elimination of the European Commission could have satisfied them. The maintenance of the "anachronism" legalized the domination of the powers over the Romanian delta. The rest of the *Statut* was simply ignored and the entire treaty dismissed. Romania's moral stance on behalf of its rights failed; the "small nation" again was forced to succumb to the wishes of the great powers.

The historiographical themes presented above approach the Danube Conference as a continuation of a century-long process aimed at furthering the influence of the great powers over the Danube's affairs. Each study builds upon the conclusions of previous works. This situation not only leads to the distorted view of a mass outpouring of public sentiment but also hides the real outcome of the conference and the drafting of the *Statut Définitif:* the treaty represented a major diplomatic victory for Romania.

Although the Foreign Ministry initially hoped that the conference would lead to the destruction of the European Commission and thus extend the idea of *Dunărea noastră* to the maritime Danube, it was quickly evident that this position would fail. Although Romania had managed operations in the delta since 1915, the powers were unwilling to sanction that condition on a permanent basis. In the face of steadfast opposition to their demand that the European agency be disbanded, Romania's delegates had the choice of either withdrawing from the convention or insisting on a program for the International Commission that upheld full riparian rights. The first alternative could only have led to failure. The other conferees would have formulated the *Statut* without Romanian participation and, faced with the mandate of the League of Nations, Romania would have had little choice but to comply with the treaty's provisions. Thus, Romania's only option at Paris was to pursue a strong policy regarding the fluvial Danube.

The question of the fluvial Danube therefore received the Romanian delegation's principal attention. Under no circumstances could the situation that prevailed in the delta, that is, a regulatory agency dominated by the powers, be allowed to extend beyond Galați. The diplomatic stance, devised by Ionescu, Stelian, and Conțescu, was the real Romanian program at Paris and it succeeded. On each major issue the Romanian view prevailed: the powers of taxation and policing, the right of a riparian to station warships on the river, the individual riverine's power to control cabotage, and the administration of the Iron Gates. Between Brăila and the Gates, Romania's concept of *Dunărea noastră* was upheld. The Romanian positions regarding the fluvial Danube now became part of accepted international law.

Romanian national pride remained scarred by the continuation of the European Commission, a fact reflected in Romanian historiography. But in the diplomatic struggle over the future administration of the Danube this wound to Romanian pride was but a temporary setback. The major struggle was won. After seven decades the fluvial Danube was internationalized and the administration designated by the Paris Conference legitimized full riparian rights. As such, the Danube Conference can be viewed as nothing less than a foreign policy success for Romania.

NOTES

Notes to Chapter I

1. Georges Kaeckenbeeck, *International Rivers: A Monograph Based on Diplomatic Documents* (London: Sweet and Maxwell, Limited, 1918), p. 1.
2. Ibid., pp. 9-10.
3. Ibid., p. 14.
4. Ibid., p. 19.
5. Ibid.
6. Ibid., p. 16.
7. Ibid., p. 15.
8. Romania did not receive admission to the European Commission until 1878.
9. The term used is derived from the title of a book by N. Dascovici published in 1927. It conveys the general attitude of Romanians toward the issue.
10. Charles and Barbara Jelavich, *The Establishment of the Balkan National States 1804-1920* (Seattle: University of Washington Press, 1977), p. 25.

Notes to Chapter II

1. Hugo Hajnal, *The Danube: Its Historical, Political and Economic Importance* (The Hague: Martinus Nijhoff, 1920), pp. 3-5.
2. Gordon Sherman, "The International Organization of the Danube," *American Journal of International Law*, XVIII (1923), p. 443.
3. Hajnal, *Danube*, p. 26.
4. Ibid., p. 46.
5. Ibid., p. 47.
6. D. Sturdza, *Recueil de Documents relatifs à la Liberté de Navigation du Danube* (Berlin: Puttkammer and Mulbrecht, 1904), p. 4.

7.   Commission Européenne du Danube, *La Commission Européenne du Danube et son oeuvre de 1856 à 1931* (Paris: Imprimerie Nationale, 1931), p. 5.

8.   C. P. Chamberlain, *The Regime of the International Rivers: Danube and Rhine* (New York: Columbia University Press, 1923), p. 36.

9.   Paul Cernovodeanu, "An unpublished British source concerning the international trade through Galatz and Brăila between 1837 and 1848," *Revue Roumaine d'Histoire*, XVI (1977), p. 517.

10.   Paul Cernovodeanu, "Anglo-American Trade Relations During the Second Half of the Nineteenth Century," Unpublished paper delivered at the Anglo-Romanian History Colloquium, London, May, 1978, p. 3.

11.   Hajnal, *Danube*, p. 58.

12.   British and Austrian commercial representatives, in an attempt to find a solution, gave momentary consideration to the construction of a canal between Cernavoda (south of Brăila) and Constanța. Following the Crimean War, the British Danube and the Black Sea Railway Co., Ltd. built a railroad bridge over this area.

13.   Chamberlain, *Regime*, p. 39.

14.   Ibid., pp. 43-4.

15.   Hajnal, *Danube*, p. 78.

16.   Ibid., p. 78.

17.   During the war a number of rock-laden ships were sunk at the mouth of the river by the opposing forces in order to slow any advances by the enemy as well as to block supply lines.

18.   Sturdza, *Documents*, p. 33.

19.   Ibid., p. 33.

20.   Chamberlain, *Regime*, p. 51.

21.   Sturdza, *Documents*, p. 63.

22.   Kaeckenbeeck, *International Rivers*, pp. 107-9.

23.   Lt. Col. Sir Henry Trotter, *Operations of the European Commission of the Danube During the Years 1894-1906* (London: Harrison and Sons, St. Martin's Press, 1906), p. 3. In the 1880s Hartley returned to work for the Commission. He began work shortening the Sulina by four miles (near the present town of Crișan), a task accomplished in 1893.

24.   Cernovodeanu, "Anglo-American Trade," p. 5.

25.   Galați was a free port until 1883.

26.   Chamberlain, *Regime*, p. 57.

27.   Ibid., pp. 93-6.

28.   Ibid., p. 59.

29.   Sturdza, *Documents*, pp. 108-9.

30.   Another riparian state, Serbia, was also granted independence at the Congress of Berlin.

31.   Sturdza, *Documents*, p. 123.

32.   Chamberlain, *Regime*, p. 73.

33.   Hajnal, *Danube*, p. 99.

34.   Ibid., p. 100.

35.   Chamberlain, *Regime*, p. 78.

36.   Cernovodeanu, "Anglo-American Trade," p. 8.

37.   Ivan T. Berend and György Ránki, *Economic Development in East Central Europe in the 19th and 20th Centuries* (New York: Columbia University Press, 1974), p. 88.

38.   Ibid., p. 36.

39.   Colonel Slucovici to Vasile Boerescu (undated), Biblioteca Centrală de Stat (BCS), Fond St. Georges, Doc. Nr. 2, PXXXIX, 13.

40.   Dinu C. Arion, *Chestia Dunării* (București: Tipografia "Cooperativa," 1916), p. 20.

41.   Cernovodeanu, "Anglo-American Trade," p. 13.

42.   Voyslav M. Radovanovitch, *Le Danube Maritime et le règlement du différend relatif aux competences de la Commission européenne sur le secteur Galatz-Braila* (Geneva: Georg et Cie, S.A., 1932), p. 19.

43.   Ibid., p. 19.

44.   R. Franasovici, *Chestia Dunării: Discurs rostit în Adunarea Deputăților în ședința dela 5 Martie 1920* (București: Imprimeria Statului, 1923), p. 45.

45.   Ibid., p. 46.

46.   M. Kogălniceanu, *Chestia Dunării* (București: Tipografia Academiei Române, 1882), p. 6.

47.   Vintilă C. Brătianu, *Chestia Dunării: expunere făcută în Adunarea Deputăților* (București: Imprimeria Statului, 1920), p. 27.

48.   Sherman, *American Journal*, p. 450.

Notes to Chapter III

1.   Arhivele Statului Galați, Fond Comisia Europeană a Dunării (henceforth listed as ASG/CED), Nr. 50, file 238.

2. ASG/CED, Nr. 51, file 1919/51, Session extraordinaire, October 15-17, 1919, protocol 1.

3. Ibid.

4. ASG/CED, Nr. 49, file 425, protocol 864, October 24, 1914.

5. The Commission met regularly twice a year. In the interim, an executive committee, made up of representatives of all the members, had full authority to make decisions, subject to the approval of the entire Commission when it reconvened.

6. ASG/CED, Nr. 51.

7. Ibid.

8. ASG/CED, Nr. 54, file 425, protocols 879, 880.

9. ASG/CED, Nr. 51.

10. Ibid.

11. ASG/CED, Nr. 56.

12. ASG/CED, Nr. 51.

13. Ibid.

14. Ibid.

15. This argument is presented especially by current Romanian legal theorists.

16. Arhivele Statului, Fond Președinţea Consiliului de Ministri (henceforth listed as AS/PCM), Dosar Nr. 8/1919, file 9.

17. ASG/CED, Nr. 51.

18. Constantin Kiriţescu, *Istoria Războiului pentru întegirea României 1916-1919* (București: Editura Casei Școalelor, 1920), vol. 1, p. 398.

19. Ibid., vol. II, pp. 10-293.

20. Norman Stone, *The Eastern Front* (London: Hodder and Stoughton, 1975), p. 279.

21. General Erich von Falkenhayn, *The German General Staff and Its Decisions: 1914-1916* (New York: Dodd, Mead and Co., 1920), p. 316.

22. Stone, *Eastern Front*, p. 265.

23. Foreign Ministry to Duiliu Zamfirescu (September 8/21, 1916), Arhivele Ministerului Afacerilor Externe (henceforth listed as AMAE), Fond 71/1914 E. 2, vol. 36, file 9; all dates have been converted from the Julian Calendar in the text. Romania did not change to the Gregorian system until March 1919. Some ambiguity is possible in documents before this date, especially regarding communications between Romanian representatives

and Western members of the Commission. Although this opens the possibility of error, all efforts have been made to ensure the accuracy of all dates.

24.   Foreign Ministry to Engineer-resident Magnussen (September 8/21, 1916), AMAE, Fond 71/1914 E. 2, vol. 36, file 24. The date of entry could not be verified by the author; the date shown was chosen because of a similarity in events.

25.   John Baldwin to Zamfirescu (September 8/21, 1916), AMAE, Fond 71/1914 E. 2, vol. 36, file 23.

26.   Zamfirescu to the Foreign Ministry (October 14/27, 1916), AMAE, Fond 71/1914 E. 2, vol. 36, file 35.

27.   Emanoil Porumbaru to C. Diamondy (October 19/31, 1916), AMAE, Fond 71/1914 E. 2, vol. 36, file 39.

28.   Ibid.

29.   Italian legation in Galați to Porumbaru (December 8, 1916), AMAE, Fond 71/1914 E. 2, vol. 36, file 63.

30.   Many members of the foreign legations left Romania during the next few months. No records exist, however, regarding the numbers that left.

31.   ASG/CED, Nr. 51.

32.   This was the first time that a Romanian national was head of this important post.

33.   Report by the Romanian military on the situation in Sulina (February 28/March 12, 1917), AMAE, Fond 71/1914 E. 2, vol. 36, files 75-77.

34.   Report by Duiliu Zamfirescu to the Foreign Ministry (May 18/31, 1917), AMAE, Fond 71/1914 E. 2, vol. 36, files 133-136.

35.   Vintilă Brătianu to Duiliu Zamfirescu (March 20/April 2, 1917), AMAE, Fond 71/1914 E. 2, vol. 36, file 91.

36.   Ibid.

37.   Constantin I. Baicoianu, *Dunărea vazută prin prizma tractatului din București* (București: Tipografia Universala, 1921), p. 10.

38.   Report by Captain Commander Mihail (April 18/31, 1917), AMAE, fond 71/1914 E. 2, vol. 36, files 108-9.

39.   Ibid.

40.   Report by Duiliu Zamfirescu (May 18/31, 1917), AMAE, Fond 71/1914 E. 2, vol. 36, files 133-136.

41.   Report by Engineer-Chief I. N. Georgescu on the Russian-Romanian Agreement of June 1917, AMAE, Fond 71/1914 E. 2, vol. 36, unpaged.

42. Report by Captain Commander Mihail (June 1917), AMAE, Fond 71/1914 E. 2, vol. 36, files 174-78.

43. Ibid.

44. ASG/CED, Nr. 51.

45. Duiliu Zamfirescu to Vintilă Brătianu (June 17/30, 1917), AMAE, Fond 71/1914 E. 2, vol. 36, files 203-6.

46. Ibid. As an ominous final note, Zamfirescu added to the growing concern over events in Romania. He stated that Romania must avoid, at all costs, the "contagion" spreading through Russian ranks.

47. ASG/CED, Nr. 51; Report by John Foscolo (October 2, 1917), AMAE, Fond 71/1914 E. 2, vol. 37, file 193.

48. Ioan Chiper and Ion Alexandrescu, et al, Chronological History of Romania (Bucharest: Editura Enciclopedia Româna, 1974). Used as a source of date verification.

49. AS/PCM, Dosar 32/1918, file 434.

50. Ibid.

51. Ibid.

52. Ibid.

53. Ibid.

54. Ibid.

55. Report of the arrival of Vilfan in Sulina (March 18/31, 1918), AMAE, Fond 71/1914 E. 2, vol. 36, files 294-5.

56. Duiliu Zamfirescu to Franjo Vilfan (undated), AMAE, Fond 71/ 1914 E. 2, vol. 36, file 298.

57. Ibid.

58. Dinu C. Arion to Duiliu Zamfirescu (March 14/27, 1918), AMAE, Fond 71/1914 E. 2, vol. 36, file 318.

59. Report on Protocol of June 14, 1918, AMAE, Fond 71/1914 E. 2, vol. 36, files 333-9.

60. The Russian delegate was released by the Central Powers and expelled from Romania in July 1918.

61. Report by German Minister Anderheiden (July 19, 1918), AMAE, Fond 71/1914 E. 2, vol. 36, file 361.

62. ASG/CED, Nr. 51, file 1919/51.

63. Ibid.

Notes to Chapter IV

1. There is no documentary evidence that specifically points to this situation. Nevertheless all archival research on the question, as well as an examination of the major Romanian newspapers, points to this conclusion.

2. Joseph Rothschild, *East Central Europe Between the Two World Wars* (Seattle: University of Washington Press, 1974), p. 281.

3. This, of course, excludes those extreme nationalists who sought even further extensions of the country's borders.

4. Constantin Kirițescu, *Istoria Razboiului*, vol. 1, p. 39.

5. See: Vintilă Brătianu, *Note asupra viitoarelor nevoi economice și financiare ale României* (Iași, 1917) as a preview of the economic ideals of the National Liberals.

6. Professor Doctor I. N. Angelescu, *Politica economică a României fața de politica economică imperialistă* (București: "Tipografiile Române Unite," 1923), p. 9.

7. This attitude remains to the present a fundamental argument in Romanian historiography.

8. Rothschild, *East Central Europe*, p. 283.

9. Ibid., p. 284.

10. Ibid., p. 286.

11. The best study of Romanian politics between the wars remains: Henry L. Roberts, *Rumania: The Political Problems of an Agrarian State* (New Haven: Yale University Press, 1951).

12. Mircea Mușat and Ion Ardeleanu, *Viața politică în România 1918-21* (București: Editura politică, 1976), p. 112.

13. Ibid., p. 362.

14. Roberts, *Rumania*, p. 24.

15. Gheorghe M. Dobrovici, *Istoricul desvoltării economice și financiare a României și împrumuturile 1823-1933* (București: Tipografia: Ziarul "Universul," 1934), p. 408.

16. L. S. Stavrianos, *The Balkans Since 1453* (New York: Holt, Rinehart and Winston, 1958), p. 691.

17. Rothschild, *East Central Europe*, p. 285.

18. David Mitrany, *The Land and Peasant in Rumania* (New York: Greenwood Press, 1968), p. 575.

19. Dobrovici, *Istoricul desvoltării*, pp. 354-363.

20.   Institutul Central de Cercetări Economice, *Progresul economic in România 1877-1977* (București: Editura politică, 1977), p. 217.

21.   Ibid., p. 219.

22.   Ibid., pp. 218-19.

23.   Angelescu, *Politica*, p. 19.

24.   Institutul Central, *Progresul*, p. 219.

25.   Dispatches relative to this effort to obtain foreign loans may be found in: Biblioteca Centrală de Stat (BCS), Fond St. Georges, DR. 3, PXLII.

Notes to Chapter V

1.   ASG/CED, Nr. 56.

2.   ASG/CED, Nr. 58.

3.   See Charles Maier, *Recasting Bourgeois Europe* (Princeton: University of Princeton Press, 1975).

4.   Walter D. Hines, *Report on Danube Navigation submitted to the Advisory and Technical Committees for Communication and Transit of the League of Nations* (Geneva).

5.   Ibid., p. 70.

6.   Ibid., p. 87.

7.   Ibid., p. 89.

8.   No records exist regarding these losses due to the chaos and destruction caused by the war. They do, however, represent reliable estimates based on property losses.

9.   ASG/CED, Nr. 51. The coefficient represents official Commission calculations. No source could be found to clarify the figures.

10.   ASG/CED, Nr. 51.

11.   One of the representatives, Mehmed Sefa Feizi Bey, a Turk, in 1916 was granted permission to remain in Galați even after Romania's declaration of war because he was responsible for his small children. Now, despite the intercession of Burghele, he was forcibly arrested and later expelled.

12.   ASG/CED, Nr. 51.

13.   Report by Magnussen (January 1919), AMAE, Fond 71/1914, vol. 37, file 30.

14.   Docan to British, French and Italian legations in Bucharest (November 24, 1918), AMAE, Fond 71/1914, vol. 37, file 23.

15.   Report by Herbert Hoover (July 4, 1919), AMAE, Fond 8 Conv. D 18, vol. I (II), file 25.

16.   Report by the French Chief of Naval Mission in Romania (April 25, 1920), Biblioteca Academiei, Fond Arhivele N. Docan. The report is highly anti-Trowbridge in nature, portraying him as a demagogue who sought to control both the Danube and the Dardanelles for British commercial and military interests.

17.   Admiral Belloy to MAE (June 5, 1919), AMAE, Fond 8 Conv. D 18, vol. I (II), files 16-19.

18.   French Ministry of War to d'Esperey (May 19, 1919), AMAE, Fond 8 Conv. D 18, vol. I (II), unpaged.

19.   General order 2009/4 (June 21, 1919), AMAE, Fond 8 Conv. D 18, vol. I (II), unpaged.

20.   Sherman David Spector, *Rumania at the Paris Peace Conference: A Study of the Diplomacy of Ioan I. C. Brătianu* (New York: Bookman Associates, Inc., 1962). Spector's book, despite its problems stemming from the inaccessibility of Romanian archives, remains the only reliable source in English on Romanian activities in Paris. Good contemporary accounts in Romanian have been written by Gheorghe and Vintilă Brătianu.

21.   F. S. Marston, *The Peace Conference of 1919: Organization and Procedure* (London: Oxford University Press, 1944), pp. 78-9.

22.   Report to Ports, Waterways and Railways Commission (March 1919), AMAE, Fond 8 Conv. D 17, vol. 1, files 1-3.

23.   Ibid.

24.   Ibid.

25.   Ibid.

26.   For the best analysis of the overall Peace Conference, see: H. W. V. Temperley, *A History of the Peace Conference of Paris* (London: Henry Frowde, and Hodder and Stoughton, 1920).

27.   Stephen Gorove, *Law and Politics of the Danube* (The Hague: Martinus Nijhof, 1964), p. 28.

28.   Conțescu's background is obscure. No account of his early career is contained in the standand works on Romania's diplomatic corps, nor was any information available in newspapers.

29.   Report to MAE (February 22, 1919), AMAE, Fond 71/1914 E. 2, vol. 37, file 44.

30.   Ibid.

31.   Report to MAE (February 22, 1919), AMAE, Fond 71/1914 E. 2, vol. 37, file 49.

32.   Foreign Ministry to British, French and Italian legations in Bucharest (March 15, 1919), AMAE, Fond 71/1914 E. 2, vol. 37, files 64-5.

33.   March report, AMAE, Fond 71/1914 E. 2, vol. 37, file 93.

34.   Conţescu to Pherekyde (March 31, 1919), AMAE, Fond 71/1914 E. 2, vol. 37, files 77-9. Eclamans was also appointed as the French delegate to the European Commission on March 31. He never formally took the post.

35.   Report of March 19, 1919, AMAE, Fond 71/1914 E. 2, vol. 37, file 24; Conţescu to Herter (ad-Interim Captain of the Port of Sulina) (May 15, 1919), AMAE, Fond 71/1914 E. 2, vol. 41, file 24.

36.   Conţescu to the Ministers of War and Public Works (May 26, 1919), AMAE, Fond 71/1914 E. 2, vol. 37, files 85, 128.

37.   Report of June 10, 1919, AMAE, Fond 71/1914 E. 2, vol. 37, files 167-68. Georgescu later became Engineer-resident after the death of Magnussen in July.

38.   Report of May 15, 1919, AMAE, Fond 71/1914 E. 2, vol. 40, file 251.

39.   Report of June 15, 1919, AMAE, Fond 71/1914 E. 2, vol. 37, file 169.

40.   Report of May 15, 1919, AMAE, Fond 71/1914 E. 2, vol. 40, file 251.

41.   ASG/CED, Nr. 51.

42.   Report of June 15, 1919, AMAE, Fond 71/1914 E. 2, vol. 37, files 174-79.

43.   Report of June 15, 1919, AMAE, Fond 71/1914 E. 2, vol. 37, file 180.

44.   Ibid.

45.   Ibid.

46.   Conţescu to all Commission department heads (June 3, 1919), AMAE, Fond 71/1914 E. 2, vol. 37, files 170-71.

47.   Rey to all Commission members (July 5, 1919), AMAE, Fond 71/1914 E. 2, vol. 37, files 227-29.

48.   French legation in Bucharest to Brătianu (September 17, 1919), AMAE, Fond 71/1914 E. 2, vol. 38, file 2.

49.   Docan to St. Aulaire (October 10, 1919), AMAE, Fond 71/1914 E. 2, vol. 38, file 4.

50.   Conţescu to General of the Army Văitoianu (October 3, 1919), AMAE, Fond 71/1914 E. 2, vol. 38, file 5.

51.   ASG/CED, Nr. 51.

52.   There is no data that supports the Romanian claim that these currency restrictions did, in fact, hinder trade. Yet, based on simple economic principles, it is an assertion based on a valid hypothesis.

53.   ASG/CED, Nr. 51.

54.   Ibid.

55.   After Ward returned, the depth of the river's arms fell. Of course, this was a coincidence. Periodically, the flow of the Danube quickens, thus creating more fill. Yet, Conţescu saw a correlation in the two events and attributed the problems to Ward. "I have formed the absolute conviction that he is not a man who justifies the confidence of the Commission in situations of extreme crises of navigation. . . . " AMAE, Fond Conv. D 17, vol. 1, files 93-4.

56.   Romania was occupying Budapest at that time.

57.   Conţescu to Legrand (November 21, 1919), AMAE, Fond 71/1914 E. 2, vol. 38, file 37.

58.   Conţescu to Legrand (January 27, 1919), AMAE, Fond 71/1914 E. 2, vol. 38, files 245-54.

59.   Docan to Conţescu (December 22, 1919), AMAE, Fond 71/1914 E. 2, vol. 38, files 44-56.

60.   Conţescu to Vaida-Voievod (December 15, 1919), AMAE, Fond 71/1914 E. 2, vol. 38, files 58-62. These estimates would later vary.

61.   Conţescu to Vaida-Voievod (January 10, 1919), AMAE, Fond 71/1914 E. 2, vol. 38, files 181-86.

62.   In 1879 (the example to which Conţescu constantly referred) Britain adamantly opposed any rise in taxes, believing that such an action would result in a decrease in trade.

63.   Conţescu to Vaida-Voievod (December 15, 1919), AMAE, Fond 71/1914 E. 2, vol. 38, files 58-62.

64.   Conţescu to Vaida-Voievod (January 10, 1919), AMAE, Fond 71/1914 E. 2, vol. 38, files 181-86.

65.   Conţescu to Vaida-Voievod (December 20, 1919), AMAE, Fond 71/1914 E. 2, vol. 38, files 150-51. Trowbridge was appointed as British

"delegate" to the Commission on June 2 with full powers to act in that capacity until Baldwin returned. His military authority, used to enforce the new taxes, exacerbated the ill-feeling with Romania, Frank Rattigan to MAE (June 2, 1919), AMAE, Fond 71/1914 E. 2, vol. 37, files 125-26.

66. Conţescu to Vaida-Voievod (January 6, 1920), AMAE, Fond 71/1914 E. 2, vol. 38, file 178.

67. Report of March 10, 1920, AMAE, Fond 71/1914 E. 2, vol. 38, files 309-10.

68. Conţescu to Vaida-Voievod (December 15, 1919), AMAE, Fond 71/1914 E. 2, vol. 38, files 58-62.

69. Conţescu to Legrand (January 27, 1920), AMAE, Fond 71/ 1914 E. 2, vol. 38, files 245-54. The March session was delayed until May.

70. Conţescu to Legrand (December 15, 1919), AMAE, Fond 71/ 1914 E. 2, vol. 38, file 63.

71. ASG/CED, Session of May 17, 1920.

72. Ibid.

73. MAE to Paris legation (June 9, 1919), AMAE, Fond 8 Conv. D 18, vol. I (II), files 11-15.

74. Ibid.

75. Memo to Lansing, Tittoni, Clemenceau and the President of the Supreme Economic Council (June 29, 1919), AMAE, Fond 8 Conv. D 18, vol. I (II), files 2-10.

76. General order 3692/4 (August 25, 1919), AMAE, Fond 8 Conv. D 18, vol. I (II), file 56. Admiral Belloy had long favored this action.

77. Romanian delegation to Supreme Council (November 21, 1919), AMAE, Fond 8 Conv. D 18, vol. I (II), files 81-4.

78. General Cinoski to MAE (October 22, 1919), AMAE, Fond 8 Conv. D 18, vol. I (II), file 85.

79. Trowbridge to MAE (December 9, 1919), AMAE, Fond 8 Conv. D 18, vol. I (II), file 124.

80. Conţescu to Vaida-Voievod (December 20, 1919), AMAE, Fond 71/1914 E. 2, vol. 38, files 150, 151, 158. In this memo, Conţescu also expressed great bitterness toward those in the Foreign Ministry who would not allow him to attend the Paris meeting in October, thereby tying his hands and embarassing him in front of his colleagues.

81.   Docan to Paris Legation (December 27, 1919), AMAE, Fond 71/1914 E. 2, vol. 38, file 157.

82.   Docan to Carp (November 28, 1919), AMAE, Fond 8 Conv. D 18, vol. I (II), file 95.

83.   Carp to MAE (December 2, 1919), AMAE, Fond 8 Conv. D 18, vol. I (II), file 103. Dates regarding the Carp affair are contradictory. One memo places him in Budapest at the time of the conference. Whatever his exact location, there was an undeniable breakdown in communication. This fact is reflected in his replacement on December 5.

84.   France postponed the meeting two days in order to give Romania additional time to send a delegate.

85.   London legation to MAE (March 22, 1920), AMAE, Fond 8 Conv. D 18, vol. I (II), file Dosar D.

86.   The minutes are contained in *Procès Verbaux a Reunions a Belgrade a bord du Sofia* (November 29-December 2, 1919), AMAE, Fond 8 Conv. D 18, vol. I (II), files 138-75.

87.   MAE to Paris legation (January 3, 1920), AMAE, Fond 8 Conv. D 18, vol. I (II), files 178-82.

88.   London (Cantacuzino) to Docan (January 13, 1920), AMAE, Fond 8 Conv. D 18, vol. I (II), file 185. This allegation was based, Cantacuzino claimed, on a conversation with Trowbridge's aide, Stead.

Notes to Chapter VI

1.   Conțescu to Take Ionescu (August 1, 1921), AMAE, Fond 8 Conv. D 19 II, files 562-64.

2.   Conțescu to G. Popescu (February 13, 1920), AMAE, Fond 71/1914 E. 2, vol. 38, file 295.

3.   Conțescu to Lebre (February 13, 1920), AMAE, Fond 71/1914 E. 2, vol. 38, file 297.

4.   This situation was rooted in the ill-feeling that developed between the two after Rey's visit in 1919.

5.   Conțescu to Zamfirescu (March 22, 1920), AMAE, Fond 71/1914 E. 2, vol. 38, file 311.

6.   Conțescu to Zamfirescu (March 22, 1920), AMAE, Fond 71/1914 E. 2, vol. 38, file 326.

7.   Frank Rattigan to MAE (February 19, 1920), AMAE, Fond 71/1914 E. 2, vol. 38, file 301.

8.   Report of March 10, 1920, AMAE, Fond 71/1914 E. 2, vol. 38, files 302-10.

9.   Ibid.

10.   MAE to Stelian (July 30, 1920), AMAE, Fond 8 Conv. D 19 I, unpaged.

11.   Ionescu to Belgrade legation (August 4, 1920), AMAE, Fond 8 Conv. D 19 I, unpaged.

12.   Trowbridge to Cantacuzino (July 21, 1920), AMAE, Fond 8 Conv. D 18, 1/I, file 29.

13.   Romania attributed this lack of cooperation in bilateral negotiations to an absence of essential materials and personnel in "Serbia." Cantacuzino to Trowbridge (August 20, 1920), AMAE, Fond 8 Conv. D 18, 1/I, file 30.

14.   Ibid.

15.   Cantacuzino to Ionescu (August 14, 1920), AMAE, Fond 8 Conv. D 18, 1/I, files 27-8.

16.   MAE to Cantacuzino (August 20, 1920), AMAE, Fond 8 Conv. D 18, 1/I, file 31.

17.   Ionescu to Stelian (September 15, 1920), AMAE, Fond 8 Conv. D 19 I, unpaged.

18.   Conférence Internationale du Danube (henceforth listed as CID), Protocole 1, session of August 2, 1920.

19.   Ibid.

20.   I. Popovici to MAE (January 13, 1920), AMAE, Fond 8 Conv. D 19 I, unpaged. Popovici was also at odds with Conţescu over the latter's demand for the tugboat "Dragos."

21.   Ibid.

22.   Royal Decree 2818 (July 3, 1920), AMAE, Fond 8 Conv. D 19 I, file 20.

23.   Popovici to MAE (January 13, 1920), AMAE, Fond 8 Conv. D 19 I, unpaged.

24.   Paris legation to MAE (June 16, 1920), AMAE, Fond 8 Conv. D 19 I, unpaged.

25.   CID, Protocole 1, August 2, 1920.

26.   CID, Annexe 1, Protocole 1, August 2, 1920, Article V.

27.   Ibid., Article VII.

28.   Ibid., Article XII.

29.   Ibid., Article XVIII.

30.   Ibid., Article XXIV.

31.   Ibid., Article XXVI.

32.   CID, Protocole 2, August 4, 1920.

33.   Ibid.

34.   Ibid.

35.   Ibid.

36.   CID, Protocole 3, August 5, 1920.

37.   Stelian to Take Ionescu (August 7, 1920), AMAE, Fond 8 Conv. D 19 I, files 40-2.

38.   This pre-conference alliance, to which Stelian alluded, did not contribute to any closer relationships among those states.

39.   Stelian to Ionescu (August 7, 1920), AMAE, Fond 8 Conv. D 19 I, files 40-2.

40.   Ibid.

41.   Take Ionescu to Belgrade legation (August 29, 1920), AMAE, Fond 8 Conv. D 19 I, unpaged.

42.   Take Ionescu to Prime Minister Venizelos (August 23, 1920), AMAE, Fond 8 Conv. D 19 I, unpaged.

43.   Take Ionescu to the Romanian legation in Rome, London, and Paris (August 25, 1920), AMAE, Fond 8 Conv. D 19 I, unpaged.

44.   Take Ionescu to Stelian (September 12, 1920), AMAE, Fond 8 Conv. D 19 I, unpaged.

45.   Minister to Belgrade Langa-Rascano to Ionescu (August 29, 1920), AMAE, Fond 8 Conv. D 19 I, unpaged.

46.   Take Ionescu to Stelian (August 25, 1920), AMAE, Fond 8 Conv. D 19 I, unpaged.

47.   The Greek project included Athens' representation on both commissions, extension of the International Commission's jurisdiction to all branches of the Danube (Morava, Inn, Tisza, Drava, and Temes) and maintained the basic supervisory powers contained in the original Legrand project.

Ristic´ sought representation (oral voice) for all riparians on the International Commission. The agency would be housed in Belgrade and grant the individual riparian great leeway over most operations.

48.   Stelian to Ionescu (September 10, 1920), AMAE, Fond 8 Conv. D 19 I, unpaged.

49.   CID, Protocole 4, September 6, 1920.

50.   Stelian to Ionescu (September 10, 1920), AMAE, Fond 8 Conv. D 19 I, unpaged.

51.   CID, Protocole 4, September 6, 1920.

52.   Stelian to Ionescu (September 11, 1920), AMAE, Fond 8 Conv. D 19 I, unpaged.

53.   Ibid.

54.   Stelian described Coromilas as a "bandit" (referring to his actions —which are never spelled out—in Salonika against the Macedonians). This personal animosity caused him to exaggerate the strength of his dealings with Ristić and Muller.

55.   Stelian to Ionescu (September 11, 1920), AMAE, Fond 8 Conv. D 19 I, unpaged. Stelian again exaggerated his arrangements with the others, claiming that "from the beginning I have been closer to the Serb and Slovak." BCS, Fond St. Georges, DR 7 PVIII, unpaged. Other dispatches refute this assertion of amiability. Stelian used this only for convenience.

56.   Ibid.

57.   Ionescu to Stelian (September 12, 1920), AMAE, Fond 8 Conv. D 19 I, unpaged.

58.   Ibid.

59.   Ionescu to Stelian (September 15, 1920), AMAE, Fond 8 Conv. D 19 I, unpaged.

60.   Stelian to Ionescu (undated, registered on March 17, 1921), AMAE, Fond 8 Conv. D 19 II, unpaged.

61.   Ionescu to Stelian (September 15, 1920), AMAE, Fond 8 Conv. D 19 I, unpaged.

62.   Ionescu to Stelian (September 12, 1920), AMAE, Fond 8 Conv. D 19 I, unpaged.

63.   Ibid.

64.   Ionescu to Stelian (September 15, 1920), AMAE, Fond 8 Conv. D 19 I, unpaged.

65.   Stelian to Ionescu (September 10, 1920), AMAE, Fond 8 Conv. D 19 I, unpaged.

66.   O. Brustrom to Take Ionescu (September 15, 1920), BCS, Papers of Take Ionescu, Fond St. Georges, DR 7 PVIII.

67.   CID, Protocole 5, September 8, 1920.

68.   Ibid.

69. Ibid.

70. Ibid. Legrand hoped that this provision would pertain to the use of police vessels rather than actual warships. Despite the opposition of the riparians, he would continue to press for the river's neutralization.

71. Ibid.

72. CID, Protocole 7, September 20, 1920. Speech by the Bulgarian representative, M. Lazaroff.

73. Ibid.

74. CID, Protocole 7, 8, and 9, September 20-24, 1920.

75. CID, Protocole 10, September 30, 1920.

76. Ibid.

77. Ibid.

78. Ibid.

79. Ibid.

80. Ibid.

81. This also denied Greece a seat on the International Commission because, according to Stelian, article 347 of Versailles stipulated that the agency would be composed of all riparians plus the members of the European Commission. Stelian to Ionescu (undated), AMAE, Fond 8 Conv. D 19 II, unpaged.

82. This did not really end the dispute. The question would ultimately go before the International Court of Justice.

83. See, for example, N. Dascovici, *Dunărea noastră* (Bucureşti: Editura Fundaţiei, 1927).

84. CID, Protocole 11, October 1, 1920.

85. CID, Protocole 12, October 6, 1920.

86. CID, Protocole 13, October 10, 1920.

87. Ibid.

88. CID, Protocole 14, October 11, 1920.

89. Ibid.

90. CID, Protocole 16, October 15, 1920.

91. Ibid.

92. Ibid.

93. Ibid.

94. Ibid.

95. CID, Protocole 18, October 20, 1920.

96. CID, Protocole 19, October 22, 1920.

97. CID, "Texte adopte en premiére lecture."

98. CID, Protocole 20, October 25, 1920.

99. CID, Protocole 19 and Protocole 20, October 22/25, 1920.

100. CID, Protocole 24, November 6, 1920.

101. CID, Protocole 25, November 8, 1920.

102. Ibid.

103. Delegation to Legrand (November 9, 1920), AMAE, Fond 8 Conv. D 19 I, unpaged.

104. CID, Protocole 27, November 12, 1920.

Notes to Chapter VII

1. Legrand opened the second session by asking his fellow conferees to act with dispatch in completing their work. CID, Protocole 30, April 5, 1921. Ionescu believed that the second session would be concluded rapidly. In a conversation with Stelian he remarked that Romania would be ready ". . . before the next session of the Danube Conference which will be much shorter than the first." Take Ionescu to Stelian (undated, part of a conversation recorded by Constantin Conțescu), AMAE, Fond 8 Conv. D 19 I, unpaged.

2. Council of Ministers report of March 23, 1921, AMAE, Fond 8 Conv. D 19 II, unpaged.

3. Ionescu to Stelian (undated, part of a conversation recorded by Conțescu), AMAE, Fond 8 Conv. D 19 I, unpaged.

4. CID, Protocole 31, April 8, 1921.

5. Ibid.

6. Ibid. Barcelona actually changed little from the ideas contained in the Vienna provisions of 1815.

7. CID, Protocole 32, April 11, 1921.

8. CID, Protocole 33, April 13, 1921.

9. N. Dascovici, *Interesele și drepturile României în texte de drept internaționale public* (Iași: Tipografia concesionara "Alexandru Țerek," 1936).

10. Ionescu to London, Paris and Rome legations, telegram 9412 (March 18, 1921), AMAE, Fond 8 Conv. D 19 II, file 7.

11. Ionescu to London legation (March 30, 1921), AMAE, Fond 8 Conv. D 19 II, unpaged.

12.   Ibid. Ionescu was referring to an article published by Stelian in a Transylvanian newspaper (IZBANDA). In this article, Stelian gave his opinions of the first session. This was a breach of the pact of silence which the delegates made in November. The article (oddly, the only significant reference to the conference in the Romanian press) angered the British Foreign Office which believed that the publication was countenanced by Ionescu. There is no evidence to support this conclusion however. It appears to have caught the Foreign Ministry by surprise. It did have a beneficial side-effect however, as it contributed to a further British mis-reading of Romanian public sentiment.

13.   M. Boerescu to Ionescu (April 2, 1921), AMAE, Fond 8 Conv. D 19 II, file 38.

14.   Boerescu to Ionescu (April 8, 1921), AMAE, Fond 8 Conv. D 19 II, unpaged.

15.   Boerescu to MAE (undated), AMAE, Fond 8 Conv. D 19 II, unpaged.

16.   Conțescu to Ionescu (April 10, 1921), AMAE, Fond 8 Conv. D 19 II, files 58-62.

17.   S. P. Waterlow to Boerescu (May 9, 1921), AMAE, Fond 8 Conv. D 19 II, files 149-54. Privately Ionescu referred to the former Central Powers as "criminals of devastation of our country." Memo (undated), AMAE, Fond 8 Conv. D 19 II, file 162.

18.   Conțescu to Ionescu (April 10, 1921), AMAE, Fond 8 Conv. D 19 II, files 58-62.

19.   Ibid.

20.   Conțescu to MAE (May 17, 1921), AMAE, Fond 8 Conv. D 19 II, file 144.

21.   Conțescu to Ionescu (August 1, 1921), AMAE, Fond 8 Conv. D 19 II, files 562-64.

22.   CID, Protocole 33, April 13, 1921. Subject of speeches by the delegates from Austria, Czechoslovakia, Bulgaria, and the Kingdom of the Serbs, Croats, and Slovenes.

23.   Ibid. Speech by Conțescu.

24.   Conțescu to Ionescu (April 22, 1921), AMAE, Fond 8 Conv. D 19 II, files 121-27.

25.   CID, Protocole 34, April 15, 1921.

26.   Ibid. Speech by Gheorghe Popescu.

27.   CID, Protocole 33 and Protocole 34, April 13/15, 1921.

28.   CID, Protocole 33, April 13, 1921.

29.   Conțescu saw Baldwin as "intransigent" and acting "in many questions unfavorable to our interests," suspicions that were similar to those he held during the controversies of 1919. Conțescu to Ionescu (August 1, 1921), AMAE, Fond 8 Conv. D 19 II, files 562-64.

30.   This quarrel (as well as a number of others) created difficulties in reaching agreement on the final protocol.

31.   CID, Protocole 42, May 4, 1921.

32.   CID, Protocole 43, May 6, 1921.

33.   CID, Protocole 51, May 25, 1921.

34.   CID, Protocole final, Article XV.

35.   Report by Conțescu (August 1, 1921), AMAE, Fond 8 Conv. D 19 II, files 477-516. Other measures involving taxes on navigation would be moderate and be based solely on the weight of the merchandise transported. Furthermore, customs could not be regulated by the International Commission because, as Conțescu argued, the conference was capable of regulating navigation only, not commerce. CID, Protocole 45, May 10, 1921.

36.   Greek legation in Bucharest to MAE (registered May 31, 1921), AMAE, Fond 8 Conv. D 19 II, unpaged. Ionescu left the question of honoring the pledge completely in Conțescu's hands. Ionescu to Conțescu, AMAE, Fond 8 Conv. D 19 II, file 187.

37.   Report by Conțescu (August 1, 1921), AMAE, Fond 8 Conv. D 19 II, files 477-516.

38.   Conțescu to Ionescu (June 8, 1921), AMAE, Fond 8 Conv. D 19 II, file 204.

39.   CID, Protocole 55, June 1, 1921.

40.   Report by Conțescu (August 1, 1921), AMAE, Fond 8 Conv. D 19 II, files 477-516.

41.   CID, Protocole 59, June 8, 1921.

42.   Ibid. Legrand attempted to modify this by suggesting the inclusion of a representative from Czechoslovakia. This proposal was also rejected by the co-riverines.

43.   CID, Protocole 59, June 8, 1921.

44.   Ibid.

45.   Ibid.

46.　Ibid.

47.　Ibid.

48.　Ionescu to Conțescu (June 16, 1921), AMAE, Fond 8 Conv. D 19 II, file 235.

49.　Report of June 16, 1921, AMAE, Fond 8 Conv. D 19 II, file 238.

50.　CID, Protocole 64, June 20, 1921.

51.　Ibid.

52.　Ibid.

53.　Ibid.

54.　Ibid.

55.　Conțescu to Ionescu (June 21, 1921), AMAE, Fond 8 Conv. D 19 II, file 240.

56.　CID, Protocole 65, June 22, 1921.

57.　Ibid.

58.　Ibid.

59.　Ionescu to Conțescu (June 30, 1921), AMAE, Fond 8 Conv. D 19 II, file 264.

60.　At first, Rome and Belgrade refused to ratify the *Statut*. The former opposed the tax provisions and Belgrade continued to seek admission to the European Commission. Italy did sign the treaty on July 30, but Ristić was not authorized to sign until September 1921.

61.　Atti Parlimentari Sessione 1924, Camaradei Deputate 139, 15 November, 1924 (Legislatura XXVII); Senato del Regno (Legislatura XXVII, a sessione 1924-5, 5 February, 1925).

62.　Conțescu to Ionescu (June 29, 1921), AMAE, Fond 8 Conv. D 19 II, files 430-39.

63.　"Expunere de Motive" to Parliament, AMAE, Fond 8 Conv. D 19 II, files 556-61.

64.　Conțescu to Ionescu (August 1, 1921), AMAE, Fond 8 Conv. D 19 II, files 562-64.

65.　Ibid.

Notes to Chapter VIII

1.　S. P. Waterlow to M. Boerescu (May 9, 1921), AMAE, Fond 8 Conv. D 19 II, files 149-54.

2.   This is a consensus definition. For one example, see Francis Graham Wilson, *A Theory of Public Opinion* (Chicago: Henry Regnery Co., 1962).

3.   Most works totally ignore the question of public opinion in nondemocratic environments or dismiss its impact with little discussion.

4.   Of course, such apathy toward foreign policy matters is prevalent in all countries. However, in less developed agricultural societies, in which the bulk of the population has limited input in the processes of government, interest in an issue such as riparian rights is probably nonexistent.

5.   Other examples are the 1907 Peasant Revolt, celebrations over unification in 1918-19, and labor strikes during the 1920s.

6.   Rothschild, *East Central Europe*, p. 285.

7.   Stavrianos, *Balkans*, p. 707.

8.   No publication figures on these works are available.

9.   In the other major Romanian newspapers, an average of only 5-6 articles on the Danube was published during these years. Most articles took the form of references to the Straits Question and the comparison of the Danube with the Straits.

10.   *Viitorul*, (December 17, 1920), Nr. 3532.

11.   Ibid.

12.   *Viitorul*, (January 17, 1920), Nr. 3578.

13.   *Viitorul*, (August 13, 1920), Nr. 3720.

14.   *Viitorul*, (September 16, 1920), Nr. 3748.

15.   I. D. Popovici, *Situaţia creită României prin noul regim al Dunărei* (Galaţi: Camera de Comerţ şi Industrie din Galaţi, 1924), p. 6.

16.   Ibid., p. 10.

17.   Jean Bart (Eugene Botez), *Cum se desleaga Chestiunea Dunării?* (Chişinau: Tipografia "Glasul Ţării," 1919), p. 23.

18.   Grigore Antipa, *Dunărea şi problemele ei stiinţifice, economice şi politice* (Bucureşti: Librăriile "Cartea Româneasca," 1921), p. 2.

19.   (M. Burghele), *Memoire du Gouvernement Roumain dans la Question du Danube* (Bucharest: Imprimerie de l'etat, 1925), p. 3.

20.   Vintilă C. Brătianu, *Chestia Dunării* (Bucureşti: Imprimerea Statului, 1920), pp. 3-5.

21.   The idea of the "rights of a small nation" is one of the most prevalent themes concerning the fight against the Commission. Any discussion of the Question inevitably evokes this argument.

22.   Gheorghe Popescu, *Freedom of Navigation on International Rivers: The Most Suitable Administration* (London: Billings and Sons, Ltd., 1935), p. 1.

23.   Ibid.

24.   Ibid., p. 2.

25.   Ibid., p. 3.

26.   Romanian opinion on this varies. Some authors refuse to acknowledge the need for the agency, ignoring Ottoman financial and technical deficiencies.

27.   Bart, *Cum se desleaga*, p. 3.

28.   It is doubtful, considering the lack of sources, whether any judgment on Romanian capabilities in this regard can be determined. Nevertheless, the ease with which the agency was able to generate capital through foreign loans does lend credence to the view that Bucharest could have raised the funds.

29.   Grigore Antipa, *Die Donau: Ihre Politische und Wirtschaftliche Bedeutung im Leben des Rumänischen Volkes* (Bukarest: Die Dacia Bücher, 1941), p. 24.

30.   Bart, *Cum se desleaga*, p. 23.

31.   Ibid.

32.   Brătianu, *Chestia*, p. 9.

33.   (Burghele), *Memoire*, p. 5.

34.   Ibid.

35.   N. Dascovici, *Dunărea noastră* (București: Editura Fundației, 1927), p. 110.

36.   For the most strident attack on the Trowbridge agency and the admiral's character, see: Iulian Cârțână and Ilie Seftiuc, *Dunărea în istoria poporului român* (București: Editura Stiințifică, 1972), chapter 3. This work must be used with caution, however. A number of archival sources cited by the authors could not be verified either by this author or archivists at the Foreign Ministry, the State Archives or the two central libraries in Bucharest.

APPENDIX 1

CONTRIBUTIONS TO THE EUROPEAN COMMISSION
OF THE DANUBE, 1915-1916

1915	Month	Country	Contribution (in francs)
	June	Britain	200,000
	July	Austria	200,000
	July	Germany	200,000
	October	Britain	200,000
	November	Italy	200,000
	December	France	400,000
1916	May	Germany	200,000
	May	Austria	200,000
	May	Turkey	400,000
	June	Italy	200,000
	September	Russia	400,000

Source: Arhivele Statului Galați, Fond Comisia Europeană a Dunării, Nr. 51, protocol 1.

APPENDIX 2

Romanian Cabinet Fluctuations: January 1918-January 1922

1918
January 29/February 10

General Al. Averescu: President, Council of Ministers, ad-interim Minister of Foreign Affairs

General I. Culcer: Minister of Public Works

C. I. Argetoianu: Minister of Justice

Fotin Enescu: Minister of Finance and ad-interim Minister of Agriculture

I. Luca Niculescu: Minister of Industry and Commerce ːce

February 8/21
C. Garoflid: Minister of Agriculture

February 19/March 5
Fotin Enescu: Minister of Agriculture

March 5/18

Al. Marghiloman: President, Council of Ministers and Minister of the Interior

C. C. Arion: Minister of Foreign Affairs

C. Meisner: Minister of Industry and Commerce

G. Dobrescu: Minister of Justice

M. Seulescu: Minister of Finance

March 25/April 7
N. Ghica-Comănești: Minister of Public Works

June 4/16
I. Mitileneu: Minister of Justice

Gr. G. Cantacuzino: Minister of Industry and Commerce

C. Garoflid: Minister of Agriculture

October 24/November 6

General C. Coandă: President, Council of Ministers and Minister of Foreign
  Affairs
Fotin Enescu: Minister of Agriculture and ad-interim Minister of Finance
General A. Văitoianu: Minister of the Interior and ad-interim Minister of
  Justice
General E. Grigorescu: Ad-interim Minister of Industry
A. Saligny: Minister of Public Works

October 28/November 10

D. Buzdugan: Minister of Justice

October 29/November 11

O. Chiriacescu: Minister of Finance
Al. Cotescu: Minister of Industry and Commerce

November 29/December 10

Ioan I. C. Brătianu: President, Council of Ministers and Minister of For-
  eign Affairs
Al. Constantinescu: Minister of Industry and Commerce
Fotin Enescu: Minister of Agriculture

December 12/25

I. G. Duca: Minister of Agriculture

1919

February 14/27

Al. Constantinescu: Minister of Public Works

September 27

General A. Văitoianu: President, Council of Ministers, Minister of the
  Interior, ad-Interim Minister of Foreign Affairs
Ioan Popovici: Minister of Public Works
I. Popescu: Minister of Industry and Commerce and ad-Interim Minister
  of Finance

E. Miclescu: Minister of Justice

October 6
I. Angelescu: Minister of Finance

October 15
N. Mişu: Minister of Foreign Affairs

December 1
Al. Vaida-Voievod: Prime Minister and Minister of the Exterior

December 5
Aurel Vlad: Minister of Finance and ad-Interim Minister of Industry and
    Commerce
V. Bontescu: Minister of Agriculture
M. Popovici: Minister of Public Works
Ion Pelivan: Minister of Justice

December 16
Ion Mihalace: Minister of Agriculture

1920

March 13
General Al. Averescu: Prime Minister and Minister of the Interior
C. Argetoianu: Minister of Finance and ad-Interim Minister of Finance
Duiliu Zamfirescu: Minister of Foreign Affairs
Gh. Văleanu: Minister of Public Works
O. Tăslăoanu: Minister of Industry and Commerce
T. Cudalbu: Minister of Agriculture

June 13
General Al. Averescu: President, Council of Ministers, without portfolio
C. Argetoianu: Minister of the Interior
Take Ionescu: Minister of Foreign Affairs
Nicolae Titulescu: Minister of Finance
D. Greceanu: Minister of Public Works

August 27
D. Greceanu: ad-Interim Minister of Justice
M. Cantacuzino: Minister of Justice

November 16
General Al. Averescu: named titular head of Commerce and Industry
D. Greceanu: Minister of Justice

1921

January 1
V. Antonescu: Minister of Justice
Ioan Petrovici: Minister of Public Works

December 17
Take Ionescu: President, Council of Ministers and Minister of Finance
Gh. Derussi: Minister of Foreign Affairs
Ion Cămărașescu: Minister of the Interior
Gh. Lucasievici: Minister of Public Works
D. Dumitescu: Minister of Agriculture
S. Popescu: Minister of Justice
M. Oromulu: Minister of Industry and Commerce

1922

January 2
V. D. Hortopan: ad-Interim Minister of Industry and Commerce

January 19

Cabinet of Ioan I. C. Brătianu
(Chart only includes changes in major cabinet positions and does not reflect
rotation of other functionaries including Ministers without Portfolio.)

Source: Mircea Mușat and Ion Ardeleanu, *Viața politică în România
1918-1921* (București: Editura Politică, 1976), pp. 354-361.

APPENDIX 3

Seats obtained in Parliamentary elections of
1919, 1920, and 1921

Party	1919	1920	1921
Conservative-Progressive	16	4	0
National Liberal	103	9	227
National Romanian	199	34	25
Peasant	130	44	40
People's	7	224	12
National-Democrat	27	3	3
Others	86	51	62

Source: Mircea Muşat and Ion Ardeleanu, *Viaţa politică în România 1918-1921* (Bucureşti: Editura politică, 1976), p. 362.

APPENDIX 4

Ships and Total Tonnage Using Sulina Facilities
1911-1921

Year	Total Ships	Aggregate Tonnage
1911	1,532	3,726,747
1912	1,008	1,788,156*
1913	936	1,742,907*
1914	721	1,364,320
1915	96	102,647
1916	128	184,677
1917	142	146,373
1918	212	302,465
1919	574	795,924
1920	648	958,563
1921	753	1,156,344

* reflects the effects of the First and Second Balkan Wars

Source: Arhivele Statului Galaţi: Fond Comisia Europeană a Dunării, Nr. 56.

APPENDIX 5

Shipping by Origin of Registry: 1912-1921
(tonnage in parentheses)

COUNTRY	1912	1913	1914	1915	1916
Germany	29 ships (68,982)	23 (57,927)	21 (59,630)	––	––
Austria-Hungary	143 (310,974)	158 (313,219)	82 (161,677)	––	––
Belgium	30 (44,068)	26 (39,894)	26 (46,786)	––	––
France	18 (33,374)	28 (54,779)	14 (26,173)		
Britain	247 (548,217)	278 (669,589)	187 (461,810)	––	––
Greece	299 (558,666)	––	––	2 (5,043)	3 (1,865)
Hungary	4 (9,637)	8 (18,729)	2 (5,250)	––	––
Italy	26 (40,916)	118 (181,860)	70 (98,896)	5 (10,438)	1 (265)
Romania	40 (47,703)	57 (77,547)	42 (78,211)	12 (27,349)	29 (59,053)
Russia	61 (52,310)	66 (65,979)	68 (60,395)	63 (53,075)	91 (122,048)
Turkey	83 (33,860)	38 (13,216)	34 (4,719)	––	––

APPENDIX 5 (continued)

COUNTRY	1917	1918*	1919* **	1920**	1921
Germany	——	82 (103,592)	——	——	——
Austria	——	89 (138,662)	——	——	——
Belgium	——	——	1 (892)	5 (8,215)	16 (33,363)
France	——	——	53 (70,398)	38 (63,680)	101 (133,568)
Britain	——	1 (3,012)	62 (143,332)	122 (271,454)	158 (346,350)
Greece	——	——	98 (64,290)	126 (118,721)	144 (137,887)
Hungary	——	——	——	11 (25,978)	23 (42,673)
Italy	——	——	44 (97,689)	123 (178,182)	106 (172,147)
Romania	——	14 (19,580)	192 (240,316)	86 (91,360)	78 (103,230)
Russia	142 (122,048)	5 (3,782)	55 (83,114)	56 (44,095)	31 (10,777)
Turkey	——	——	25 (1,321)	3 (104)	2 (118)

* does not reflect ships using Commission port facilities but evading taxes
** In 1919, six "Inter-Allied" ships passed through Sulina carrying 19,305 tons; in 1920 an additional sixteen (22,957 tons) vessels used these facilities.

Source: Arhivele Statului Galați: Fond Comisia Europeană a Dunării, Nr. 56.

APPENDIX 6

Percentage of Tonnage by Category of Ship (Capacity)

	0-200	201-400	401-600	601-800	801-1000	1001-1500	1500+
1912	3.97	3.67	6.84	3.08	3.97	11.31	67.16
1913	2.56	1.50	8.76	5.34	4.70	7.37	69.77
1914	4.44	1.66	5.27	8.60	5.00	6.10	68.93
1915	11.46	7.29	14.58	11.46	17.71	12.50	25.00
1916	3.91	1.56	3.90	5.47	19.50	24.22	41.41
1917	0.70	7.04	26.76	10.56	10.57	28.17	16.20
1918	15.57	17.45	2.36	7.55	—	14.15	42.92
1919	11.50	6.80	9.76	14.81	6.79	14.98	35.36
1920	9.26	5.25	7.25	10.18	8.03	16.66	43.36
1921	8.23	5.98	9.56	6.91	6.91	12.61	49.80

Tonnage by % of Capacity

1912	.18	.60	2.04	1.20	1.99	8.14	85.85
1913	.07	.26	2.52	1.98	2.26	4.86	88.05
1914	.16	.23	1.48	2.98	2.33	3.81	88.91
1915	.57	2.12	7.06	7.99	14.55	14.04	53.67
1916	.13	.28	1.49	2.67	11.72	19.46	64.25
1917	.13	2.10	13.62	7.46	9.14	32.74	34.81
1918	1.41	3.55	.89	3.53	—	12.81	77.81
1919	.64	1.52	3.46	7.46	4.37	13.97	68.58
1920	.49	1.13	2.49	4.82	4.85	14.59	71.63
1921	.60	1.25	3.15	3.12	4.06	10.43	77.39

Source: Arhivele Galați: Fond Comisia Europeană a Dunării, No. 58.

156

APPENDIX 7

CONFÉRENCE INTERNATIONALE DU DANUBE

Belgique
M. Brunet, Ministre plénipotentiare, Directeur général au Ministère des Affaires Étrangères.

France
M. Albert Legrand, Ministre plénipotentiare, Représentant de la France à Commission européennee du Danube et à la Commission internationale du Danube.

Grande-Bretagne
M. John Grey Baldwin, Ministre plénipotentiare, Représentant de la Grand-Bretagne à la Commission européennee du Danube, à la Commission centrale du Rhin et aux Commissions internationales de l'Elbe et de l'Oder.

Grèce
M. Lambros Coromilas, Envoyé extraordinaire et Ministre plénipotentiare de S.M. le Roi des Hellènes à Rome.

Italie
M. Vittore Siciliani, Ministre plénipotentiare, Représentant de l'Italie a la Commission européenne de Danube.

Roumanie
M. Thomas Stelian, ancien Ministre d'État.

Royaume des Serbes, Croates, Slovenes
M. Mihailo G. Ristitch, Ministre plénipotentiare, Représentant du Royaume des Serbes, Croates, Slovènes à la Commission internationale de Danube.

Tcheco-Slovaquie
M. l'Ingénieur Bohuslav Muller, Secretaire d'État au Ministère des Travaux Publics.

Allemagne
M. le Dr. Seelinger, Envoyé extraordinaire et Ministre plénipotentiare.

Autriche
M. le Dr. Victor Ondraczek, Chef de section au Département des Voies et Communications.

Bulgarie
M. Georges Lazaroff, Directeur général des constructions des Chemins de fer et des Ports.

Hongrie
M. Edmond Miklós de Miklosvar, Conseiller intime actual, Secrétaire d'État, Membre de la Chambre des Magnats.

APPENDIX 8
ANNEXE AU PROTOCOLE N° 1.

———

PROJET DE CONVENTION

PRÉSENTÉ PAR LE PLENIPOTENTIAIRE DE FRANCE.

————

La Belgique, la France, la Grande-Bretagne, la Grèce, l'Italie, la Roumanie, le Royaume des Serbes, Croates et Slovènes et l'État Tchéco-Slovaque,

Voulant déterminer d'un commun accord, conformément aux stipulations des Traités de Versailles, de Saint-Germain, de Neuilly et de Trianon, les règles générales suivant lesquelles sera assurée d'une manière définitive la libre navigation du Danube international,

Ont décidé de conclure la présente convention et ont, à cet effet, désigné pour leurs Plénipotentiaires, savoir :

. . . .

. . . .

lesquels, après avoir échangé leurs pleins pouvoirs trouvés en bonne et due forme, ont arrêté, en présence des Représentants de l'Allemagne (pour la Bavière et le Wurtemberg), de l'Autriche, de la Bulgarie et de la Hongrie, les stipulations suivantes :

I. Administration générale du Danube.

———

Article I.

La navigation du Danube est libre et ouverte à tous les pavillons dans des conditions d'égalité complète sur tout le cours navigable du fleuve, c'est-à-dire d'Ulm à la mer Noire.

Art. II.

Deux Commissions internationales distinctes sont chargées de l'administration et du contrôle de la navigation sur le Danube.

Art. III.

La partie du Danube comprise entre Ulm et Braila, dite Danube fluvial, et ses affluents qui seront déclarés internationaux dans les conditions prévues par les articles 331 du Traité de Versailles, 291 du Traité de Saint-Germain, 219 du Traité de Neuilly et 275 du Traité de Trianon, sont placés sous l'administration de la *Commission internationale du Danube*.

Art. IV.

La partie du fleuve comprise entre Braila et la mer, dite Danube maritime, avec toutes ses embouchures, est maintenue sous l'administration de la *Commission européenne du Danube*.

II. Commission européenne.

Art. V.

La Commission européenne du Danube est composée des Représentants de la France, de la Grande-Bretagne, de l'Italie et de la Roumanie à raison d'un Délégué par Puissance. La Grèce est admise à s'y faire représenter dans les mêmes conditions.

Art. VI.

La juridiction de ladite Commission s'étend, comme il est dit à l'article IV, sur toute la partie du fleuve accessible aux navires de haute mer, c'est-à-dire de Braila à la mer Noire.

Art. VII.

Il n'est rien changé aux droits, attributions et immunités que la Commission européenne tient des actes internationaux qui l'ont constituée et des traités qui ont confirmé ses pouvoirs.

Art. VIII.

Les pouvoirs de la Commission européenne ne pourront être modifiés ou prendre fin que par l'effet d'un arrangement international auquel tous les États signataires de la présente Convention auraient été appelés à participer.

Toutefois, la composition de ladite Commission, telle qu'elle est fixée à l'article V, pourra être modifiée avec le consentement unanime des États qui y sont représentés

Le siège légal de la Commission est fixé à Galatz.

III. Commission internationale.

Art. IX.

La Commission internationale du Danube est composée, à raison d'un Délégué par Puissance, par les Représentants des États mentionnés aux articles 347 du Traité de Versailles, 302 du Traité de Saint-Germain, 230 du Traité de Neuilly et 286 du Traité de Trianon, à savoir de l'Autriche, de la Bavière, de la Bulgarie, de la Hongrie, du Royaume des Serbes, Croates, Slovènes, de la Roumanie, de l'État Tchéco-Slovaque et du Wurtemberg et par un Délégué de chacun des États non-riverains représentés à la Commission européenne du Danube.

Art. X.

La juridiction de la Commission internationale s'étend sur la partie du Danube comprise entre Ulm et Braila et sur ceux de ses affluents qui seront déclarés internationaux, dans les conditions prévues à l'article III, par un acte additionnel à la présente Convention.

Art. XI.

La Commission internationale a un pouvoir supérieur de contrôle sur la partie du Danube comprise dans sa juridiction. Elle veille à ce qu'aucun obstacle quelconque ne soit mis, du fait d'un ou de plusieurs États riverains, à la libre navigation du fleuve, à ce qu'une égalité complète de traitement soit maintenue entre tous les pavillons qui le fréquentent et, d'une manière générale, à ce qu'aucune atteinte ne soit portée au caractère international que les traités ont assigné au Danube.

Art. XII.

La Commission internationale établit le programme d'ensemble des travaux qu'elle juge nécessaire d'entreprendre sur le fleuve pour l'entretien et l'amélioration de sa navigabilité. Elle en surveille l'étude et l'exécution.

Art. XIII.

Les travaux nécessaires pour le maintien et l'amélioration de la navigabilité du Danube seront entrepris soit par les États riverains intéressés, avec l'approbation préalable de la Commission, soit par la Commission elle-même, de sa propre initiative. Dans le cas où un État riverain se trouverait hors d'état d'entreprendre lui-même les travaux d'entretien et d'amélioration que la Commission aura jugés nécessaires, celle-ci peut les exécuter par ses propres moyens ; l'État riverain sera tenu dans ce cas de fournir à la Commission toutes les facilités nécessaires à l'exécution desdits travaux.

Aucun ouvrage de caractère public ou privé susceptible de modifier la profondeur du fleuve ou les conditions de sa navigabilité, ce dont la Commission sera seule juge, ne peut être entrepris sans son assentiment préalable.

ART. XIV.

La Commission internationale établira des règlements de navigation qui, dans la mesure du possible, seront uniformes pour la partie du Danube placée sous son administration.

ART. XV.

A l'effet de surveiller et de contrôler l'exécution desdits règlements, la Commission entretient sur le fleuve un Inspecteur en chef et des Inspecteurs dont l'autorité s'exercera à l'égard de tous les pavillons sans distinction. Ces agents seront responsables de l'application des règlements et auront le droit, dans l'exercice de leurs fonctions, de recourir à l'assistance des autorités locales toutes les fois qu'ils le jugeront nécessaire.

L'Inspecteur en chef ou, en son absence, l'Inspecteur d'une section fluviale, prononcera en première instance les peines applicables aux infractions aux règlements.

Appel de ces jugements pourra être porté devant un tribunal de navigation constitué ou désigné par la Commission internationale.

ART. XVI.

Indépendamment des agents de contrôle mentionnés à l'article ci-dessus, la Commission peut nommer tels fonctionnaires ou agents qu'elle jugerait nécessaire pour l'administration et l'entretien du Danube.

ART. XVII.

Par dérogation aux dispositions qui précèdent, le secteur des Portes de Fer, compris entre Orsova et Bazias, étant donné ses difficultés naturelles et l'importance qu'il présente pour la libre navigation du Danube, sera soumis à un régime particulier.

Une Sous-Commission, où les États riverains seront obligatoirement représentés, sera nommée par la Commission internationale et chargée de prendre dans ce secteur les mesures d'administration directe que la Commission aura jugées nécessaires.

Elle disposera d'un personnel et d'un matériel qui lui seront propres, y compris le matériel prévu à l'article 288 du Traité de Trianon, et pourra percevoir certaines taxes, organiser et surveiller le pilotage et réglementer l'utilisation des forces hydrauliques des Portes de Fer.

Un règlement spécial élaboré par la Commission internationale fixera dans leur détail la composition et les pouvoirs de cette Sous-Commission.

Art. XVIII.

La Commission internationale est autorisée à établir et à percevoir sur la navigation des taxes, d'un taux modéré, dont le montant servira exclusivement à subvenir aux dépenses d'administration et à l'exécution des travaux d'entretien et d'amélioration de la navigabilité. Elle déterminera elle-même les modalités de la perception et de la comptabilité de ces taxes, en veillant à ce qu'elles ne puissent jamais, sous une forme quelconque, constituer un traitement différentiel entre les divers pavillons.

Art. XIX.

Les droits de douane et d'octroi et autres taxes sur les marchandises établis par les États riverains devront être perçus de manière à n'apporter aucune entrave à la navigation. Ces droits et taxes ne peuvent être perçus que sur les marchandises débarquées sur les rives du Danube ; ils ne peuvent, sous aucun prétexte, être perçus sur les marchandises en transit.

Art. XX.

La Commission internationale examinera la question et, s'il est nécessaire, décidera de la création de ports francs, ou de zones franches dans les ports où le transbordement est généralement ou nécessairement pratiqué. Les règlements relatifs à l'usage des ports francs ou des zones franches seront soumis à l'approbation de la Commission.

Art. XXI.

La Commission fixe elle-même l'ordre de ses travaux dans un règlement établi en session plénière. Elle arrête le nombre et le lieu de ses sessions périodiques et constitue, si elle le juge utile, un Comité exécutif permanent chargé de surveiller l'exécution des dispositions qu'elle a adoptées en plenum.

Les décisions de la Commission internationale seront prises à la majorité des voix des membres présents. En cas de partage, la voix du Président sera prépondérante.

Le siège légal de la Commission est fixé à Budapesth.

Art. XXII.

La Commission internationale du Danube jouit, tant pour ses installations que pour la personne de ses membres et de ses agents, des mêmes privilèges et immunités qui sont reconnus en temps de paix comme en temps de guerre aux agents et aux établissements de la Commission européenne.

Elle a le droit d'arborer sur ses navires et sur ses immeubles un pavillon dont elle détermine elle-même la forme et les couleurs.

Art. XXIII.

Les pouvoirs de la Commission internationale ne pourront être modifiés ou prendre fin que par l'effet d'un arrangement international auquel tous les États signataires de la présente Convention auraient été appelés à participer.

IV. Coordination entre les deux Commissions.

Art. XXIV.

La Commission internationale et la Commission européenne du Danube prendront toutes dispositions nécessaires pour assurer, dans la mesure où cela sera possible et utile, l'uniformité du régime administratif du Danube.

Elles échangeront régulièrement à cet effet toutes informations, tous documents, procès-verbaux, études et projets pouvant intéresser l'une et l'autre. Elles pourront, en cas de besoin, se réunir en sessions mixtes pour arrêter d'un commun accord certaines règles identiques concernant la navigation et la police du fleuve.

V. Dispositions générales.

Art. XXV.

Dans le cas où une infraction grave serait commise aux dispositions de la présente Convention, ou dans le cas où un litige survenu entre deux États riverains menacerait de compromettre la libre navigation du Danube, la Commission intéressée aura le droit, après avoir épuisé tous les moyens d'avertissement et de conciliation, de porter l'affaire devant le Conseil de la Société des Nations.

Art. XXVI.

Tous les traités, conventions, actes et arrangements relatifs au régime des fleuves internationaux en général, et au Danube et à ses embouchures en particulier, sont maintenus dans toutes celles de leurs dispositions qui ne sont pas abrogées ou modifiées par les stipulations qui précèdent.

Art. XXVII.

La présente Convention sera établie en un seul exemplaire qui sera déposé dans les archives du Gouvernement de la République française. Il en sera fait autant de copies certifiées conformes que de Parties Contractantes. Ses dispositions entreront en vigueur à dater du jour de sa signature.

En foi de quoi...

ANNEXE AU PROTOCOLE N° 2.

COMMISSION POUR L'ÉTUDE DE LA LIBERTÉ DES COMMUNICATIONS
ET DU TRANSIT.

PROJET DE CONVENTION
SUR LE RÉGIME INTERNATIONAL DES VOIES NAVIGABLES.
(Texte adopté dans la séance du 30 mars 1920.)

La Conférence générale des communications et du transit de la Société des Nations,

Convoquée à   par

Après avoir décidé d'adopter diverses propositions relatives au régime international des voies navigables, question formant le deuxième point de l'ordre du jour de la session de la Conférence tenue à   et

Après avoir décidé que ces propositions seraient rédigées sous forme d'un projet de convention internationale,

Adopte le projet de convention ci-après à ratifier par les Membres de la Société des Nations, ainsi que par toutes autres Puissances qui en auraient reçu communication officielle du Conseil de la Société des Nations; ceux desdits Membres et desdites Puissances qui ratifieront le présent objet étant désignés ci-après comme Hautes Parties Contractantes.

PRÉAMBULE.

Principe de la Convention. — Les Hautes Parties Contractantes, désireuses de mettre en application sur les voies d'eau placées sous leur souveraineté ou leur autorité, le principe de la liberté des communications, conformément à l'article 23 e) du Pacte de la Société des Nations, arrêtent les dispositions de la présente Convention touchant le régime de certaines de ces voies, définies comme internationales à l'article 1er ci-après.

Elles déclarent, en outre, quant aux voies d'eau non définies comme internationales en vertu dudit article, leur intention de s'inspirer du même principe en l'appliquant autant que possible dans chaque cas particulier, étant entendu que, dès à présent et sans préjudice des dispositions de la Convention sur la liberté du transit, il ne devra être établi aucune différenciation entre les Hautes Parties Contractantes en raison du pavillon, en ce qui concerne les transports d'importation et d'exportation directe sans transbordement, et que le présent alinéa ne fait pas obstacle à l'établissement de services publics de remorquage ou autres moyens de traction monopolisés.

CONFÉR. DANUBE. — T. I.

165

TITRE I.
Voies d'eau internationales.

ARTICLE PREMIER.

Définition. — Pour l'application de la présente Convention, seront considérées comme « voies d'eau internationales » :

1° Toutes parties naturellement accessibles depuis la mer d'une voie d'eau qui dans son cours naturellement accessible depuis la mer sépare ou traverse différents États ainsi que toutes parties d'une autre voie d'eau naturellement accessibles depuis la mer et reliant à la mer une voie d'eau rentrant dans la définition ci-dessus.

En vue de cette définition, il est entendu :

a) Que la possibilité d'un transbordement d'un navire ou d'un bateau à un autre n'est pas exclue par les mots « accessibles depuis la mer » ;

b) Que les affluents doivent être considérés comme des voies d'eau séparées ;

c) Que les canaux latéraux établis en vue de suppléer aux imperfections d'une voie d'eau sont assimilés à cette dernière.

2° Les voies d'eau ou partie de voies d'eau, naturelles ou artificielles, désignées expressément comme devant être soumises au régime de la présente Convention dans des actes unilatéraux ou dans des accords comportant notamment le consentement du ou des États sous la souveraineté ou l'autorité desquels se trouveraient placées les voies d'eau ou parties de voies d'eau considérées.

TITRE II.
Liberté de navigation.

ART. 2.

Libre exercice de la navigation. — Sous réserve des stipulations des articles 4, 14 et 16, chacune des Hautes Parties Contractantes accordera sur les parties de voies d'eau ci-dessus désignées qui seraient placées sous sa souveraineté ou sous son autorité le libre exercice de la navigation aux navires et bateaux battant pavillon de l'une quelconque des autres Parties Contractantes.

ART. 3.

Égalité de traitement. — Dans ledit exercice de la navigation et sous réserve des stipulations visées à l'article 2, les ressortissants, les biens et les pavillons de toutes les Parties Contractantes seront, sous tous les rapports, traités sur le pied d'une parfaite égalité, de telle sorte qu'aucune distinction ne soit faite entre les ressortissants, les biens et les pavillons des différents États riverains, y compris l'État riverain sous la souveraineté ou l'autorité duquel serait placée la partie de voie d'eau considérée, ou entre les ressortissants, les biens et les pavillons des États rive-

rains et ceux des non-riverains; étant entendu qu'en conséquence, il ne sera accordé sur
lesdites voies d'eau aucun privilège exclusif de navigation à des sociétés ou à des particuliers, et que, pour l'application du présent article, les Hautes Parties Contractantes
reconnaîtront le pavillon maritime des navires et bateaux de toute Partie Contractante qui
n'a pas de littoral maritime, lorsqu'ils sont enregistrés en un lieu unique déterminé, situé
sur son territoire et constituant pour ces navires et bateaux le port d'enregistrement.

Art. 4.

Restrictions. — Toutefois, dans les cas où un ensemble de considérations économiques,
techniques et topographiques le justifieraient exceptionnellement, celles d'entre les Hautes
Parties Contractantes qui se trouveraient riveraines d'une même voie d'eau internationale
pourront refuser, sous réserve de l'accord unanime des États riverains ou représentés à la
Commission internationale de ladite voie d'eau, s'il en existe une, le droit d'exécution des
transports locaux de voyageurs et de marchandises entre les ports situés sur cette voie d'eau
et placés sous des souverainetés ou des autorités différentes, aux pavillons de toutes les
Parties Contractantes non-riveraines.

Art. 5.

Mesures administratives. — Chacune des Hautes Parties Contractantes se réserve, sur les
voies d'eau visées à l'article 1er et placées sous sa souveraineté ou sous son autorité, tous droits
existants d'édicter les dispositions et de prendre les mesures nécessaires à la police générale
du territoire, à l'application des lois et règlements concernant les douanes, les prescriptions
sanitaires, les précautions contre les maladies des animaux et des végétaux, l'émigration,
l'immigration et l'importation ou l'exportation des marchandises prohibées; étant entendu
que ces dispositions et ces mesures, raisonnables et appliquées sur un pied de parfaite
égalité aux ressortissants, aux biens et aux pavillons de l'une quelconque des Parties
Contractantes, y compris la Partie Contractante qui les édicte, ne devront pas, sans motif
valable, entraver le libre exercice de la navigation.

TITRE III.

Redevances.

Art. 6.

Redevances ayant le caractère de rémunération. — Sur le parcours comme à l'embouchure
des voies d'eau internationales, il ne pourra être perçu de redevances d'aucune espèce,
autres que les redevances ayant le caractère de rétributions et destinées exclusivement à
couvrir d'une manière équitable les frais d'entretien de la navigabilité ou d'amélioration de
la voie d'eau et de son accès ou à subvenir à des dépenses faites dans l'intérêt de la
navigation. Le tarif en sera calculé sur ces frais et dépenses et affiché dans les ports. Ces
redevances seront établies de manière à ne pas rendre nécessaire un examen détaillé de la
cargaison si ce n'est lorsqu'il y a soupçon de fraude ou de contravention, et à faciliter
autant que possible, tant par leurs conditions d'application que par leurs tarifs, le trafic
international.

TITRE IV.
Transit, importation, exportation, ports.

Art. 7.

Formalités douanières. — Le transit des navires et bateaux, des voyageurs et des marchandises, sur les voies d'eau internationales, s'effectuera dans les conditions fixées par la Convention sur la liberté du transit ; les dispositions complémentaires ci-après lui seront en outre applicables :

Lorsque les deux rives d'une voie d'eau internationale font partie d'un même État, les formalités douanières imposées aux marchandises en transit ne pourront excéder la mise sous scellés ou sous la garde d'un agent des douanes. Lorsque la voie d'eau internationale forme la frontière entre deux États, les navires et bateaux, les voyageurs et les marchandises en transit devront être en cours de route exempts de toute formalité douanière sauf le cas où, pour des raisons valables d'ordre pratique et sans porter atteinte à la facilité de la navigation, l'accomplissement des formalités douanières se ferait en un point de la partie du fleuve formant frontière.

Le transit des navires et bateaux, des voyageurs et des marchandises sur ces voies d'eau internationales ne pourra donner lieu à la perception des droits prévus et autorisés à l'article 3 de la Convention sur la liberté du transit.

Art. 8.

Utilisation des ports. — Les ressortissants, les biens et les pavillons de toutes les Hautes Parties Contractantes jouiront, sous réserve des dispositions des articles 4, 14 et 16, dans tous les ports situés sur une voie d'eau internationale et sous le rapport de l'utilisation de ces ports, notamment en ce qui concerne les droits et charges de ports, d'un traitement égal à celui des ressortissants, des biens et des pavillons de l'État riverain sous la souveraineté ou l'autorité duquel le port est placé ; étant entendu que les biens auxquels s'applique le présent alinéa sont les biens ayant pour origine, provenance ou destination l'une quelconque des Hautes Parties Contractantes.

Les installations des ports situés sur une voie d'eau internationale et les facilités offertes dans ceux-ci à la navigation ne pourront être soustraites à l'usage public que dans une mesure raisonnable et pleinement compatible avec le libre exercice effectif de la navigation.

Tous droits de douane, d'octroi local ou de consommation perçus à l'occasion de l'importation ou de l'exportation des marchandises par lesdits ports devront être les mêmes, que le pavillon du navire ou bateau ayant effectué ou devant effectuer le transport soit le pavillon national ou celui de l'une quelconque des Hautes Parties Contractantes. A moins de motif exceptionnel justifiant raisonnablement, pour des nécessités économiques, une dérogation, ces droits devront être établis sur les mêmes bases et d'après les mêmes taux que les droits similaires appliqués aux autres frontières douanières de l'État intéressé, et toutes les facilités qui seraient accordées par les Hautes Parties Contractantes sur d'autres voies de terre ou d'eau ou dans d'autres ports pour l'importation et l'exportation des marchandises seront également concédées à l'importation ou à l'exportation par la voie d'eau internationale et les ports visés ci-dessus.

TITRE V.
Travaux.

***

Art. 9.

Travaux d'entretien et d'amélioration. — A défaut d'une organisation spéciale ou d'accords particuliers relatifs à l'entretien et à l'amélioration d'une voie d'eau internationale, tout État riverain de cette voie est tenu de s'abstenir de toutes mesures susceptibles de porter atteinte à la facilité de la navigation, ainsi que de prendre toutes dispositions utiles pour écarter les obstacles et dangers pour la navigation, et d'exécuter tous travaux nécessaires d'entretien de la voie d'eau, ou, sous réserve d'une répartition des dépenses entre les États intéressés proportionnelle à l'intérêt auxdits travaux, de les laisser exécuter.

Tout État riverain est également tenu, dans les mêmes conditions, et sauf motifs valables d'opposition fondés sur des intérêts autres que ceux de la navigation, tels que notamment le maintien du régime normal des eaux, la nécessité de l'irrigation ou de l'utilisation de la force hydraulique, d'exécuter ou laisser exécuter tous travaux d'amélioration de la voie d'eau au cas où les États qui en feraient la demande offriraient d'en couvrir les frais.

Les dispositions du présent article ne pourront être invoquées en aucun cas contre un État riverain qui justifierait agir ou avoir agi avec le consentement unanime de tous les États riverains de la voie d'eau internationale ou représentés à la Commission internationale de ladite voie d'eau, s'il existe une telle Commission.

TITRE VI.
Administration.

***

Art. 10.

Réglementation de la navigation. — Sauf dispositions contraires d'un accord ou traité particulier, l'administration des voies d'eau internationales est exercée par chacun des États riverains sous la souveraineté ou l'autorité duquel cette voie d'eau est placée. Chacun desdits États riverains a notamment pouvoir et est tenu d'édicter la réglementation de la navigation sur la voie d'eau et de veiller à son application; ladite réglementation devant être établie et appliquée de telle manière que soit facilité le libre exercice de la navigation, dans les conditions prévues à la présente Convention; les règles de procédure touchant notamment la constatation, la poursuite et la répression des délits de navigation devront, en particulier, être aussi expéditives que possible.

Toutefois les Hautes Parties Contractantes reconnaissent hautement désirable une entente entre États riverains d'une même voie d'eau internationale en ce qui concerne son administration et particulièrement l'adoption d'une réglementation de la navigation aussi uniforme, sur tout le parcours de cette voie d'eau, que le permet la diversité des circonstances locales.

Art. 11.

Commissions fluviales. — Dans le cas où un des accords du traité particulier visés à l'article précédent aurait confié ou confierait certaines fonctions à une Commission internationale, comprenant des représentants d'États autres que les États riverains de la voie d'eau internationale, une telle Commission s'inspirera exclusivement, sous réserve des dispositions de l'article 9, des intérêts de la navigation, et sera considérée comme un des organismes prévus à l'article 24 du Pacte de la Société des Nations; étant entendu par là qu'elle échangera directement avec les organes de la Société des Nations toutes informations utiles et fera parvenir un rapport annuel à la Société des Nations.

Les attributions des Commissions prévues à l'alinéa précédent seront déterminées dans l'Acte de navigation de chaque voie d'eau et comporteront au moins les attributions suivantes :

1° La Commission aura qualité pour élaborer les règlements de navigation qu'elle jugerait nécessaire d'élaborer elle-même et recevra communication de tous autres règlements de navigation ;

2° Elle inspectera ou fera inspecter périodiquement la voie d'eau et signalera aux États riverains les travaux utiles pour l'entretien des ouvrages et le maintien de la navigabilité ;

3° Elle recevra de chacun des États riverains communication officielle de tous projets d'amélioration de la voie d'eau ;

4° Au cas où l'Acte de navigation ne comprendrait pas une réglementation spéciale quant à la perception des redevances, elle aura qualité pour approuver la perception de redevances, en appliquant les dispositions de l'article 6 de la présente Convention.

TITRE VII.

Dispositions diverses.

Art. 12.

Application de la Convention en temps de guerre. — Les stipulations de la présente Convention subsistent en temps de guerre dans toute la mesure compatible avec les droits et les devoirs des belligérants et des neutres.

Art. 13.

Relations entre les présentes obligations et les autres obligations des Membres de la Société des Nations. — La présente Convention n'impose à aucune des Hautes Parties Contractantes une obligation qui irait à l'encontre de ses droits et obligations en tant que Membre de la Société des Nations.

Art. 14.

Bâtiments de guerre, etc. — La présente Convention doit être entendue comme n'affectant en aucune manière, sauf stipulation contraire d'un accord ou traité particulier relatif à une voie d'eau déterminée, la navigation des navires et bâtiments de guerre, de police, de contrôle et, en général, de tous bâtiments exerçant, au nom d'un État souverain, une autorité quelconque de puissance publique.

Art. 15.

Relations avec les États non-adhérents. — Chacune des Hautes Parties Contractantes s'engage à ne conclure avec un État non adhérent à la présente Convention aucun accord relatif à la navigation sur une voie d'eau internationale qui ne soit licite entre Parties Contractantes aux termes de la présente Convention.

Art. 16.

Transports locaux. — La présente Convention ne doit pas être entendue comme visant aucunement le droit d'exécution des transports locaux de voyageurs et de marchandises entre ports placés sous la souveraineté ou l'autorité d'un même État.

Art. 17.

Relations avec les traités donnant des facilités plus grandes. — La présente Convention ne doit pas être entendue comme impliquant aucunement le retrait de facilités plus grandes accordées au libre exercice de la navigation, telles que, par exemple, l'absence de toutes redevances, sur une voie d'eau internationale quelconque, dans des conditions compatibles avec le principe d'égalité entre les ressortissants, les biens et les pavillons de toutes les Parties Contractantes, tel qu'il est défini et appliqué à la présente Convention, non plus que l'interdiction d'en accorder dans l'avenir de semblables.

Art. 18.

Relations entre la présente Convention et les Traités de Paix. — La présente Convention ne fait pas obstacle à l'application des Traités de Versailles, Saint-Germain, Neuilly, etc., entre les Puissances signataires de ces Traités.

Art. 19.

Juridiction. — A défaut d'entente directe entre les Parties, tous différends relatifs à l'interprétation et à l'application des articles de la présente Convention seront portés tout d'abord devant la Commission internationale visée à l'article 11, s'il en existe une pour la voie d'eau considérée. S'il n'existe pas de telle Commission internationale, comme dans le cas où les conclusions de cette Commission ne seraient pas acceptées par l'un des États, tout État intéressé pourra saisir le Comité permanent des communications et du transit et pourra éventuellement faire appel, dans les délais fixés, à la Cour permanente de justice internationale, dans les conditions prévues dans la résolution de l'Assemblée de la Société des Nations, en date du   , et du règlement d'organisation de la Conférence générale et du Comité permanent des communications et du transit, en date du   .

Ces différends bénéficieront, en cas d'urgence, d'une procédure expéditive et pourront faire l'objet de la part de la Commission internationale, du Comité permanent des communications et du transit et de la Cour permanente de justice internationale, sans préjudice des conclusions, de l'avis et du jugement définitifs touchant le fond du litige, de conclusions, d'un avis et d'un jugement provisoire pouvant prescrire toutes mesures provisionnelles destirées notamment à rendre à la navigation les facilités dont elle jouissait avant l'acte ou le fait donnant lieu au différend.

Le présent article ne fait pas obstacle au règlement de différends, soit par arbitrage, soit de toute autre manière, en vertu de conventions spéciales entre États intéressés, sauf en ce qui concerne les voies d'eau soumises à la juridiction des Commissions internationales visées à l'article 11.

Art. 20.

Sanctions. — Dans le cas où l'une des Hautes Parties Contractantes ne se conformerait pas aux conclusions de la Commission ou à l'avis du Comité permanent des communications et du transit, ou, en cas d'appel, au jugement de la Cour permanente de justice internationale, toute Haute Partie Contractante pourra saisir la Cour permanente de justice internationale, afin d'obtenir de la Cour déclaration des mesures que chacune des Hautes Parties Contractantes sera fondée à prendre en l'espèce.

Art. 21.

Ratification. — Le Secrétaire général de la Société des Nations communiquera une copie certifiée conforme du présent projet de Convention à chacun des Membres de la Société des Nations, ainsi qu'à chacune des Puissances auxquelles le Conseil de la Société des Nations déciderait de donner communication du présent projet de Convention.

Les ratifications officielles de la présente Convention seront notifiées au Secrétaire général de la Société des Nations et par lui enregistrées.

Art. 22.

Notification. — Aussitôt que les ratifications de trois des Membres ou des Puissances visées à l'article précédent auront été enregistrées au Secrétariat, le Secrétaire général notifiera le fait à tous les Membres ou Puissances visés à l'article précédent.

Art. 23.

Mise en vigueur de la Convention. — La présente Convention entrera en vigueur trente jours après la date où cette notification aura été effectuée par le Secrétaire général de la Société des Nations. Elle ne liera que les Membres ou les Puissances qui auront fait enregistrer leur ratification au Secrétariat, ou dont l'adhésion serait déjà acquise. Par la suite, la présente Convention entrera en vigueur au regard de tout Membre ou de toute autre Puissance trente jours après la date où la ratification de ce Membre ou de cette Puissance aura été enregistrée au Secrétariat.

Art 24.

Délai d'application de la Convention. — Tout Membre qui ratifie la présente Convention s'engage à appliquer ses dispositions au plus tard le 1ᵉʳ juillet 1922 et à prendre telles mesures qui seront nécessaires pour rendre effectives ces dispositions.

Toute Puissance qui ratifie la présente Convention après avoir reçu communication du Conseil de la Société des Nations s'engage à appliquer ses dispositions au plus tard dix-huit mois après la date de ladite communication et à prendre telles mesures qui seront nécessaires pour rendre effectives ses dispositions.

Art. 25.

Dénonciation. — Tout Membre ou toute Puissance ayant ratifié la présente Convention peut la dénoncer à l'expiration d'une période de dix années après la date de la mise en vigueur de la Convention par un acte communiqué au Secrétaire général de la Société des Nations et par lui enregistré.

La dénonciation ne prendra effet qu'une année après avoir été enregistrée au Secrétariat.

Art. 26.

Revision. — Le Comité permanent des communications et du transit devra au moins une fois par dix années présenter à la Conférence générale des communications et du transit un rapport sur l'application de la présente Convention et décidera s'il y a lieu d'inscrire à l'ordre du jour de la Conférence la question de la revision ou de la modification de ladite Convention.

Art. 27.

Texte officiel. — Les textes français et anglais de la présente Convention feront foi l'un et l'autre.

ANNEXE V.

PROJET PRÉSENTÉ PAR LE PLÉNIPOTENTIAIRE DE ROUMANIE.

La Belgique, la France, la Grande-Bretagne, la Grèce, l'Italie, la Roumanie, le Royaume des Serbes, des Croates et des Slovènes et la Tchéco-Slovaquie,

Désireux de se conformer aux dispositions des Traités :

de Versailles (Art. 331 à 338 et 349),

de Saint-Germain (Art. 291 à 300 et 304),

de Neuilly (Art. 219 à 232),

et de Trianon (Art. 275 à 283, 288) relatives à la navigation ;

et considérant le but poursuivi par lesdits Traités d'assurer la libre navigation et l'uniformité des régimes sur toutes les eaux fluviales internationales, but en vue duquel la Commission pour l'étude de la liberté des communications et du transit, instituée conformément à l'article 23 du Pacte de la Société des Nations, a élaboré le projet de convention sur le régime international des voies navigables, ont décidé de conclure la présente Convention et, à cet effet, ont désigné leurs Délégués Plénipotentiaires, savoir :

. . . .

Les Délégués Plénipotentiaires, après avoir échangé leurs pleins pouvoirs, trouvés en bonne et due forme, ont arrêté, en présence des Représentants de l'Allemagne (pour la Bavière et le Wurtemberg), de l'Autriche, de la Bulgarie et de la Hongrie, les stipulations suivantes, lesquelles seront, de droit, et sans l'intervention d'aucun des États signataires de la présente Convention, modifiées et remplacées par les dispositions contraires ou différentes qui seront comprises dans le statut de la navigation sur le Rhin.

Régime général du Danube.

ARTICLE PREMIER.

La navigation sur tout le cours navigable du Danube, c'est-à-dire d'Ulm à Soulina (mer Noire) est libre et ouverte, sous le rapport du commerce, à tous les pavillons des États riverains ou non-riverains sans distinction aucune.

ART. 2.

Toutefois, l'exercice des transports habituels ou par lignes locales régulières, de voyageurs et de marchandises indigènes ou indigénées, entre les ports d'un même pays riverain du Danube, est réservé au pavillon national respectif, sauf le cas d'autorisation spéciale accordée à d'autres pavillons.

Art. 3.

Les pays riverains seront libres d'édicter et d'appliquer le long du Danube les dispositions nécessaires concernant la police générale de leur territoire, les douanes, les prescriptions sanitaires, les mesures préventives contre les maladies infectieuses des animaux et des végétaux, l'émigration, l'immigration, l'importation et l'exportation des marchandises prohibées, etc.

Toutes ces mesures seront appliquées de manière à ne jamais entraver le libre exercice de la navigation.

Art. 4.

La partie navigable du Danube, ainsi que les canaux et les affluents déclarés internationaux par les articles 331 du Traité de Versailles, 291 du Traité de Saint-Germain, 219 du Traité de Neuilly et 275 du Traité de Trianon, sont placés, au point de vue de la navigation, sous la surveillance et le contrôle de la Commission internationale du Danube.

Composition et attributions de la Commission internationale du Danube.

Art. 5.

La Commission internationale du Danube est composée, à raison d'un Délégué par Puissance, par les Représentants des États mentionnés aux articles 347 du Traité de Versailles, 302 du Traité de Saint-Germain, 230 du Traité de Neuilly et 286 du Traité de Trianon, à savoir : la Bulgarie, la Hongrie, le Royaume des Serbes, des Croates et des Slovènes, la Roumanie, la Tchéco-Slovaquie, l'Autriche, la Bavière, le Wurtemberg et par un Délégué de chacun des États non-riverains prévus par les articles 346 du Traité de Versailles, 301 du Traité de Saint-Germain, 229 du Traité de Neuilly et 285 du Traité de Trianon, ainsi que par un Délégué de la Belgique.

Art. 6.

Elle veille à ce qu'aucune entrave, d'aucun genre, ne soit apportée, du fait d'un ou de plusieurs États riverains ou non riverains, à la libre navigation du fleuve ; elle assure l'égalité complète du traitement de tous les pavillons ; elle veille, d'une manière générale, à ce qu'aucune atteinte ne soit portée au caractère international que les Traités ont assigné au Danube.

Art. 7.

Les travaux nécessaires au maintien et à l'amélioration de la navigation du Danube seront entrepris par les États riverains intéressés, selon un programme élaboré par eux et approuvé, après examen préalable, par la Commission internationale du Danube.

Dans le cas où un État riverain ne se trouverait pas en mesure d'entreprendre lui-même les travaux dont il s'agit, la Commission internationale du Danube pourra les confier à l'État riverain voisin le plus indiqué, ou les faire exécuter par ses propres moyens.

Art. 8.

La Commission internationale du Danube a qualité pour examiner et approuver, dans leur ensemble et dans un esprit de parfaite égalité envers tous les États riverains, les plans des travaux d'entretien et d'amélioration de la navigation, qui lui seraient soumis par lesdits États pour les portions du Danube comprises entre leurs frontières.

Art. 9.

Les États riverains sont libres d'exécuter sur leurs territoires respectifs tous les ouvrages ayant un caractère public ou privé, notamment les travaux de défense des villes contre l'inondation, les endiguements des terrains inondables, l'irrigation, l'utilisation des forces hydrauliques, etc..., à la condition, cependant, que ces travaux n'apportent pas le moindre changement au régime de navigabilité du fleuve.

Ces plans seront également communiqués à la Commission internationale du Danube.

Art. 10.

La Commission internationale est chargée de l'élaboration des règlements de navigation, lesquels seront uniformes pour tout le cours navigable du Danube.

Ces mêmes règlements seront appliqués par tous les pays riverains dans leurs eaux territoriales.

Art. 11.

A l'effet de surveiller et d'assurer l'application de ces règlements d'une façon égale pour tous les pavillons, la Commission internationale du Danube entretient deux Inspecteurs généraux appartenant à des nationalités européennes non représentées à la Commission, aidés de plusieurs Inspecteurs et sous-Inspecteurs, recrutés parmi les nationaux des États riverains, chargés d'exercer leurs fonctions dans les eaux territoriales de l'État auquel ils appartiennent.

Art. 12.

Les Inspecteurs constatent les infractions aux règlements et les signalent à la fois à l'Inspecteur général et aux autorités respectives de l'État riverain, lesquelles autorités ont seules qualité pour instruire l'affaire, dresser les actes judiciaires nécessaires et juger.

Un résumé du dossier avec une copie de la sentence seront communiqués au Secrétariat de la Commission internationale du Danube.

Des instructions spéciales, à ce sujet, seront données aux Inspecteurs par la Commission internationale du Danube.

Art. 13.

La Commission internationale pourra inspecter elle-même périodiquement la voie d'eau et signaler aux États riverains les travaux techniques qu'elle jugerait utiles dans l'intérêt de la navigation.

ART. 14.

Le siège de la Commission internationale du Danube, ainsi que de son Secrétariat général, est fixé à Galatz.

Le fonctionnement de la Commission et de son Secrétariat général sera déterminé par un règlement élaboré par elle en séance plénière.

ART. 15.

Au siège de la Commission, il y aura un Comité exécutif permanent, composé d'au moins trois des membres de la Commission désignés d'avance à tour de rôle.

Le Comité est chargé de veiller à l'application des dispositions adoptées par la Commission ou d'en prendre d'autres, dont le caractère urgent réclamerait une solution immédiate.

Les décisions d'ordre général sont toutefois strictement réservées au plenum de la Commission.

ART. 16.

La Commission internationale du Danube jouit, tant pour ses installations que pour la personne de ses membres, des mêmes privilèges et immunités qui sont reconnus par le droit des gens aux représentants diplomatiques des États.

Elle a le droit d'avoir son propre pavillon.

ART. 17.

Les pouvoirs de la Commission internationale du Danube pourront être revisés après une période de dix ans de fonctionnement, par la Société des Nations, sur la demande d'un des États signataires de la présente Convention.

Les Portes de Fer et les Bouches du Danube.

ART. 18.

Deux Comités techniques différents auront la charge de prendre toutes les dispositions nécessaires en vue de l'entretien et de l'amélioration de la navigation, de l'organisation du pilotage, de la réglementation des forces hydrauliques, etc., l'un, roumano-serbe aux Portes de Fer, pour la portion comprise entre Turnu-Severin et O'Moldova, ayant son siège à Orsova; l'autre roumain, pour la portion comprise entre Soulina et Galatz, avec son siège à Soulina.

Dans chacun de ces deux Comités, la Commission se fera représenter par un Délégué technique appartenant à un des États non-riverains du Danube et ayant les mêmes pouvoirs que les autres membres du Comité.

Ces deux Comités posséderont le matériel et le personnel qui leur sont propres, y compris le matériel technique prévu par l'article 288 du Traité de Trianon et travailleront suivant le programme des travaux que la Commission internationale pourra élaborer elle-même à l'aide de spécialistes ou de techniciens consultants, appartenant à d'autres nationalités.

Un règlement spécial établi par la Commission internationale du Danube indiquera les détails de l'administration de ces deux secteurs, tant au point de vue technique qu'à celui de la liberté absolue de la navigation pour tous les pavillons, liberté que les pays riverains sont tenus à respecter et à garantir.

Redevances.

Art. 19.

Aucune taxe de navigation ne sera perçue sur tout le parcours navigable du Danube. Toutes les dépenses nécessitées par l'entretien courant du chenal navigable, des travaux de balisage, etc., seront à la charge des États riverains qui les auront effectués.

Néanmoins, en ce qui concerne les travaux techniques importants effectués aux embouchures ou aux Portes de Fer, ainsi que dans un secteur quelconque du Danube, la Commission internationale du Danube examinera leur importance et fixera les droits qui devront être perçus par l'État riverain intéressé. Ces droits seront fixes, raisonnables, et les mêmes pour tous les pavillons sans distinction aucune; leur montant servira exclusivement à couvrir les frais occasionnés par les travaux effectués et ils seront revisés périodiquement.

La Commission internationale du Danube établira la modalité de la perception et pourra contrôler, à l'aide de ses organes financiers, la marche de ses opérations de caisse.

Tous les États représentés à la Commission internationale seront obligés de contribuer d'une façon égale aux frais généraux d'entretien et de fonctionnement de la Commission internationale du Danube, établis par son budget annuel.

Transit, importation, exportation, ports.

Art. 20.

Tout navire et bateau de commerce ou de voyageurs en cours de route est exempt de toutes formalités douanières et aucune taxe, sous aucun prétexte, ne sera perçue sur les marchandises en transit.

Néanmoins, sur la partie du fleuve dont les deux rives appartiennent à un même État, le transit peut faire exceptionnellement l'objet d'une surveillance de la part de cet État, soit par la mise sous scellés de la cargaison, soit par la garde d'un agent de douane, et sans que cette formalité fasse retarder les transports.

En général, pour le transit sur le Danube, les dispositions à adopter seront les mêmes que celles que la Société des Nations aura définitivement adoptées pour la Convention sur la liberté du transit.

Art. 21.

Les ressortissants, les biens et les navires de toutes les nations jouiront dans tous les ports du Danube, sous la réserve des dispositions des articles 2 et 3, d'un traitement absolument égal.

Les installations des ports, ainsi que tout leur outillage, seront mis par ordre d'inscription à la disposition des navigateurs, selon les règlements locaux, et sans aucune distinction quant au pavillon.

Art. 22.

Tous droits de douane ou d'octroi dus à l'occasion de l'importation ou de l'exportation des marchandises dans les ports danubiens, seront perçus, sans distinction de pavillon, en conformité des tarifs et des conventions commerciales en vigueur dans les pays respectifs.

Les États riverains auront le droit de percevoir dans leurs ports des taxes modérées, exclusivement destinées à couvrir les frais de construction, d'entretien, d'administration et d'amélioration des quais et des ports.

Ces taxes seront publiées dans tous les ports et appliquées de la même façon à l'égard de tous les pavillons.

Navires de guerre.

Art. 23.

Cette Convention doit être entendue comme n'affectant en aucune manière la navigation des navires et bâtiments de guerre, de police, de contrôle et, en général, de tous les bâtiments exerçant au nom d'un État souverain une autorité de puissance publique.

La navigation dans les eaux territoriales des pays riverains de tels navires ou bâtiments, n'est permise que par autorisation spéciale de la part des États riverains respectifs.

Dispositions générales.

Art. 24.

Dans le cas où une infraction grave aux stipulations de la présente Convention ou un conflit sérieux survenu entre deux États riverains menacerait de compromettre la libre navigation sur le Danube, la Commission internationale du Danube a le droit — après avoir épuisé tous les moyens de conciliation, — de porter le différend devant le Conseil de la Société des Nations.

Art. 25.

Tous les traités, actes et arrangements relatifs au régime des fleuves internationaux en général, et au Danube et à son embouchure en particulier, sont maintenus dans toutes celles de leurs dispositions qui ne sont ni abrogées, ni modifiées par les stipulations qui précèdent.

Art. 26.

La Commission européenne du Danube, remplacée par la Commission internationale du Danube, lui transmettra tous ses biens, meubles et immeubles, ses installations, son matériel flottant, son actif et son passif, ainsi que son personnel, selon les modalités que ses membres actuels auront fixées.

I. Régime général du Danube.

———

Article I.

La navigation du Danube est libre et ouverte à tous les pavillons dans des conditions d'égalité complète sur tout le cours navigable du fleuve, c'est-à-dire entre Ulm et la mer Noire, et sur tout le réseau fluvial internationalisé ainsi qu'il est déterminé à l'article suivant, de telle sorte qu'aucune distinction ne soit faite, au détriment des ressortissants, des biens et du pavillon d'une Puissance quelconque, entre ceux-ci et les ressortissants, les biens et le pavillon de l'État riverain lui-même ou de l'État dont les ressortissants, les biens et le pavillon jouissent du traitement le plus favorable.

Ces dispositions doivent s'entendre sous réserve des stipulations contenues dans les articles XXII et XLIII de la présente Convention.

Art. II.

Le réseau fluvial internationalisé mentionné à l'article précédent est composé de :

La *Morava* et la *Thaya* dans la partie de leur cours constituant la frontière entre l'Autriche et la Tchéco-Slovaquie;

La *Drave* depuis Barcs;

La *Tisza* depuis l'embouchure du *Szamos;*

Le *Maros* depuis Arad;

Les canaux latéraux ou chenaux qui seraient établis, soit pour doubler ou améliorer des sections naturellement navigables dudit réseau, soit pour réunir deux sections naturellement navigables d'un de ces mêmes cours d'eau.

Art. III.

La liberté de la navigation et l'égalité entre les pavillons sont assurées par deux Commissions distinctes, à savoir la *Commission européenne du Danube*, dont la compétence, telle qu'elle est déterminée au Chapitre II, s'étend sur la partie du fleuve dite Danube maritime, et la *Commission internationale du Danube*, dont la compétence, telle qu'elle est déterminée au Chapitre III, s'étend sur le Danube fluvial navigable, ainsi que sur les voies d'eau déclarées internationales par l'article II.

II. Danube maritime.

Art. IV.

La Commission européenne du Danube est composée provisoirement des Représentants de la France, de la Grande-Bretagne, de l'Italie et de la Roumanie, à raison d'un Délégué par Puissance.

Toutefois, tout État européen qui justifiera à l'avenir d'intérêts commerciaux maritimes et européens suffisants aux embouchures du Danube pourra, sur sa demande, être admis à se faire représenter dans la Commission sur une décision unanime prise par les Gouvernements qui y sont eux-mêmes représentés.

Art. V.

La Commission européenne exerce les pouvoirs qu'elle avait avant la guerre.

Il n'est rien changé aux droits, attributions et immunités qu'elle tient des Traités, Conventions, Actes et Arrangements internationaux relatifs au Danube et à ses embouchures.

Art. VI.

La compétence de la Commission européenne s'étend, dans les mêmes conditions que par le passé et sans aucune modification à ses limites actuelles, sur le Danube maritime, c'est-à-dire depuis les embouchures du fleuve jusqu'au point où commence la compétence de la Commission internationale.

Art. VII.

Les pouvoirs de la Commission européenne ne pourront prendre fin que par l'effet d'un arrangement international conclu par tous les États représentés à la Commission.

Le siège légal de la Commission demeure fixé à Galatz.

III. Danube fluvial.

Art. VIII.

La Commission internationale du Danube est composée, conformément aux articles 347 du Traité de Versailles, 302 du Traité de Saint-Germain, 230 du Traité de Neuilly et 286 du Traité de Trianon, par deux Représentants des États allemands riverains, un Représentant de chacun des autres États riverains et un Représentant de chacun des États non-riverains représentés à la Commission européenne du Danube ou qui pourraient l'être à l'avenir.

Art. IX.

La compétence de la Commission internationale s'étend sur la partie du Danube comprise entre Ulm et Braila et sur le réseau fluvial déclaré international en vertu de l'article II. Aucune voie d'eau, autre que celles qui sont mentionnées à l'article II, ne pourra être placée sous la compétence de la Commission internationale sans le consentement unanime de ladite Commission.

Art. X.

Sur la partie du Danube et sur le réseau fluvial placés sous sa compétence, et dans la limite des pouvoirs qu'elle tient de la présente Convention, la Commission internationale veille à ce qu'aucun obstacle quelconque ne soit mis, du fait d'un ou de plusieurs États, à la libre navigation du fleuve, à ce que, tant pour le passage que pour l'usage des ports, de leurs installations et de leur outillage, les ressortissants, les biens et les pavillons de toutes les Puissances soient traités sur le pied d'une complète égalité et, d'une manière générale, à ce qu'aucune atteinte ne soit portée au caractère international que les Traités ont assigné au réseau internationalisé du Danube.

Art. XI.

Sur la base des propositions et des projets qui lui sont présentés par les États riverains, la Commission internationale établit le programme général des grands travaux d'amélioration qui doivent être entrepris dans l'intérêt de la navigabilité du réseau fluvial international et dont l'exécution peut être échelonnée sur une période de plusieurs années.

Le programme annuel des travaux courants d'entretien et d'amélioration du réseau fluvial est élaboré par chaque État riverain, pour ce qui concerne son domaine territorial, et communiqué à la Commission, qui appréciera si ce programme est conforme aux exigences de la navigation; elle pourra le modifier si elle le juge utile.

Dans toutes ses décisions, la Commission tiendra compte des intérêts techniques, économiques et financiers des États riverains.

Art. XII.

Les travaux compris dans ces deux programmes seront exécutés par les États riverains dans les limites de leurs frontières respectives. La Commission s'assurera de l'exécution des travaux et de leur conformité avec le programme où ils sont prévus.

Dans le cas où un État riverain ne serait pas en mesure d'entreprendre lui-même les travaux qui sont de sa compétence territoriale, cet État sera tenu de les laisser exécuter par la Commission internationale elle-même dans les conditions qu'elle déterminera et sans qu'elle puisse en confier l'exécution à un autre État, sauf en ce qui concerne les parties du réseau fluvial formant frontière. Dans ce dernier cas, la Commission déterminera les modalités de l'exécution des travaux en tenant compte des stipulations spéciales des Traités.

Les États riverains intéressés sont tenus de fournir à la Commission ou à l'État exécutant, suivant les cas, toutes les facilités nécessaires à l'exécution desdits travaux.

Art. XIII.

Les États riverains auront le droit d'entreprendre, dans les limites de leurs frontières respectives, sans l'approbation préalable de la Commission internationale, les travaux qui pourraient être nécessités par une circonstance imprévue et urgente. Ils devront toutefois aviser sans délai la Commission des raisons qui ont motivé ces travaux, en lui en fournissant une description sommaire.

Art. XIV.

Les États riverains feront parvenir à la Commission internationale une description sommaire de tous travaux qu'ils considèrent comme nécessaires à leur développement économique, notamment les travaux de défense contre les inondations, ceux qui concernent les irrigations et l'utilisation des forces hydrauliques, et qui seraient à exécuter sur la voie d'eau comprise dans les limites de leurs frontières respectives.

La Commission ne peut interdire de tels travaux qu'en tant qu'ils seraient de nature à porter atteinte à la navigabilité du fleuve.

Si, dans le délai de deux mois à dater de la communication, la Commission n'a formulé aucune observation, il pourra être procédé sans autres formalités à l'exécution desdits travaux. Dans le cas contraire, la Commission devra prendre une décision définitive dans le plus bref délai possible et, au plus tard, dans les quatre mois qui suivront l'expiration du premier délai.

Art. XV.

Les frais des travaux courants d'entretien sont à la charge des États riverains respectifs.

Toutefois, lorsque l'État exécutant sera en mesure d'établir que les dépenses qui lui incombent du chef de l'entretien du chenal navigable dépassent notablement ce qu'exigeraient les besoins de son propre trafic, il pourra demander à la Commission de répartir équitablement ces dépenses entre lui et les États riverains directement intéressés à l'exécution desdits travaux. La Commission, dans ce cas, fixera elle-même la part contributive de chaque État et en assurera le règlement.

Si la Commission entreprend elle-même des travaux d'entretien dans les limites des frontières d'un État, elle recevra de cet État le montant de la dépense qui lui incombe.

Art. XVI.

Quant aux travaux d'amélioration proprement dits et aux travaux s'appliquant à l'entretien des travaux d'amélioration d'une importance particulière, l'État qui les entreprendra pourra être autorisé par la Commission à se couvrir de leurs frais par la perception de taxes sur la navigation.

Si la Commission exécute elle-même des travaux de cette catégorie, elle pourra se couvrir de ses dépenses par la perception de taxes.

Art. XVII.

En ce qui concerne les parties du Danube formant frontière, l'exécution des travaux et la répartition des dépenses seront réglées par entente entre les États riverains respectifs.

A défaut d'entente, la Commission déterminera elle-même, en tenant compte des stipulations des traités, les conditions de l'exécution desdits travaux et éventuellement la répartition des dépenses occasionnées par leur exécution.

Art. XVIII.

Les taxes, lorsqu'il en sera perçu sur la navigation, seront d'un taux modéré. Elles seront calculées sur la jauge du bateau et ne pourront en aucun cas être basées sur les marchandises transportées. A l'expiration d'une période de cinq ans, ce système d'assiette des taxes pourra être revisé si la Commission en décide ainsi à l'unanimité de ses membres.

Le produit des taxes sera exclusivement affecté aux travaux qui ont donné naissance à leur établissement. La Commission internationale en déterminera et en publiera les tarifs; elle en contrôlera la perception et l'affectation.

Ces taxes ne devront jamais constituer un traitement différentiel basé soit sur le pavillon des bateaux ou la nationalité des personnes et des biens, soit sur la provenance, la destination ou la direction des transports; elles ne devront en aucun cas procurer un revenu à l'État percepteur ou à la Commission, ni rendre nécessaire un examen détaillé de la cargaison, à moins qu'il y ait soupçon de fraude ou de contravention.

Au cas où la Commission internationale prendrait à sa charge l'exécution des travaux, elle percevra, par l'entremise de l'État riverain intéressé, le montant des taxes correspondant à ses dépenses.

Art. XIX.

Les droits de douane et d'octroi et autres taxes établies par les États riverains sur les marchandises à l'occasion de leur embarquement ou de leur débarquement dans les ports ou sur les rives du Danube seront perçus sans distinction de pavillon et de manière à n'apporter aucune entrave à la navigation.

Les droits de douane ne pourront être supérieurs à ceux qui sont perçus aux autres frontières douanières de l'État intéressé sur les marchandises de même nature, de même provenance et de même destination.

Art. XX.

Les ports et lieux publics d'embarquement et de débarquement établis sur le réseau fluvial international, avec leur outillage et leurs installations, seront accessibles à la navigation et utilisés par elle sans distinction de pavillon, de provenance et de destination et sans qu'une priorité de faveur puisse être accordée par les autorités locales compétentes à un bateau au détriment d'un autre, sauf dans des cas exceptionnels où il serait manifeste que les nécessités du moment et les intérêts du pays réclament une dérogation. La priorité, dans ces cas, devra être concédée de manière à ne pas constituer une entrave réelle au libre exercice de la navigation, ni une atteinte au principe de l'égalité des pavillons.

Les mêmes autorités veilleront à ce que toutes les opérations nécessaires au trafic, telles que l'embarquement, le débarquement, l'allègement, l'emmagasinage, le transbordement, etc., soient exécutées dans des conditions aussi faciles et aussi rapides que possible et de manière à n'apporter aucune entrave à la navigation.

L'utilisation des ports et lieux publics d'embarquement et de débarquement peut donner lieu à la perception de taxes et redevances raisonnables et égales pour tous les pavillons, correspondant aux dépenses d'établissement, d'entretien et d'exploitation des ports et de leurs installations. Les tarifs en seront publiés et portés à la connaissance des navigateurs. Ils ne seront applicables qu'en cas d'utilisation effective des installations et outillage en vue desquels ils ont été fixés.

Les États riverains ne feront pas obstacle à ce que toutes les entreprises de navigation entretiennent sur leur territoire les agences indispensables à l'exercice de leur trafic, sous réserve de l'observation des lois et règlements du pays.

Art. XXI.

Dans le cas où les États riverains auraient décidé de créer des ports francs ou des zones franches dans les ports où le transbordement est nécessaire ou généralement pratiqué, les règlements relatifs à l'usage desdits ports ou zones seront communiqués à la Commission internationale.

Art. XXII.

Le transport de marchandises et de voyageurs entre les ports des différents États riverains ainsi qu'entre les ports d'un même État est libre et ouvert à tous les pavillons, dans des conditions d'égalité complète, sur le réseau internationalisé du Danube.

Toutefois, l'établissement d'un service local régulier de transport de voyageurs et de marchandises indigènes ou indigénées entre les ports d'un seul et même État ne pourra être effectué par un pavillon étranger qu'en conformité des règlements nationaux et d'accord avec les autorités de l'État riverain intéressé.

Art. XXIII.

Le passage en transit des bateaux, radeaux, voyageurs et marchandises est libre sur le réseau internationalisé du Danube, que ce transit s'effectue directement ou après transbordement ou après mise en entrepôt.

Il ne sera perçu aucun droit de douane ou autre droit spécial basé uniquement sur le fait de ce transit.

Lorsque les deux rives de la voie d'eau font partie d'un même État, les marchandises en transit pourront être mises sous scellés, sous cadenas ou sous la garde d'agents des douanes.

L'État transité aura le droit d'exiger du capitaine ou patron une déclaration écrite, faite au besoin sous serment, et affirmant s'il transporte ou non des marchandises dont la circulation est réglementée ou dont l'importation est prohibée par l'État transité. La liste de ces marchandises sera communiquée le plus tôt possible à la Commission internationale à titre d'information.

La production du manifeste ne pourra être exigée par les autorités compétentes de l'État transité, si ce n'est dans les cas où le capitaine ou patron est convaincu d'avoir tenté la contrebande ou lorsque les clôtures douanières ont été brisées. Si, dans ces cas, on découvre une différence entre la cargaison et le manifeste, le capitaine ou patron ne peut invoquer la liberté du transit pour mettre soit sa personne, soit la marchandise qu'il a voulu transporter frauduleusement, à l'abri des poursuites dirigées contre lui par les employés de la douane conformément aux lois du pays.

Lorsque la voie d'eau forme frontière entre deux États, les bateaux, radeaux, voyageurs et marchandises en transit seront exempts de toute formalité douanière.

Art. XXIV.

La Commission internationale élaborera, en s'inspirant des propositions qui lui seront présentées par les États riverains, un règlement de navigation et de police qui, dans la mesure du possible, sera uniforme pour la partie du réseau fluvial placée sous sa compétence.

Chaque État mettra ce règlement en vigueur sur son propre territoire par un acte de législation ou d'administration et sera chargé de son application, sous réserve des pouvoirs de surveillance reconnus à la Commission internationale par les articles XXVII à XXX.

Pour les parties du fleuve formant frontière, l'exécution du règlement de navigation et de police sera assurée sous les mêmes réserves par accord entre les États riverains et, à défaut d'accord, par chaque État riverain dans les limites de sa souveraineté.

Art. XXV.

L'exercice de la police générale sur le réseau fluvial internationalisé appartient aux États riverains, qui en communiquent les règlements à la Commission internationale pour lui permettre de constater que leurs dispositions ne portent pas atteinte à la liberté de la navigation.

Art. XXVI.

Tous les bâtiments affectés spécialement par les États riverains au service de la police fluviale seront tenus d'arborer à côté de leur pavillon national un insigne distinctif et uniforme. Leurs nom, signalement et numéro seront portés à la connaissance de la Commission internationale.

Art. XXVII.

En vue de l'accomplissement de la tâche qui lui est confiée par les dispositions du présent statut, la Commission internationale constituera tous les services administratifs, techniques, sanitaires et financiers qu'elle jugera nécessaires. Elle en nommera et rétribuera le personnel et elle en fixera les attributions.

La Commission pourra établir à son siège central, notamment :

1° Un Secrétariat général permanent, dont le chef sera choisi parmi les ressortissants d'un État non-riverain représenté à la Commission ;

2° Un Service technique, dont le chef sera nommé à la majorité statutaire des suffrages s'il appartient à un État non-riverain représenté ou non à la Commission, et à l'unanimité s'il est ressortissant d'un État riverain du Danube ;

3° Un Service de la navigation, dont le chef sera choisi parmi les ressortissants d'un État européen non représenté à la Commission ;

4° Un Service de la comptabilité générale et du contrôle de la perception des taxes, dont le chef sera choisi parmi les ressortissants d'un État riverain ou d'un État non-riverain représenté ou non à la Commission.

Ces chefs de service seront assistés par des fonctionnaires choisis, de préférence et autant que possible d'une manière égale, parmi les ressortissants des États riverains. Ce personnel est international ; il est nommé et rétribué par la Commission et ne pourra être révoqué que par elle.

Art. XXVIII.

Chaque État riverain désignera, pour ce qui le concerne, des agents appropriés chargés, dans les limites de ses frontières, de prêter le concours de leur compétence et de leurs bons offices aux agents supérieurs de la Commission internationale et de leur faciliter l'exercice de leur mission.

Art. XXIX.

Les États riverains donneront aux fonctionnaires de la Commission toutes les facilités nécessaires pour accomplir les actes de leurs fonctions. Ces fonctionnaires, munis du brevet de la Commission constatant leur qualité, auront notamment le droit de circuler librement sur le fleuve et dans les ports et lieux publics de débarquement ; les autorités locales de chaque État riverain leur prêteront aide et assistance pour remplir leur mission. Les formalités de police et de douane auxquelles ils auraient à se soumettre seront accomplies à leur égard de manière à ne pas entraver l'exercice de leurs fonctions.

Art. XXX.

Les fonctionnaires dûment qualifiés de la Commission signaleront toute infraction au règlement de navigation et de police aux autorités locales compétentes, qui sont tenues d'appliquer les sanctions appropriées et de faire connaître à la Commission la suite donnée à la plainte dont elles ont été saisies.

Chaque État riverain désignera à la Commission les juridictions qui seront chargées de connaître, en première instance et en appel, des infractions mentionnées à l'alinéa précédent. Devant ces juridictions, dont le siège devra être aussi voisin du fleuve que possible, le fonctionnaire de la Commission qui a signalé l'infraction sera entendu, s'il y a lieu.

Art. XXXI.

Dans les actions judiciaires relatives à la navigation du Danube, portées devant un tribunal d'un État riverain, il ne pourra être exigé des étrangers aucune caution *judicatum solvi* à raison de leur nationalité ou à raison du fait qu'ils n'ont pas de domicile ou de résidence dans le pays où est établi le tribunal ou qu'ils n'y possèdent pas de biens.

Le capitaine ou patron ne pourra être empêché de poursuivre son voyage à raison d'une procédure engagée contre lui, dès qu'il aura fourni le cautionnement exigé par le juge pour l'objet du débat.

Art. XXXII.

A l'effet de maintenir et d'améliorer les conditions de la navigation dans le secteur du Danube compris entre Turnu-Severin et Moldova, dit des Portes-de-Fer et des Cataractes, il sera constitué, de commun accord entre les deux États co-riverains et la Commission internationale, des services techniques et administratifs spéciaux qui auront leur siège central à Orsova, sans préjudice des services auxiliaires qui pourraient être en cas de besoin installés sur d'autres points du secteur. A l'exception des pilotes, qui pourront être choisis parmi les ressortissants de toutes les nations, le personnel de ces services sera fourni et nommé par les deux États co-riverains; il sera dirigé par des chefs de service désignés par les mêmes États et agréés par la Commission internationale.

Art. XXXIII.

La Commission décidera, sur la proposition des services prévus à l'article précédent, les mesures utiles à l'entretien et à l'amélioration de la navigabilité et à l'administration du secteur ainsi que les taxes ou éventuellement toutes autres ressources destinées à y faire face, sans qu'il puisse en résulter l'obligation d'un concours financier de la part des Gouvernements représentés.

Elle fixera par un règlement spécial le fonctionnement des services, le mode de perception des taxes et la rétribution du personnel.

Elle mettra à la disposition de ces services les équipements, édifices et installations prévus à l'article 288 du Traité de Trianon.

Lorsque les difficultés naturelles qui ont motivé l'institution de ce régime spécial auront disparu, la Commission pourra en décider la suppression et replacer le secteur sous les dispositions qui régissent, en ce qui concerne les travaux et les taxes, les autres parties du fleuve formant frontière entre deux États.

Art. XXXIV.

La Commission pourra, si elle le juge utile, appliquer un régime administratif analogue aux autres parties du Danube et de son réseau fluvial qui présenteraient pour la navigation les mêmes difficultés naturelles, et le supprimer dans les conditions prévues à l'article précédent.

Art. XXXV.

La Commission internationale fixe elle-même l'ordre de ses travaux dans un règlement établi en session plénière. Au moment de l'établissement de son budget annuel, elle détermine les ressources nécessaires pour couvrir les frais généraux de son administration. Elle fixe le nombre et le lieu de ses sessions périodiques ordinaires et extraordinaires et constitue un Comité exécutif permanent, composé des Délégués présents au siège ou de leurs suppléants, et chargé de surveiller l'exécution des décisions adoptées en *Plenum* ainsi que la bonne marche des services.

La présidence de la Commission est exercée pour une période de six mois par chaque Délégation, en vertu d'un roulement déterminé suivant l'ordre alphabétique des États représentés.

La Commission ne peut délibérer valablement que lorsque les deux tiers de ses membres sont présents.

Les décisions sont prises à la majorité des deux tiers des membres présents.

Art. XXXVI.

Le siège légal de la Commission internationale est fixé à Bratislava pour une période de cinq années à dater du jour de la mise en vigueur de la présente Convention.

A l'expiration de cette période, la Commission aura le droit de se transporter pour une nouvelle période quinquennale dans une autre ville située sur le Danube, en vertu d'un roulement dont elle établira elle-même les modalités.

Art. XXXVII.

La Commission internationale jouit, tant pour ses installations que pour la personne de ses Délégués, des privilèges et immunités reconnus en temps de paix comme en temps de guerre aux agents diplomatiques accrédités.

Elle a le droit d'arborer sur ses bâtiments et sur ses immeubles un pavillon dont elle détermine elle-même la forme et les couleurs.

Art. XXXVIII.

La Commission doit être saisie de toute question relative à l'interprétation et à l'application de la présente Convention.

Tout État qui serait en mesure d'invoquer, contre une décision de la Commission internationale, des motifs basés sur l'incompétence ou sur la violation de la présente Convention pourra en saisir, dans un délai de six mois, la juridiction spéciale organisée par la Société des Nations. Pour tout autre motif, la requête en vue du règlement du différend ne pourrait être formée que par l'État ou les États territorialement intéressés.

Dans le cas où un État refuserait de se conformer à une décision prise par la Commission en vertu des pouvoirs qu'elle tient de la présente Convention, le différend pourra être porté devant la haute juridiction mentionnée à l'alinéa 2, dans les conditions prévues par le statut de ladite juridiction.

IV. Dispositions générales.

Art. XXXIX.

La Commission internationale du Danube et la Commission européenne du Danube prendront toutes dispositions nécessaires pour assurer, dans la mesure où cela sera possible et utile, l'uniformité du régime du Danube.

Elles échangeront régulièrement à cet effet toutes informations, tous documents, procès-verbaux, études et projets pouvant intéresser l'une et l'autre des deux Commissions. Elles pourront arrêter d'un commun accord certaines règles identiques concernant la navigation et la police du fleuve.

Art. XL.

Les États signataires de la présente Convention s'efforceront d'établir par des conventions séparées des règles uniformes d'ordre civil, commercial, sanitaire et vétérinaire relatives à l'exercice de la navigation et au contrat de transport.

Art. XLI.

Tous les traités, conventions, actes et arrangements relatifs au régime des fleuves internationaux en général et au Danube et à ses embouchures en particulier, en vigueur au moment de la signature de la présente Convention, sont maintenus dans toutes celles de leurs dispositions qui ne sont pas abrogées ou modifiées par les stipulations qui précèdent.

Art. XLII.

A l'expiration d'un délai de cinq ans à dater de sa mise en vigueur, le présent statut pourra être revisé si les deux tiers des États signataires en font la demande, en indiquant les dispositions qui leur paraissent susceptibles de revision. Cette demande sera adressée au Gouvernement de la République française, lequel provoquera dans les six mois la réunion d'une Conférence à laquelle tous les États signataires de la présente Convention seront invités à participer.

V. Disposition transitoire.

Art. XLIII.

Les stipulations de la présente Convention doivent être entendues dans ce sens qu'elles ne portent aucune atteinte aux dispositions des Traités de Paix telles qu'elles résultent des articles 327 (alinéa 3), 332 (alinéa 2) et 378 du Traité de Versailles et des articles correspondants des Traités de Saint-Germain, de Neuilly et de Trianon.

Art. XLIV.

La présente Convention sera ratifiée et les ratifications en seront déposées à Paris dans le plus bref délai possible, et au plus tard avant le 31 mars 1922.

Elle entrera en vigueur trois mois après la clôture du procès-verbal de dépôt des ratifications.

EN FOI DE QUOI les Plénipotentiaires susnommés ont signé la présente Convention, rédigée en un seul exemplaire, qui sera déposé dans les archives du Gouvernement de la République française et dont une expédition authentique sera remise à chacune des Puissances signataires.

FAIT à Paris, le 23 juillet 1921.

(L. S.) J. BRUNET.

(L. S.) A. LEGRAND.

(L. S.) John BALDWIN.

(L. S.) A. ANDRÉADÈS.

(L. S.) VANNUTELLI REY.

(L. S.) Const. CONTZESCO.

(L. S.) M. G. RISTITCH.

(L. S.) Ing. Bohuslav MULLER.

(L. S.) SEELIGER.

(L. S.) Dr ONDRACZEK.

(L. S.) Georges LAZAROFF.

(L. S.) E. de MIKLOS.

APPENDIX 12

POST-1921 DANUBE EVENTS

1921-30: Trade through the maritime ports remains at a depressed level, averaging 1,790,000 tons annually, compared to the average of 12,500,000 tons between 1895 and 1915.

1925: Baldwin complains to the Secretary General of the League of Nations that Romania is obstructing the work of the Commission between Galați and Brăila. The Secretary General hands the matter to a League subcommission. Conțescu however refuses to recognize the authority of that organization to discuss what he termed "no longer an anachronism but a scandalous defiance of the rights and sentiments of our country." The four members agree to place the issue before the International Court of Justice.

1927: The Court rules that the Commission not only is competent to act between the ports, but also holds full authority in the port of Brăila itself.

1929: The members of the Commission agree that Romania should have greater control over judicial matters in its territory. A "Tribunal of Navigation" is formed to oversee the enforcement of all laws.

1930: Italy, Britain, and France renounce the right to station warships on the Lower Danube. They had never accepted the fact that an article declaring the disarmament of the river had not been incorporated into the *Statut*.

1932: Romania receives the power to tax all vessels within the jurisdictional limits of the Commission.
The Commission agrees to abstain from supervising navigation between Galați and Brăila, thereby ending the long-standing controversy.

1934: German grain purchases in the Basin bring a renewed German interest in commerce on the Lower Danube.

1936: The Montreaux Treaty abolishes foreign relation of the Turkish Straits, thus presenting Romania with a precedent to work for the abolition of the European Commission.
Adolph Hitler denounces international river regimes and suggests that Danube trade be conducted by means of a series of bilateral agreements among the riparian states.

1938: Germany supports the idea of abolishing both commissions and replacing them with a new riparian agency.
France suggests abolishing the European Commission.
At a meeting of Romanian technicians and the Foreign Ministry, Conţescu calls for the maintenance of the European Commission as a "serious shield" against aggression. The Romanian Foreign Minister, N. Petrescu-Comnen, supports this proposal, although allowing for German admission to the Commission.

1938-39: At a special conference in Sinaia, Romania receives complete authority to regulate work, control finances, and replace most foreign workers with Romanian nationals. An autonomous Maritime Danube Board would be established by Romania. The Commission thus ceases to be "independent of territorial authorities," and becomes no more than a figurehead organization. Italy however refuses to sign the measure. Count Ciano states that a German delegate must be admitted before Italy will sign. Thus, Romania, in an attempt to protect its own interests and keep Germany at arms length, is forced to agree to German representation on the Lower Danube. The pact is signed in March 1939.

1939-44/5: German authorities supervise the river.

1948: At the Belgrade Conference a new commission, composed only of the riparian states (except for Germany), is established. The commission is dominated by the Soviet Union.

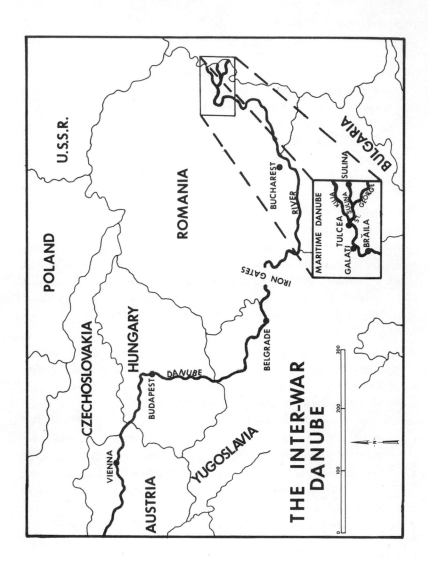

THE INTER-WAR DANUBE

POLAND

U.S.S.R.

CZECHOSLOVAKIA

HUNGARY

ROMANIA

BUCHAREST

RIVER

IRON GATES

DANUBE

BUDAPEST

BELGRADE

VIENNA

AUSTRIA

YUGOSLAVIA

BULGARIA

MARITIME DANUBE

TULCEA

SULINA

GALAȚI

BRĂILA

ST. GEORGE

SULINA

0   100   200   300

194

A NOTE ON THE SOURCES

PRIMARY SOURCES

Preparation of the text required the use of five major archival deposits in Romania: The State Archives in Galați and Bucharest (*Arhivele Statului Galați* and *Arhivele Statului*), the Foreign Ministry Archives (*Arhivele Ministerului Afacerilor Externe*), and the Central State and Academy Libraries (*Biblioteca Centrală de Stat* and *Biblioteca Academiei*), as well as a number of published collections of documents. These included the transcripts of the Paris Conference and the Romanian Parliament, and official Commission literature.

For the study of the Danube Question after World War I, the most important repository is the Foreign Ministry. It houses all documents relating to the negotiations, including the papers from the Paris and Versailles conferences. Within this collection are the dispatches of the Romanian representatives (Conțescu, Stelian, and Zamfirescu) and the authorities at the Foreign Ministry (Ionescu and Docan), as well as correspondence between Bucharest and its legations.

The archives of the European Commission are still in Galați at the State Archives, although microfilms of these records have been prepared for storage in Bucharest. Unfortunately pre-1918 files are incomplete due to the fire that engulfed the body's headquarters in 1917.

The State Archives hold the documents of the *Casa Regală* (Royal House), a disparate collection pertaining to Romanian history from the mid-1800s through the interwar epoch. A rich source of information on Romanian politics, society, and the economy, its archival deposits directly related to the Danube are limited. Most of the material has been moved to the Foreign Ministry. The same is true for material in the Central State Library. The latter, however, does house the private correspondence between N. Titulescu and Take Ionescu, Romania's outstanding interwar

195

Foreign Ministers. These letters touch on the problems of the Danube, as well as the other issues confronting Romania after 1918.

The Romanian Academy Library contains a manuscript prepared by N. Docan, the individual in the Foreign Ministry most responsible for the conduct of Romanian policy toward the Danube following the war. Although primarily devoted to pre-1914 events, the manuscript provides valuable insight into the government's conduct in the matter. The Docan collection also holds a number of letters and reports from foreign sources, including dispatches prepared by functionaries stationed in Romania. In addition, the Academy has the most complete collection of interwar Romanian newspapers.

Besides the archival deposits, there exists a number of valuable published volumes. Foremost among these is the *Conférence Internationale pour l'etablissement du Statut Définitif du Danube* (Paris: Imprimerie Nationale, 1921),which contains the records of the Danube Conference, totalling nearly 1,500 transcript pages.

For the nineteenth century, the essential documents can be found in D. Sturdza, *Recueil de Documents relatifs à la Liberté de Navigation du Danube* (Berlin, 1904). It includes all the relevant material pertaining to the Danube discussed at the major conferences, from the texts of the treaties to summaries of the critical negotiations.

Two other sources should be noted: the official publications of the European Commission (minutes of the bi-annual meetings) and *Monitorul Oficial.* The former is the authoritative source for vital statistics pertaining to the river and its commerce; the latter comprises the debates of the Romanian Parliament and is important as much for what was said about the Danube as was not said, that is, the dearth of interest in the matter by most members of Parliament after 1918.

BIBLIOGRAPHIES

Although there is no bibliographic guide specifically addressed to the river's history, two useful sources of such information are: L. Bădulescu, Gh. Canja and E. Glaser, *Contribuţii la studiul istoriei regimului internaţional de navigaţie pe Dunăre (Contributions to the Study of the History of the International Navigational Regime of the Danube) (Bucureşti, 1957);* and Iulian Cârţana and Ilie Seftiuc, *Dunărea în istoria poporului român (The Danube in the History of the Romanian People)* (București, 1972). The text of the former, it must be noted, should be read with caution, as it has a strong Stalinist-era overtone.

BOOKS AND ARTICLES
A. The Danube Before 1914

A number of standard works on Balkan history, general European diplomacy and the Eastern Question are valuable in placing the Danube issue in its proper context. Four volumes are particularly outstanding in this regard. Both L. S. Stavrianos, *The Balkans Since 1453* (New York, 1958) and the more recent Charles and Barbara Jelavich, *The Establishment of the Balkan National States 1804-1920* (Seattle, 1977) contain excellent surveys of the sweep of Balkan history as well as essential bibliographies. M. S. Anderson, *The Eastern Question* (New York, 1966) is the finest work devoted to the subject. While not addressed in any detail to the Danube Question *per se*, it nevertheless indicates the value placed upon maintaining the balance of power in the Basin. Finally, Rene Albrecht-Carrie, *A Diplomatic History of Europe Since the Congress of Vienna* (New York, 1958) remains the best general survey of European diplomacy.

Three studies written during the 1920s are the most complete analyses of the issue by Western scholars: Hugo Hajnal, *Le Droit du Danube International* (LeHaye, 1929) and *The Danube: Its Historical, Political and Economic Importance* (The Hague, 1920), and Joseph Chamberlain, *The Regime of the International Rivers: Danube and Rhine* (New York, 1923). All are well researched considering the limitations placed on documents and, although Eurocentric in nature, present superior overviews of the problem.

Other works, in turn, examine particular phases of the controversy. The formation of the European Commission and the work undertaken by Sir Charles Hartley toward restoring the channels to a navigable condition can be found in *Mémoire sur les travaux d'amelioration exécutés aux embouchures du Danube par la Commission Européenne* (Galați, 1867). Barbara Jelavich, *The Ottoman Empire, the Great Powers and the Straits Question* (Bloomington, 1973) covers the background to the Congress of Berlin and includes a twenty page analysis of the Danube issue. W. N. Medlicott, *The Congress of Berlin and After: A Diplomatic History of the Near Eastern Settlements 1878-1880* (London, 1938) looks at the Berlin accords and their effect upon the Basin. Sir Henry Trotter, *Operations of the European Commission of the Danube during the years 1894-1906* (London, 1906) is a short pamphlet that focuses on the organization during its "quiet" years at the turn of the century.

The foremost Romanian scholar on the history of the river prior to the war was Constantin Baicoianu. His *Le Danube* (Paris, 1913) and *Dunărea (The Danube)* (București, 1915), among others, are valuable studies that for the most part avoid the unfortunate trappings of other works on the Danube, that is, they are scholarly rather than prejorative. They are also a rich source of statistical analysis.

Three pamphlets by distinguished Romanians also present interesting glimpses into the problem from native eyes: D. Arion, *Chestia Dunării (The Danube Question)* (București, 1916); N. Iorga, *Chestiunea Dunării (The Danube Question)* (Valenii de Munte, 1913); and Mihail Kogălniceanu, *Chestia Dunării (The Danube Question)* (București, 1882). Both Arion and Kogălniceanu were high-ranking cabinet members and Iorga was Romania's most celebrated historian as well as a leading politician during the interwar years. Of greatest interest is the polemic by Kogălniceanu, which attacks the great powers for their conduct at Berlin and their moves toward creating the mixed-commission for the Middle Danube.

Among the numerous other books and pamphlets written by Romanian historians, each usually indistinguishable from another, two other works deserve mention. *Le Danube et les intérets économiques de l'Europe* (Paris, 1920) was an attempt to rally public opinion in the West to Romania's claims against the European Commission. Auguste Filip, *Le Regime Internationale du Danube* (Paris, 1932) was also an attempt to gain Western support, but is too superficial in comparison with the studies by Baicoianu.

B. Economic and Legal Studies

The most important studies of Danube trade during the nineteenth century are Romanian in origin; Western historians unfortunately have not approached the topic. Andrei Oțetea, *Pătrunderea comerțului românesc în circuitul internațional (The Penetration of Romanian Commerce into International Circulation)* (București, 1977) looks at the development of Romanian and Danubian trade. Constantin Baicoianu, *Handelspolitische Bestrebungen Englands zur Erschliessung der unteren Donau* (Berlin, 1913) and the recent articles by Paul Cernovodeanu of the Iorga Institute of History examines the growth of river trade between England and the Danubian Principalities. Constantin Buse, *Comerțul exterior prin Galați sub regimul de port franc (1837-1883) (External Commerce Through Galați Under the Free Port Regime)* (București, 1976) centers on the port during the developmental stages of maritime commerce.

The economic growth of the Danube Basin is generally overlooked in most economic histories of Europe. Of the few which address the development of the area's economy, one work stands out: Ivan T. Berend and György Ránki, *Economic Development in East Central Europe in the Nineteenth and Twentieth Centuries* (New York, 1974), an invaluable contribution to the study of the region. It is the only analysis of the development of all phases of the economies of the East European states, from demographic and agrarian problems to credit and transportation. Leo Pasvolsky, *Economic Nationalism in the Danubian States* (London, 1928) is dated but still a narrative of merit. Less important are the analyses prepared by the Royal Institute of International Affairs (*Southeastern Europe: A Political and Economic Survey*, London, 1939) and Frederick Hertz, (*The Economic Problem of the Danubian States*, London, 1947).

The finest study of the Romanian economy is Gheorghe Dobrovici, *Istoricul desvoltării economice și financiare a României și imprumuturile contractate 1823-1933 (The History of Romania's Economic and Financial Development and Loans Contracted 1823-1933)* (București: 1934), which includes a summary of the country's precarious financial structure after the war. A more recent volume, *Progresul economic în România 1877-1977 (Economic Progress in Romania 1877-1977)* (București, 1977) is generally too superficial and concentrates on the period after 1945. For the economic thinking prevalent at the time, one should consult the journals "Analele Statistice și Economice" and "Corespondența Economică," the works of the political economist I. N. Angelescu, especially his *Histoire Economique*, the numerous pamphlets by Vintilă Brătianu, and the studies by N. Dascovici, especially his *Politica comercială a Dunării (Danube Commercial Politics)* (București, 1926).

Georges Kaeckenbeeck, *International Rivers: A Monograph Based on Diplomatic Documents* (London, 1918), despite its date of publication,

presents the most succinct definition of the theory of internationality.
P. M. Ogilvie, *International Waterways* (London, 1920) is a reference
manual on the question of internationality and its application. Ruth E.
Bacon, "British Policy and the Regulation of European Rivers of International Concern," *British Yearbook of International Law*, 1929, pp.
158-77, examines the role of internationality as defined by British legal
theorists and the government in London. *Repetoire de Droit International* contains the principal river statutes formulated since the French
Revolution. Gordon E. Sherman, "The International Organization of the
Danube under the Peace Treaties," *American Journal of International Law*,
vol. 17, 1923, studies the background to the formation of the *Statut*. Stephen Gorove, *Law and Politics of the Danube* (The Hague, 1964) is the most
recent monograph devoted to the river's international status; Gorove,
however, is primarily interested in the river after 1945. Finally, two works
by the Yugoslav legal theorists Voyslav Radovanovitch, *Le Danube et
l'application du principe de la liberté de la navigation fluviale* (Geneva,
1925) and *Le Danube Maritime et la règlement du différend relatif aux
competences de la Commission européenne sur le secteur Galatz-Braila*
(Geneva, 1932) are straightforward studies of the two international organizations.

Considering Romania's interest in the controversy, it is not surprising
to find a proliferation of legalistic studies of the river and internationality.
Toma Stelian's manuscript, *Curs de Drept Maratim (Course in Maritime
Law)* (Biblioteca Centrală de Stat) is a collection of his lectures on international river law. N. Dascovici, *Interesele si drepturile României în texte
de drept internaționale public (Romanian Interests and Rights in Texts of
International Law)* (Iași, 1936) analyzes the texts of the major international agreements involving Romania. Constantin Georgescu, *Politica de
stat în materie de transporturi de apa (Politics of the State in Matters of
Water Transportation)* (București, 1927) and G. Meitani, *Dunărea: Studii
de drept internațional (The Danube: Studies in International Law)* (București, 1924) present the Romanian views of internationality that were
prevalent at the time of the conference. Two recent studies should also
be mentioned: Grigore Geamanu, *Dreptul internațional contemporan
(Contemporary International Law)* (București, 1965) and *Drept Internațional Fluvial (International Fluvial Law)* (București, 1973), the latter
a compilation of essays on river law prepared by the country's leading legal
theorists.

C. Romania and the Danube, 1914-22

Among the numerous studies of Eastern Europe after 1914, one work stands out: Joseph Rothschild's *East Central Europe Between the Two World Wars* (Seattle, 1974). Rothschild looks at each country individually with great insight into the major problems confronting the region after 1918. It is an essential tool in comprehending any issue facting the states of the Basin during the interwar years.

For the study of Romania, there is also one volume that is the outstanding work on the period. Henry L. Roberts, *Rumania: The Political Problems of an Agrarian State* (New Haven, 1951) presents a superior analysis of Romanian history during the twentieth century, paying particular attention to the political malaise that plagued the country. Other works on Romanian history include: N. Iorga, *Histoire des Roumains*, 10 vols. (București, 1945), a highly nationalistic survey of the sweep of the nation's history; Andrei Oţetea, *The History of the Romanian People* (București, 1970); *Istoria României*, prepared by the Romanian Academy; and Mircea Muşat and Ion Ardeleanu, *Viaţa Politică în România 1918-1921 (Political Life in Romania, 1918-1921)* (București, 1976), the best volume in the current series on Romanian political life and an indispensable reference for the topsy-turvy era.

The war years on the Balkan front generally are given minimal attention by historians. Although the works by Lidell Hart, Marc Ferro, and Norman Stone are first-rate studies, they avoid the Romanian front almost entirely. Considering the importance of the other theaters perhaps this is understandable. However, this vacuum in scholarship means that the Romanian front is discussed solely in works by native historians. Of these, Constantin Kiriţescu's three volume *Istoria Războiului pentru întegirea României 1916-1919 (The History of the War for the Unification of Romania 1916-1919)* (București, 1927) proves to be a satisfactory narrative. Despite its attempts to glorify even the most miniscule military success, it also mentions the country's shortcomings, a rarity for a contemporary publication.

As background to the war and Romanian intervention one should consult Şerban Rădulescu-Zoner, *România şi Tripla Alianţa la inceputul secolului al XX-lea (Romania and the Triple Alliance at the Beginning of the 20th Century)* (București, 1977), Constantin Nuţu, *România în anii neutralitaţii (Romania in the Years of Neutrality)* (București, 1972), and

Glenn Torrey, "Rumania's Decision to Intervene," *Rumanian Studies* 2 (1971-72), pp. 3-29. Although none of these deal with the Danube Question, they are helpful in understanding the divisions within the country during this period.

Vintilă Brătianu, *Pacea de Robire (Peace of Theft)* (Bucureşti, 1919) is a strident attack on the former Central Powers for their actions during the war and the terms of the Treaty of Bucharest. Constantin Baicoianu, *Dunărea vazuta prin prizma tractatului din Bucureşti (The Danube as Seen through the Treaty of Bucharest)* (Bucureşti, 1921) examines the effect of the treaty upon the river in a relatively dispassionate manner considering the anti-German mood after the war.

The work and effects of the peace settlements have been covered in detail. For the history of the entire conference the most important work remains H. W. V. Temperley, *A History of the Peace Conference of Paris* (London, 1920), which analyzes all phases of the treaties. Arno J. Mayer, *Politics and Diplomacy of Peacemaking: Containment and Counterrevolution at Versailles 1918-1919* (New York, 1967) concentrates on the fears of Bolshevism which affected the outcome at Versailles and enabled Brătianu, for example, to obtain significant territorial gains by presenting Romania as a bulwark against Bolshevism. Frank S. Marston, *The Peace Conference of 1919: Organization and Procedure* (London, 1944) contains an informative account of the complicated committee structure employed at Versailles. The Romanian position at the conference is assessed in Sherman David Spector, *Rumania at the Paris Peace Conference: A Study in the Diplomacy of Ioan I. C. Brătianu* (New York, 1962).

Most of the secondary sources devoted to the Danube Question after 1914-18 are contemporary to the era. With few exceptions, no significant work has appeared since the 1930s. This is especially true for non-Romanian sources. Most histories of the river therefore are badly outdated and are based on scanty documentation. In fact, save for the aforementioned studies by Joseph Chamberlain and Hugo Hajnal, little has been written on the controversies following the war. The short account prepared by the Secretary General of the International Commission *(Dix Ans de Regime International sur le Danube Fluvial 1920-30)* is little more than a pamphlet extolling the virtues of the agency. Likewise, *Le Commission Européenne et son oeuvre de 1856 á 1931* (Paris, 1931) praises the work of the maritime body; it does however include a section of valuable charts. Walter Hines, *Report on Danube Navigation submitted to the*

Advisory and Technical Committees for Communications and Transit of the League of Nations (Geneva, 1925), in contrast, is a substantive examination of the problems facing commerce after the war.

The views of one of the non-voting states at the Danube Conference can be found in E. von Kvassai, *Le Danube et la Hongrie* (Budapest, 1921). Like most of its Romanian counterparts, however, it is more prejorative than it is scholarly.

In contrast to this paucity of works outside Romania, Romanian histories of the river and its administration abound. Although most of these books center on pre-1914 events, numerous pamphlets and monographs address postwar events as well.

The best volume is N. Dascovici, *Dunărea noastră (Our Danube)* (București, 1927). Dascovici looks at the development of the conflict in a realistic manner that separates histrionics from the realities of great power politics. Additional works by Dascovici include *Libertatea navigației în Mediterana și Interesele noastre naționale (Liberty of Navigation in the Mediterranean and Our National Interests)* (Iași, 1938) and "Dunărea Internațională și Ținutul Românesc al Gurilor," ("The International Danube and the Romanian Region of the Mouth"), *Analele Dobrogei,* 1920, IX, pp. 771-77.

Eugene Botez, the Captain of the Port of Sulina during the war, published three pamphlets under the pseudonym "Jean Bart" (as well as writing a well-regarded novel entitled *Europolis* based upon a river society and derived from his experiences in the delta). His "histories" include *La question du Danube et sa solution* (Galați, 1920), *Memorii asupra Comisiei Europeană Dunărene din punct de vedere politic și militar (Statements on the European Commission of the Danube from a Military and Political Point of View)* (Galați, 1913), and *Cum se desleaga Chestiunea Dunării? (How to Untie the Danube Question)* (Chișinau, 1919). All are almost identical attacks upon the Commission as a threat to Romanian sovereignty. Another Commission functionary, Gheorghe Popescu, the technical delegate to the Conference, was also a pamphleteer and, like Bart, expressed indignation at the continuation of the "anomaly." His works, including *Freedom of Navigation on International Rivers: The Most Suitable Administration* (London, 1935), *L'internationalisation des fleuves navigables: Le Danube et la Roumanie* (Paris, 1919), and *Libertate comunicației pe Caile Navigabile și Regimul Dunărei (The Liberty of*

Communication on Navigable Routes and the Danube Regime) (Bucureşti, 1920), among others, are generally more thought-provoking than the works of his compatriots. A third Commission employee, I. D. Popovici, published a study of the *Statut* entitled *Situaţia creită României prin noul regim al Dunărei (The Situation Created in Romania by the New Danube Regime)* (Galaţi, 1924) which concentrated on the European Commission rather than the successful outcome of the Conference for Romania. Other works include: Vintilă Brătianu, *Chestia Dunării (The Danube Question)* (Bucureşti, 1923); R. Franasovici, *Chestia Dunării (The Danube Question)* (Bucureşti, 1923); M. Burghele, *Memoire du Gouvernement Roumain dans la Question du Danube* (Bucureşti, 1925); Grigore Antipa, *Die Donau: Ihre Politische und Wirtschaftliche Bedeuteung im Leben des Rumänischen Volkes* (Bukarest, 1941); and the collection of essays prepared by E. Porumbaru, V. Brătianu, C. I. Baicoianu, and N. Stefănescu, *Memoire sur la question du Danube.*

More recent studies are G. G. Florescu, *Navigaţia în Marea Neagră prin strîmtori şi pe Dunăre (Navigation in the Black Sea through the Straits and on the Danube)* (Bucureşti, 1975) and Paul Gogeanu, *Dunărea în relaţiile internaţionale (The Danube in International Affairs)* (Bucureşti, 1970), neither of which presents any significant new insights into the field. On the other hand, Iulian Cârţână and Ilie Seftiuc, *Dunărea în istoria poporului român (The Danube in the History of the Romanian People)* uses archival sources previously inaccessible to historians. However, the book should be read with caution as the use of those archives is spotty and, more importantly, the authors cite a source (the Fond Biblioteca Ioan I. C. Brătianu) that could not be located by the author, archivists in Bucharest, or a leading member of the Iorga Institute of History.

SELECTED BIBLIOGRAPHY

Primary Sources

I. ARCHIVES—Bucharest, Romania

Arhivele Ministerului Afacerilor Externe, Fond 71/1914; Fond 8 Conv. D
Arhivele Statului (București), Fond Casa Regală
Arhivele Statului Galați, Fond Comisia Europeană a Dunării
Biblioteca Academiei R.S.R., Fond Arhivele N. Docan
Newspapers:
Adevărul, Dimineața, Universul, Viitorul
Biblioteca Centrală de Stat (București), Fond St. Georges

II. PUBLISHED DOCUMENTS

Conférence Internationale pour l'établissement du Statut Définitif du Danube. Paris: Imprimerie Nationale, 1921.

D. Sturdza, *Recueil de Documents relatifs à la Liberté de Navigation du Danube.* Berlin: Puttkammer and Muhlbrecht, 1904.

D. A. Sturdza, *Les travaux la Commission Europeenne du Danube 1865-1911: Actes et Documents.* Vienna, 1913.

Secondary Sources

Academia de Stiințe Sociale și Politice a Republicii Socialiste România. *Drept internațional fluvial.* București: Editura Academiei R.S.R., 1973.

Academia Republicii Populare Române. *Istoria Rominiei.* București: Editura Academiei R.P.R., 1964.

Albrecht-Carrie, Rene. *A Diplomatic History of Europe Since the Congress of Vienna.* New York: Harper and Row Publishers, 1958.

Allen, George H. *The Great War*. vols. 4 and 5. Philadelphia: George Barrie's Sons, 1919.

Anderson, M. S. *The Eastern Question*. New York: St. Martin's Press, 1966.

Angelescu, I. N. "Criza comercială și financiară actuală în România." *Analele Statistice și Economice*, no. 4, April 1919, pp. 8-11.

Angelescu, I. N. *Histoire economique*. București, 1918.

Angelescu, I. N. *Politica economică a României fața de politica economică imperialistă*. București: "Tipografiile Române Unite", 1923.

Antipa, Gr. *Citeva probleme stiințifice și economice privitoare la Delta Dunărei*. București: Librariile Socec. și Comp., 1914.

Antipa, Grigore. *Die Donau: Ihre Politische und Wirtschaftliche Bedeutung im Leben des Rumänischen Volkes*. Bukarest: Die Dacia Bücher, 1941.

Antipa, Gr. *Dunărea și problemele ei stiințifice economice și politice*. București: Librăriile "Cartea Româneasca", 1921.

Arion, Dinu C. *Chestia Dunării*. București: Tipografia "Cooperativa", 1916.

Axenciuc, V. "Evoluția economiei românești în anii 1918-1938." *Analele Institutului de Studii Istorice și Sociale-Politice de pe linga c.c. al P.C. R.*, 6/1966, pp. 3-18.

Bacon, Ruth E. "British and American Policy and the Right of Fluvial Navigation." *British Yearbook of International Law*, 1932, pp. 76-93.

Bacon, Ruth E. "British Policy and the Regulation of European Rivers of International Concern." *British Yearbook of International Law*, 1929, pp. 158-71.

Bădulescu, L; Canja, Gh., and Glaser, E. *Contribuții la studiul istoriei regimului internațional de navigație pe Dunăre*. București: Editura Stiințifică, 1957.

Baicoianu, C. I. *Dunărea: Privire Istorică, economică și politică*. București: Tipografia "Eminescu," 1915.

Baicoianu, Constantin I. *Dunărea văzută prin prizma tractatului din București*. București: Tipografia "Universala", 1921.

Baicoianu, Constantin I. *Handelspolitische Bestrebungen Englands zur Erschliessung der unteren Donau*. Berlin: J. Schwitzer Verlag, 1913.

Baicoianu, C. I. *Le Danube*. Paris: Librairie de la Societe du Recueil Sirey, 1917.

Bart, Jean. *Cum se desleaga Chestiunea Dunării?* Chişinau: Tipografia "Glasul Ţării", 1919.

Bart, Jean. *La question du Danube et sa solution.* Galaţi: Stabilimentul Grafic "Moldova", 1920.

Basch, Antonin. *The Danube Basin and The German Economic Sphere.* New York: Columbia University Press, 1943.

Berend, Ivan T. and Gyorgy Ranki. *Economic Development in East Central Europe in the 19th and 20th Centuries.* New York: Columbia University Press, 1974.

(Botez,Eugene). *Memorii asupra Comisiei Europeană Dunărene din punct de vedere politic şi militar: Material de studii pregatitoare în vederea viitoarelor aranjamente în chestia Dunărei.* Galaţi: Tipo-Litografia: A. Friedmann, 1913.

Brătianu, Gheorghe. *Actiunea Politică şi Militară a României în 1919: In lumea corespondenţii diplomatice a lui Ion I. C. Brătianu.* Bucureşti: "Cartea Româneasca", 1939.

Brătianu, Gh. *Problemele politicii noastre externe.* Bucureşti: Editura mişcarea, 1934.

Brătianu, Vintilă C. *Chestia Dunării: expunere făcută în Adunarea Deputaţilor.* Bucureşti: Imprimeria Statului, 1920.

Brătianu, Vintilă. *Note asupra viitoarelor nevoi economice şi financiare ale României.* Iaşi, 1917.

Brătianu, Vintilă. *Pacea de Robire.* Bucureşti, 1919.

Brătianu, Vintilă. *Un pericol naţional: studiu asupra taxelor de la Porţile de Fier.* Bucureşti: "Voinţa Naţională", 1899.

(Burghele, M.). *Memoire du Gouvernement Roumain dans la Question du Danube.* Bucureşti: Imprimerie de l'etat, 1925.

Buse, Constantin. *Comerţul exterior prin Galaţi sub regimul de port franc (1832-1883).* Bucureşti: Editura Academiei R.S.R., 1976.

Cârţană, Iulian and Ilie Seftiuc. *Dunărea în istoria poporuli român.* Bucureşti: Editura Stiinţifică, 1972.

Cârţană, Iulian. *România şi Problema Dunării.* Bucureşti: Academia de Stiinţe Sociale-Politice "Stefan Gheorgiu", 1969.

Cernovodeanu, Paul. "An unpublished British source concerning the international trade through Galatz and Brăila between 1837 and 1848." *Revue Roumanie d'Histoire,* XVI, 3/1977, pp. 517-31.

Cernovodeanu, Paul. "Anglo-American Trade-Relations During the Second

Half of the 19th Century." Unpublished paper delivered at the Anglo-Romanian History Colloquium, London, May 1978.

Cernovodeanu, Paul. "British Economic Interests in the Lower Danube and the Balkan Shore of the Black Sea between 1803 and 1829." *The Journal of European Economic History*, V, 1 (Spring 1976), pp. 105-20.

Chamberlain, Joseph P. *The Regime of the International Rivers: Danube and Rhine.* New York: Columbia University Press, 1923.

Commission Européenne. *Mémoire sur les travaux d'amelioration exécutes aux embouchures de Danube par la Commission Européenne.* Galați: Imprimerie de la Commission Européenne du Danube, 1867.

Commission Européenne du Danube. *La Commission Européenne du Danube et son oeuvre de 1856 a 1931.* Paris: Imprimerie Nationale, 1931.

Dascovici, N. "Dunărea Internațională și Ținutul Românesc al Gurilor." *Analele Dobrogei*, IX/I (1920), pp. 771-77.

Dascovici, N. *Dunărea noastră.* București: Editura Fundației, 1927.

Dascovici, N. *Interesele și drepturile României în texte de drept internațional public.* Iași: Tipografia concesionara "Alexandru Țerek", 1936.

Dascovici, N. *Libertatea navigației în Mediterana și Interesele noastre naționale.* Iași: Institutul de Arte Grafice "Brawo", 1938.

Dascovici, N. *Politica comercială a Dunării.* București: Cartea Româneasca, 1926.

Dascovici, N. *Politica externă a României.* Iași: Tipografia "Alex A. Țerek", 1936.

Dascovici, N. *Politica externă și interesele naționale.* Iași: Tipografia "Alex. A. Țerek," 1938.

Demorgny, Gustave. *La question du Danube.* Paris: L. Larose and L. Tenin, 1911.

Dobrovici, Gheorghe M. *Istoricul desvoltării economice și financiare a României și imprumuturile contractate 1823-1933.* București: Tipografia: Ziarul "Universul", 1934.

Ferro, Marc. *The Great War 1914-1918.* London: Routledge and K. Paul, 1973.

Filip, Auguste I. *Le Regime International du Danube.* Paris: "Les Presses Universitaires de France", 1923.

Florescu, G. G. *Navigația în Marea Neagră prin strîmtori și pe Dunăre.* București: Editura Academiei R.S.R., 1975.

Franasovici, R. *Chestia Dunării: Discurs rostit in Adunarea Deputăților*. București: "Imprimeria Statului", 1923.

Geamănu, Grigore. *Dreptul internațional contemporan*. București: Editura Didactica și Pedagogica, 1965.

Georgescu, Constantin. *Politica de stat in materie de transporturi pe apa*. București: Imprimeriile independența, 1927.

Gogeanu, Paul. *Dunărea în relațiile internaționale*. București: Editura politică, 1970.

Gorove, Stephen. *Law and Politics of the Danube*. The Hague: Martinus Nijhoff, 1964.

Hajnal, Henri. *Le Droit du Danube International*. Le Haye: Martinus Nijhoff, 1929.

Hajnal, Henry. *The Danube: Its Historical, Political and Economic Importance*. The Hague: Martinus Nijhoff, 1920.

Hart, Liddell. *A History of the Great War 1914-1918*. London: Faber and Faber Limited, 1934.

Hertz, Frederick. *The Economic Problem of the Danubian States*. London: Victor Gollancz Ltd., 1947.

Hines, Walter D. *Report on Danube Navigation submitted to the Advisory and Technical Committee for Communication and Transit of the League of Nations*. Geneva: League of Nations, 1925.

Institutul Central de Cercetări Economice. *Progresul economic în România 1877-1977*. București: Editura Politică, 1977.

Iorga, N. *Chestiunea Dunării*. Valenii de Munte: Editura Societatii "Neamul Romanesc", 1913.

Iorga, N. *Histoire des Roumains*. București: L'Academie Roumaine, 1945.

Jelavich, Barbara. *The Ottoman Empire, the Great Powers and the Straits Question 1870-1887*. Bloomington: Indiana University Press, 1973.

Jelavich, Charles and Barbara Jelavich. *The Establishment of the Balkan National States 1804-1920*. Seattle: University of Washington Press, 1977.

Kaeckenbeeck, Georges. *International Rivers: A Monograph Based on Diplomatic Documents*. London: Sweet and Maxwell Limited, 1918.

Kirițescu, Constantin. *Istoria Războiului pentru integirea României 1916-1919*. București: Editura Casei Școalelor, 1927.

Kogălniceanu, M. *Chestia Dunării*. București: Tipografia Academiei Române, 1882.

Le Danube et les intérêts economiques de L'Europe. Paris, 1920.

Macartney, C. A. and Alan Palmer. *Independent Eastern Europe.* London: Macmillan and Co., Ltd., 1962.

Malița, Mircea. *Reprezentantele diplomatice ale României.* București: Editura Politică, 1971.

Mamatey, Victor S. *The United States and East Central Europe: A Study in Wilsonian Diplomacy and Propaganda.* Princeton: Princeton University Press, 1957.

Maier, Charles. *Recasting Bourgeois Europe.* Princeton: Princeton University Press, 1975.

Marston, F. S. *The Peace Conference of 1919: Organization and Procedure.* London: Oxford University Press, 1944.

Mayer, Arno J. *Politics and Diplomacy of Peacemaking: Containment and Counterrevolution at Versailles 1918-1919.* New York: Vintage Books, 1967.

Medlicott, W. N. *The Congress of Berlin and After: A Diplomatic History of the Near Eastern Settlements 1878-1880.* London: Methuen and Co., Ltd., 1938.

Meitani, G. *Dunărea: Studii de drept internațional.* București: Tipografia "Curierul Judicai", 1924.

(Ministerul de Industrie și Comerț) "Corespondența Economica," No. 9/15 August, 1921. Nos. 24 and 25/1, April 1922.

Ministerul Lucrărilor Publice și al Communicaților. *Noțiuni elementare asupra sectorului român al Dunărei.* București: Imprimeria Centrală, 1935.

Ministerul Regal al Afacerilor Straine. *Convențiune stabilînd Statul definitiv al Dunării încheiată la Paris la Iulie 1921.* București: Imprimeria Centrală, 1936.

Mitrany, David. *The Land and Peasant in Romania.* New York: Greenwood Press, 1968.

Mușat, Mircea and Ion Ardeleanu. *Viața politică în România 1918-1921.* București: Editura politică, 1976.

Nuțu, Constantin. *România în anii neutralității (1914-1916).* București: Editura Stiințifica, 1972.

Ogilvie, Paul Morgan. *International Waterways.* London: The MacMillan Co., 1920.

Österreichisches Institut für Wirtschaftsforschung. *Die wirtschaftliche*

Bedeutung und Entwicklung der Donauschiffahrt. Wien, 1962.

Oțetea, Andrei. *Pătrunderea comerțului românesc în circuitul internațional.* București: Editura Academiei R.S.R., 1977.

Pasvolski, Leo. *Economic Nationalism of the Danubian States.* London: George Allen and Unwinn Ltd., 1928.

"Politica economică a României Mări." *Analele Statistice și Economice,* No. 9-10 (Sept./Oct. 1919), pp. 134-44.

Popescu, Georges. *Freedom of Navigation on International Rivers: The Most Suitable Administration.* London: Billings and Sons Ltd., 1935.

Popescu, Georges. *La Navigation et la Politique Commerciale.* București: "Cartea Românească", 1926.

Popescu, Georges. *Le Relevement économique de la Roumanie.* Paris: Librarie Felix Alcan. No date.

Popescu, Gheorghe. *Libertatea comunicației pe Caile Navigabile și Regimul Dunării: Desbătut în conferința dela Paris în anii 1919-20.* București: Buletinul Societate Politicenice, 1920.

Popescu, Georges. *L 'internationalisation des fleuves navigables: Le Danube et la Roumanie.* Paris: "Dubois et Baur", 1919.

Popescu, Gh. *Navigația maritimă.* București, 1932.

Popescu, Georges. *Politica necesară pentru ridicarea importanței României în navigațiunea europeană.* București: Cartea Românească, 1928.

Popovici, Inginer I. D. *Necesitațea mărinei și organizărei porturilor noăstre.* Galați: Camera de Comerț și Industrie din Galați, 1924.

Popovici, I. D. *Situația creiată României prin noul regim al Dunărei.* Galați: Camera de Comerț și Industrie din Galați, 1924.

Porumbaru, E., V. Brătianu, C. I. Băicoianu and N. Stefănescu. *Memoire sur la question du Danube.* No date.

Radovanovitch, Voyslav M. *Le Danube et l'application du principle de la liberté de la navigation fluviale.* Geneva: Imprimerie Jent, 1925.

Radovanovitch, Voyslav M. *Le Danube Maritime et le règlement du différend relatif aux compétences de la Commission européenne sur le secteur Galatz-Braila.* Geneva: Georg et Cic, S.A., 1932.

Rădulescu-Zoner, Șerban. *România și Tripla Alianță la inceputul secolului al XX-lea 1900-1914.* București: Editura Litera, 1977.

Repetoire de Droit International. Paris, 1929.

Roberts, Henry L. *Rumania: The Political Problems of an Agrarian State.* New Haven: Yale University Press, 1951.

Rothschild, Joseph. *East Central Europe between the Two World Wars.* Seattle: University of Washington Press, 1974.

Royal Institute of International Affairs. *South-Eastern Europe: A Political and Economic Survey.* London: Oxford University Press, 1939.

Sayre, Francis Bowles. *Experiments in International Administration.* New York: Harper and Brothers Publishers, 1919.

Secretariat General de la Commission Internationale du Danube. *Dix Ans de Regime International sur le Danube Fluviale (1920-1930).* No date.

Seton-Watson, Hugh. *Eastern Europe Between the Wars 1918-1941.* New York: Harper and Row Publishers, 1967.

Sherman, Gordon E. "The International Organization of the Danube under the Peace Treaties." *American Journal of International Law,* vol. 17 (1923).

Solms-Braunfels, Dr. Franz Prinz du. *Die Volkerrechtliche Stellung der Donau.* Wurzburg-Aumuhle: Verlag Konrad Triltisch, 1935.

Stavrianos, L. S. *The Balkans Since 1453.* New York: Holt, Rinehart and Winston, 1958.

Spector, Sherman David. *Rumania at the Paris Peace Conference: A Study of the Diplomacy of Ioan I. C. Brătianu.* New York: Bookman Associates, Inc., 1962.

Stelian, Toma. *Curs de Drept Maritim.* No date.

Stere, C. *Marele răsboiul și politica României.* București: Atelierele Societății Anonime "Poporul", 1918.

Stone, Norman. *The Eastern Front 1914-1917.* London: Hodder and Stoughton, 1975.

Sugar, Peter F. and Ivo J. Lederer. *Nationalism in Eastern Europe.* Seattle: University of Washington Press, 1969.

Temperley, H. W. V. *A History of the Peace Conference of Paris.* vol. II. London: Henry Frowde, and Hodder and Stoughton, 1920.

Trotter, Lt. Col. Sir Henry. "Operations of the European Commission of the Danube during the years 1894-1906." London: Harrison and Sons, St. Martin's Press, 1906.

von Falkenhayn, General Erich. *The German General Staff and Its Decisions 1914-1916.* New York: Dood, Mead and Co., 1920.

von Kvassai, E. *Le Danube et la Hongrie.* Budapest, 1921.

Wilson, Francis Graham. *A Theory of Public Opinion.* Chicago: Henry Regnery Co., 1962.

Wolfers, Arnold. *Britain and France Between the Two Wars: Conflicting Strategies of Peace from Versailles to World War II.* New York, 1940.

INDEX

Act of Navigation (1857), 16-7, 23, 40
Adrianople, Treaty of (1829), 13
Aix-la-Chapelle, Congress of (1818), 25
Andreades, A., 90-1, 105-6
Arion, C. C., 42
Austria (see also Habsburg Empire), 12, 62, 93, 107
Averescu, A., 40, 50-1

Baldwin, J., 35-6, 67-70, 72, 80-1, 84, 91, 93-5, 99-101, 104-6, 109, 191
Barcelona Conference (1921), 87, 98-101
Belgium, 56, 60, 76, 84
Belgrade Conference (1948), 192
Belloy, Admiral, 60
Berlin, Congress of (1878), 19-20, 22-23, 37, 41, 93
Bessarabia, 14, 20, 37-8, 46-7, 87, 115
Boerescu, M., 101-2
Boerescu, V., 24
Botez, E., 36, 38-9, 68, 201
Brăila, 13, 19, 25-6, 34-6, 60-1, 80-1, 84, 86, 98-90, 103-4, 120, 123
Brătianu, Ioan I. C., 38, 40, 60, 86, 115
Brătianu, V., 35, 37-8
Bratislava, 109
Brunet, M., 90, 106
Bucharest, Treaty of (1812), 13
Bucharest, Treaty of (1918), 34, 40-1, 43-4, 50, 108, 121
Budapest, 71-3, 80, 95
Buftea, Peace Treaty (1918), 40, 42

Bulgaria, 8, 12, 21-2, 27, 34-5, 40, 47, 62, 117
Burghele, M., 42, 63, 131

Carol I, 24-5
Carp, M., 72, 136n
Carp, P., 23
Clemenceau, G., 60-1
Commission of the Mouth of the Danube, 41-3
Conference Internationale du Danube, "affluents," 95; and Barcelona Conference, 99-101; cabotage, 84, 88-9, 94-5, 105-6; European Commission, 89-91, 103-4; International Commission, 87-9, 91-6, 104-9; Iron Gates, 80, 84, 96-7, 102, 106-9; Legrand projects, 81-2, 83-4; Opposition to Legrand project, 82-4; Signing, 109-11; Taxation, 84, 88, 93; Warships, 84, 88, 93-4, 102-3, 109; Work, 80, 84, 88, 92, 105
Congo River, 94, 121
Constanța, 34, 61, 125n
Conțescu, C., 55, 59, 63-9, 72, 76-7, 80, 98-110, 123, 134n, 143n, 192
Coromilas, L., 85, 94, 105, 139n
Crimean War, 14-15, 125n
Czechoslovakia, 61, 70, 75, 77-8, 103, 105, 107

Danube River, Allied control, 59-60; Danube Question, v, vi, 1, 3-9, 12-27, 45-6, 53, 113-4, 116; de-militarization, 20, 84, 88, 93-4, 102-3, 109; during World War I, 28-

213

London, Conference of (1883), 24-6, 73, 120-1

Mackensen, E. von, 34-5, 40
Magnussen, Chief-engineer, 37, 39, 59
Marghiloman, A., 40, 50
Montreaux Treaty of (1936), 192
Muller, B., 85, 89, 93, 102-3, 105

Odessa, 13, 36, 64
Ottoman Empire, 6, 8, 12, 14-15, 19, 22, 30, 34-5, 37, 40-2, 45, 48, 119-20

Paris, Treaty of (1856), 3, 14-6, 68, 75, 93, 110, 119-20
Popescu, G., 79, 107, 201
Popovici, I., 79
Ports and Waterways Commission, 60-2, 64, 81, 121
Portugal, 12, 61
Porumbaru, E., 36
Public Act of 1865, 18-19

Rey, F., 30-1, 33-4, 58-9, 65-9, 76-7, 80
Rhine River, 10-11, 16, 62, 84, 87-8, 94
Ristic, M., 81, 84-5, 89-90, 92-3, 96, 99, 102, 106-8, 138n
River State Commission, 15-17, 19, 20, 22, 119
Romania, admission to European Commission, 19-20; and Danube Question, v, vi, 4-5, 8-11; and Middle Danube, 22-27; and World War I: neutrality, 28-33; at war, 33-40, 58; under Treaty of Bucharest, 40-44; as supporter of preliminary *Statut*, 103-11; at *Conference*, 81-111; at Versailles, 60-4; diplomacy with Greece and "Yugoslavia," 82-5; interim maneuvers, 101-2; on European

Commission, 89-91; on Iron Gates 96-7, 102, 106-9; on International Commission, 91-6, 104-9; post-war situation, 45-53; pre-conference maneuvers, 76-80; pre-war views, 23-26; public opinion, 101, 112-23; ratifies *Statut*, 109-11; replaces Stelian, 98-9; *Session extraordinaire*, 66-9, 72-3; Stelian's policy, 83-7; versus Inter-Allied Commission, 69-74; war with Hungary, 71
Russia (and Soviet Union), 6, 8, 12-15, 19-20, 23-25, 35-40, 42-3, 45, 47, 52, 121, 192

Seeliger, Dr., 105-6, 108
Serbia, 8, 21-22, 25, 27, 60, 70, 83
Sinaia Conference (1938), 192
Spa Conference (1920), 47, 53, 116
St. George channel, 13
Statut Definitif, 1, 73-5, 80-1, 88-9, 95, 98, 100-1, 104, 106, 109-112, 122-3, 191
Stefănescu, N., 61-3
Stelian, T., 79-86, 89-94, 96, 98-9, 123, 139n, 140n, 141n, 142n
Sturdza, D., 24, 72, 77
Sulina channel, 13, 17-18, 29-31, 36-8, 43, 55, 59, 65, 72, 77
Sulina, port of, 18, 36, 41, 57, 64-5, 71
Supreme Allied Commission, 54-5, 60-1, 70, 73-4

Trowbridge, Admiral E., 55, 60, 63, 68-74, 77, 86, 122, 135n, 146n
Turtucaia, 34-36

Vaida-Voievod, A., 50, 68
Venizelos, E., 83-5
Versailles, Treaties, vi, 1, 3-4, 45-7, 55, 60-4, 70-1, 85-9, 92, 95, 99-100, 103, 116
Vienna, Congress of (1815), 10, 14, 16-17, 81, 100, 119

EAST EUROPEAN MONOGRAPHS

The *East European Monographs* comprise scholarly books on the history and civilization of Eastern Europe. They are published by the *East European Quarterly* in the belief that these studies contribute substantially to the knowledge of the area and serve to stimulate scholarship and research.

Political Ideas and the Enlightenment in the Romanian Principalities, 1750-1831. By Vlad Georgescu. 1971.

America, Italy and the Birth of Yugoslavia, 1917-1919. By Dragan R. Zivjinovic. 1972.

Jewish Nobles and Geniuses in Modern Hungary. By William O. McCagg, Jr. 1972.

Mixail Soloxov in Yugoslavia: Reception and Literary Impact. By Robert F. Price. 1973.

The Historical and National Thought of Nicolae Iorga. By William O. Oldson. 1973.

Guide to Polish Libraries and Archives. By Richard C. Lewanski. 1974.

Vienna Broadcasts to Slovakia, 1938-1939: A Case Study in Subversion. By Henry Delfiner. 1974.

The 1917 Revolution in Latvia. By Andrew Ezergailis. 1974.

The Ukraine in the United Nations Organization: A Study in Soviet Foreign Policy. 1944-1950. By Konstantin Sawczuk. 1975.

The Bosnian Church: A New Interpretation. By John V. A. Fine, Jr., 1975.

Intellectual and Social Developments in the Habsburg Empire from Maria Theresa to World War I. Edited by Stanley B. Winters and Joseph Held. 1975.

Ljudevit Gaj and the Illyrian Movement. By Elinor Murray Despalatovic. 1975.

Tolerance and Movements of Religious Dissent in Eastern Europe. Edited by Bela K. Kiraly. 1975.

The Parish Republic: Hlinka's Slovak People's Party, 1939-1945. By Yeshayahu Jelinek. 1976.

The Russian Annexation of Bessarabia, 1774-1828. By George F. Jewsbury. 1976.

Modern Hungarian Historiography. By Steven Bela Vardy. 1976.

Values and Community in Multi-National Yugoslavia. By Gary K. Bertsch. 1976.

The Greek Socialist Movement and the First World War: The Road to Unity. By George B. Leon. 1976.

The Radical Left in the Hungarian Revolution of 1848. Bv Laszlo Deme. 1976.

Hungary between Wilson and Lenin: The Hungarian Revolution of 1918-1919 and the Big Three. By Peter Pastor. 1976.

The Crises of France's East-Central European Diplomacy, 1933-1938. By Anthony J. Komjathy. 1976.

Polish Politics and National Reform, 1775-1788. By Daniel Stone. 1976.

The Habsburg Empire in World War I. Robert A. Kann, Bela K. Kiraly, and Paula S. Fichtner, eds. 1977.

The Slovenes and Yugoslavism, 1890-1914. By Carole Rogel. 1977.

German-Hungarian Relations and the Swabian Problem. By Thomas Spira. 1977.

The Metamorphosis of a Social Class in Hungary During the Reign of Young Franz Joseph. By Peter I. Hidas. 1977.

Tax Reform in Eighteenth Century Lombardy. By Daniel M. Klang. 1977.

Tradition versus Revolution: Russia and the Balkans in 1917. By Robert H. Johnston. 1977.

Winter into Spring: The Czechoslovak Press and the Reform Movement 1963-1968. By Frank L. Kaplan. 1977.

The Catholic Church and the Soviet Government, 1939-1949. By Dennis J. Dunn. 1977.

The Hungarian Labor Service System, 1939-1945. By Randolph L Braham. 1977.

Consciousness and History: Nationalist Critics of Greek Society 1897-1914. By Gerasimos Augustinos. 1977.

Emigration in Polish Social and Political Thought, 1870-1914. By Benjamin P. Murdzek. 1977.

Serbian Poetry and Milutin Bojic. By Mihailo Dordevic. 1977.

The Baranya Dispute: Diplomacy in the Vortex of Ideologies, 1918-1921. By Leslie C. Tihany. 1978.

The United States in Prague, 1945-1948. By Walter Ullmann. 1978.

Rush to the Alps: The Evolution of Vacationing in Switzerland. By Paul P. Bernard. 1978.

Transportation in Eastern Europe: Empirical Findings. By Bogdan Mieczkowski. 1978.

The Polish Underground State: A Guide to the Underground, 1939-1945. By Stefan Korbonski. 1978.

The Hungarian Revolution of 1956 in Retrospect. Edited by Bela K. Kiraly and Paul Jonas. 1978.

Boleslaw Limanowski (1835-1935): A Study in Socialism and Nationalism. By Kazimiera Janina Cottam. 1978.

The Lingering Shadow of Nazism: The Austrian Independent Party Movement Since 1945. By Max E. Riedlsperger. 1978.

The Catholic Church, Dissent and Nationality in Soviet Lithuania. By V. Stanley Vardys. 1978.

The Development of Parliamentary Government in Serbia. By Alex N. Dragnich. 1978.

Divide and Conquer: German Efforts to Conclude a Separate Peace, 1914-1918. By L. L. Farrar, Jr. 1978.

The Prague Slav Congress of 1848. By Lawrence D. Orton. 1978.

The Nobility and the Making of the Hussite Revolution. By John M. Klassen. 1978.

The Cultural Limits of Revolutionary Politics: Change and Continuity in Socialist Czechoslovakia. By David W. Paul. 1979.

On the Border of War and Peace: Polish Intelligence and Diplomacy in 1937-1939 and the Origins of the Ultra Secret. By Richard A. Woytak. 1979.

Bear and Foxes: The International Relations of the East European States 1965-1969. By Ronald Haly Linden. 1979.

Czechoslovakia: The Heritage of Ages Past. Edited by Ivan Volgyes and Hans Brisch. 1979.

Prima Minister Gyula Andrassy's Influence on Habsburg Foreign Policy. By Janos Decsy. 1979.

Citizens for the Fatherland: Education, Educators, and Pedagogical Ideals in Eighteenth Century Russia. By J. L. Black. 1979.

A History of the "Proletariat": The Emergence of Marxism in the Kingdom of Poland, 1870-1887. By Norman M. Naimark. 1979.

The Slovak Autonomy Movement, 1935-1939: A Study in Unrelenting Nationalism. By Dorothea H. El Mallakh. 1979.

Diplomat in Exile: Francis Pulszky's Political Activities in England, 1849-1860. By Thomas Kabdebo. 1979.

The German Struggle Against the Yugoslav Guerrillas in World War II: German Counter-Insurgency in Yugoslavia, 1941-1943. By Paul N. Hehn. 1979.

The Emergence of the Romanian National State. By Gerald J. Bobango. 1979.

Stewards of the Land: The American Farm School and Modern Greece. By Brenda L. Marder. 1979.

Roman Dmowski: Party, Tactics, Ideology, 1895-1907. By Alvin M. Fountain, II. 1980.

International and Domestic Politics in Greece During the Crimean War. By Jon V. Kofas. 1980.

Fires on the Mountain: The Macedonian Revolutionary Movement and the Kidnapping of Ellen Stone. By Laura Beth Sherman. 1980.

The Modernization of Agriculture: Rural Transformation in Hungary, 1848-1975. Edited by Joseph Held. 1980.

Britain and the War for Yugoslavia, 1940-1943. By Mark C. Wheeler. 1980.

The Turn to the Right: The Ideological Origins and Development of Ukrainian Nationalism, 1919-1929. By Alexander J. Motyl. 1980.

The Maple Leaf and the White Eagle: Canadian-Polish Relations, 1918-1978. By Aloysius Balawyder. 1980.

Antecedents of Revolution: Alexander I and the Polish Congress Kingdom, 1815-1825. By Frank W. Thackeray. 1980.

Blood Libel at Tiszaeszlar. By Andrew Handler. 1980.

Democratic Centralism in Romania: A Study of Local Communist Politics. By Daniel N. Nelson. 1980.

The Challenge of Communist Education: A Look at the German Democratic Republic. By Margrete Siebert Klein. 1980.

The Fortifications and Defense of Constantinople. By Byron C.P. Tsangadas. 1980.

Balkan Cultural Studies. By Stavro Skendi. 1980.

Studies in Ethnicity: The East European Experience in America. Edited by Charles A. Ward, Philip Shashko, and Donald E. Pienkos. 1980.

The Logic of "Normalization:" The Soviet Intervention in Czechoslovakia and the Czechoslovak Response. By Fred Eidlin. 1980.

Red Cross. Black Eagle: A Biography of Albania's American Schol. By Joan Fultz Kontos. 1981.

Nationalism in Contemporary Europe. By Franjo Tudjman. 1981.

Great Power Rivalry at the Turkish Straits: The Montreux Conference and Convention of 1936. By Anthony R. DeLuca. 1981.

Islam Under the Double Eagle: The Muslims of Bosnia and Hercegovina, 1878-1914. By Robert J. Donia. 1981.

Five Eleventh Century Hungarian Kings: Their Policies and Their Relations with Rome. By Z.J. Kosztolnyik. 1981.

Prelude to Appeasement: East European Central Diplomacy in the Early 1930's. By Lisanne Radice. 1981.

The Soviet Regime in Czechoslovakia. By Zdenek Krystufek. 1981.

School Strikes in Prussian Poland, 1901-1907: The Struggle Over Bilingual Education. By John J. Kulczycki. 1981.

Romantic Nationalism and Liberalism: Joachim Lelewel and the Polish National Idea. By Joan S. Skurnowicz. 1981.

The "Thaw" In Bulgarian Literature. By Atanas Slavov. 1981.

The Political Thought of Thomas G. Masaryk. By roman Szporluk. 1981.

Prussian Poland in the German Empire, 1871-1900. By Richard Blanke. 1981.

The Mazepists: Ukrainian Separatism in the Early Eighteenth Century. By Orest Subtelny. 1981.

The Battle for the Marchlands: The Russo-Polish Campaign of 1920. By Adam Zamoyski. 1981.

Milovan Djilas: A Revolutionary as a Writer. By Dennis Reinhartz. 1981.

Date Due
